AN EMBARRASSMENT OF TYRANNIES

Twenty-five Years of Index on Censorship

AN EMBARRASSMENT OF TYRANNIES

Twenty-five Years of *Index on Censorship*

EDITED BY W. L. WEBB and ROSE BELL

GEORGE BRAZILLER PUBLISHER
New York

First published in the United States in 1998 by George Braziller, Inc.

Originally published in Great Britain in 1997 by Victor Gollancz

For information, please address the publisher:

George Braziller, Inc.
171 Madison Avenue
New York, NY 10016

Library of Congress Cataloging-in-Publication Data:

An embarrassment of tyrannies : twenty-five years of Index on censorship /
    edited by W. L. Webb and Rose Bell.
        p.   cm.
    ISBN 0-8076-1441-6 (hc.)
    ISBN 0-8076-1446-7 (pbk.)
    1. Censorship. I. Webb, W. L. II. Bell, Rose, 1962–
III. Index on censorship.
Z657.E43   1998
363.3'1—dc21   98-24011
                                                      CIP

Printed and bound in the United States

First Paperback Edition

Acknowledgements

'An embarrassment of tyrannies' © W. L. Webb 1977

'Letter to Europeans' © George Mangakis 1971

'With concern for those not free' © Estate of Stephen Spender 1972

'And you, candle' © Natalya Gorbanevskaya 1964, this translation © Daniel Weissbort 1972

'Instructions on how to enter a new society' © Heberto Padilla 1968, this translation © John Butt 1972, first published in Spanish in *Fuera del Juego* 1968

'Out of the game' © Heberto Padilla 1968, this translation © John Butt 1972, first published in Spanish in *Fuera del Juego* 1968

'God keep me from going mad' © Alexander Solzhenitsyn 1950–53, this translation © Michael Scammell 1972

'Interview with Joseph Brodsky' © Michael Scammell 1972

'A writer's freedom' © Nadine Gordimer 1975

'A cup of coffee with my interrogator' © Ludvík Vaculík 1977, this translation © Estate of George Theiner 1977, from original made available by Palach Press

'Cemetery of words' © Eduardo Galeano 1978, this translation © William Rowe 1978

'The sin of power' © Arthur Miller 1977

'Distractions' © Juan Gelman 1978, this translation © Jo Labanyi 1978

'Apocalypse at Solentiname' © Estate of Julio Cortázar 1979, this translation © Nick Caistor 1979

'Pale browns and yellows' © Jorge Musto 1981, this translation © Alicia and Nick Caistor 1981

'Manuscripts banned and destroyed' © Pramoedya Ananta Toer 1981, this translation © Carmel Budiardjo 1981

5

'Variation on an eternal theme' © Ivan Klíma 1981, this translation © Estate of George Theiner 1981

'Open letter to President Husák' © Tom Stoppard 1981

'A convenient illusion' © Michael Tippett 1983

'Why should music be censorable?' © Yehudi Menuhin 1983

'Madness' © Anka Kowalska 1982, this translation © Adam Czerniawski 1982

'Last chance?' © Salman Rushdie 1983

'Father Jerzy Popiełuszko: In memoriam' introduction © Writers & Scholars International 1985, this translation © Andrew Short 1985

'When they beat us, we suffer' © Dario Fo 1984

'A simple solution' © Ivan Kraus 1985, this translation © Estate of George Theiner 1985

'Stars suddenly rain down' © Irina Ratushinskaya 1985, this translation © Sally Laird 1985

'And we remain' © Irina Ratushinskaya 1985, this translation © Pamela White Hadas and Ilya Nykin 1995

'Nunca Más' © Editorial Universitaria de Buenos Aires 1984, this translation © Writers & Scholars International 1986

'Václav Havel: My temptation' © Karel Kvíždala 1986

'Trademark territory' © Ariel Dorfman 1988, this translation © George R. Shivers 1988

'So where do we go for freedom?' © John Mortimer 1988

'Jihad for freedom' © Wole Soyinka 1989, first published in the *African Guardian* 1989

'The train of wonders' © Dror Green 1989, this translation © Shirley Eber 1990

'Here is the patriotically censored news' © Phillip Knightley 1991

'LOW warspeak' © Matthew d'Ancona 1991

'Suffer the little children' © Adewale Maja-Pearce 1991

'The Lubianka's hidden treasure: an interview with Vitaly Shentalinsky' © Irena Maryniak 1991

'From wimps to warriors' © Anthony Sampson 1991

'Should *Index* be above the battle?' © Stuart Hampshire 1992

'China is a world problem' © Fang Lizhi 1992

'Not a special case' © Ursula Ruston 1992

'Gentle Reader' © Judy Blume 1993

'Goodnight, Croatian writers' © Dubravka Ugrešić 1993, this translation © Celia Hawkesworth 1993

'A new map of censorship' © Ronald Dworkin 1994

'Sweet home of liberty' © Noam Chomsky 1994

'Standing in the queue' © Nadine Gordimer 1994

'The Bosnian bull' © Irfan Horozovic 1994, this translation © Christina Pribichevich-Zoric 1994

'The last despot and the end of Nigerian history?' © Wole Soyinka 1994

'Daring to speak one's name' © Alberto Manguel 1995

'The dark cloud over Turkey' © Yaşar Kemal 1995, this translation © Judith Vidal-Hall 1995

'A bright, shining hell' © Mumia Abu-Jamal 1995

'Rewriting history' © Felipe Fernández-Armesto 1995

'Beyond 2001' © Arthur C. Clarke 1995

'No end in sight' © Philip French 1995

'Market takes all' © Ken Loach 1996, revised 1997

'After Chernobyl: confusion and deceit' © Anthony Tucker 1996

'A liquidator's story' © Mikhail Byckau 1996, this translation © Vera Rich 1996

'Bosnian diary: Who goes home?' © W. L. Webb 1996

'No room for books' © Salman Rushdie 1996

'Urbicides, massacres, common graves' © Juan Goytisolo 1996, this translation © Peter Bush 1996

'Astrakhan on the Kremlin towers' © Victor Pelevin 1995, this translation © Arch Tait 1996, first published in Russian in *Ogonyok* No 42, 1995

'The truth, the whole truth and nothing but . . .' © Pieter-Dirk Uys 1996

'Articles of faith' © Michael Ignatieff 1996

'Cost of a miracle' © John Gittings 1997

'Whatever happened to Soviet childhood?' © Irena Maryniak 1997

Every effort has been made to trace all the copyright holders, but if any have been inadvertently overlooked the Publishers will be pleased to make the necessary arrangements at the first opportunity.

Contents

CONTENTS

Contents

11

CONTENTS

Contents

URSULA OWEN

Preface

'Let us drink to the success of our hopeless endeavour' goes the old toast of Soviet dissidents. And perhaps for *Index* to have been truly successful it should have made itself redundant. But the world being what it is, that is unthinkable. So thank God, alas, we are still in business, circulation rising, readership broader than ever. The geography of silencing may have altered since Stephen Spender founded the magazine, but there is still plenty of it – as our running chronicle *Index* Index continues to document in every issue.

It was in May 1972 that *Index* published its first issue, in response to Soviet dissidents Pavel Litvinov and Larisa Bogoraz Daniel, protesting against show trials in Moscow. The idea was to make public the circumstances of those who are silenced in their own countries, wherever that may be, and publish their work. In 1989, the Berlin Wall fell and the world was turned upside down. As a result, maps have been redrawn and the world has had to cope with a strategic and intellectual cataclysm. But though ideologies have been discredited and borders altered, there are still many parts of the world where the old familiar forms of censorship – the blue pencil, imprisonment, forced exile, assassination – are alive and well. And now new and troubling questions have surfaced, some of them challenging the primacy of free expression itself: religious extremism, relative values and cultural difference, the rise of nationalism, the rewriting of history, words that kill, pornography, violence on television, freedom on the Internet – all these are argued and anguished over, in and out of the media. As this turbulent century ends, *Index*, more than ever, must remain the forum for difficult debates.

Writing a preface to this fine collection, I am deeply conscious of the photographs on our office walls, the documents in the drawers, the range of talent and commitment among its writers, its editors, its staff over the years, the unique accumulated archive, of the fact that

Index has published some of the best and most exciting contemporary writing over the past 25 years. What remain the most moving reassurances that we are doing something useful are the letters from silenced, exiled and marginalized writers, journalists, lawyers, teachers, saying that *Index* makes them feel visible, part of the human race, that their lives *matter*, that their writings have not disappeared into the dark.

Stephen Spender once said that 'the opposite of censorship is self-expression, which we call literature', and from the very beginning *Index* ranged itself on the side of the 'scribblers'. That remains our task. But now, eight years after the fall of Communism, we have to address very different worlds at one and the same time. Release from tyranny turns out not, on the whole, to have led to an upsurge of creativity. We have to concern ourselves with how freedom is used as well as its suppression, and there are certainly freedoms lost by us in the West, the 'spoilt brats of civilisation', when we allow ourselves to be dominated by the mediocrity of media moguls and the bottom line.

But there are still plenty of dictatorships and fanaticisms, sacred as well as profane, which turn writers involuntarily into public heroes and martyrs. These writers know the price of being forced to abandon their real work – of grappling with inwardness, with language itself. As Günter Grass has told us, 'without the storytellers the history of humanity has not been fully told, but is at an end.' We at *Index* will continue to defend, everywhere, the right of people to tell their stories, the right of the imagination to flourish.

W. L. WEBB

An embarrassment of tyrannies

'Wake up!' Solzhenitsyn taunted the Kremlin's geriatrics after the invasion of Czechoslovakia in 1968: 'Your clocks are slow in relation to our times!' *Index*, a child of the better ideals and aspirations of the sixties, was a response to that impatience at the stalling of yet another turning point of history. What moved Stephen Spender and some of his writer and scholar friends was not so much the dramas lately enacted on the political barricades, but the appeals from writers and other intellectuals in eastern Europe and the Soviet Union, driven by frustration at the holding back of change, asking directly and openly for help and solidarity from their peers in the West. The cases they described were disturbing enough, like that of Andrei Sinyavsky, and the trial in Moscow of Yuri Galanskov and Aleksander Ginzburg, which Pavel Litvinov in a brave and unprecedented letter to *The Times* called 'a wild mockery of . . . the accused . . . and of the witnesses unthinkable in the twentieth century'. What Spender thought remarkable, however, was that Litvinov, Andrei Amalrik and the other Russian human rights campaigners, as he wrote in the first issue of *Index* in the Spring of 1972, 'seemed to take it for granted that in spite of the ideological conditioning of the society in which they live, there is nevertheless an international community of scientists, writers and scholars thinking about the same problems and applying to them the same human values . . .'

Solzhenitsyn and others had spoken about the especial horror for writers of having their writings disappear with them into the dark of a lawless imprisonment, vanishing as though they had never been, like cherished children strangled in infancy. 'The idea behind *Index*,' wrote another of the founders, Stuart Hampshire, in the twentieth anniversary issue, 'was to ensure that . . . the tyrant's concealments of oppression and of absolute cruelty, should always be challenged. There should be the noise of publicity outside every detention centre and concentration

17

camp, and a published record of every tyrannical denial of free expression.' In this way, imprisoned or exiled writers would know at least that 'their names, and the names of their works, would remain among the names of the living'. As for their persecutors, what was aimed at was 'the embarrassment of tyranny, wherever it appears'.

Index kept faith with Pavel Litvinov, Amalrik and their kind, kept up the noise, kept the spotlight of publicity trained on the barbed wire, the prison window, the torture chamber in the basement, the shameful 'treatment' rooms of psychiatric clinics in which the KGB had taken to incarcerating citizens suffering from independent thought. As well as letters of protest, and the smuggled testimonies of exile and abuse, they gave us the banned literary texts not only of Solzhenitsyn, Sinyavsky and other established, if little published, novelists and essayists, but of younger writers like Joseph Brodsky, for whose marvellous talent the Soviet literary and legal establishments found no use. (After all, as Spender said in his introductory manifesto, by most informed reckoning the work that was being censored – in Greece, South Africa and South America, as well as in the Soviet bloc – was among the most exciting being written. In this, too, opening windows on the complacent provincialism of British literary life, *Index* was ahead of the game, widening the horizons of British publishing and leading the way for followers like *Granta*.) The magazine also kept an eye on the work and welfare of Václav Havel and the other Czech Chartists, in and out of prison; and when Polish tanks went on the streets of Warsaw and Gdansk in December 1981, and Solidarity's activists disappeared into prisons and detention centres, General Jaruszelski was not spared the embarrassment of Adam Michnik's scathing texts and other unwelcome attentions *Index* was able to bring to bear.

It was not until 1989 that history and the Kremlin were ready to turn at last. What a mistake it would have been for *Index* to suppose that with the Cold War 'won', and the end of history ushering in the eternal day of economic liberalism, its job was largely done, though many a politician and police chief must have wished devoutly that it had been so. But then its editors and writers never did think of themselves as enlisted men and women in the Cold War, and '. . . tyranny, wherever it appears' was never a false or empty piety.

That, from the beginning, is the flag under which Index has sailed. Of course the grim suppressions of the Communist world were not neglected. The first issue contained Solzhenitsyn's moving memorial for Alexander Tvardovsky, poems by Natalya Gorbanevskaya, herself lately released from a psychiatric prison, and a fine story by Milovan Djilas, banned in his own country since 1963. (Also a review, I note, with some pride at the connection, of *Writers Against Rulers*, Dušan Hamšik's account of the Czechoslovak writers' role in the Prague Spring, for which I had written an introduction. That brought in another impulse important to Index: to celebrate the liberating effect of the human voice speaking plainly and directly to power, as Ludvík Vaculík had done to the outraged Czech leadership, refusing to employ the blank and evasive dialect Party etiquette required.)

But even that first Index made just as much disconcerting noise under the windows of the Greek colonels, of Pakistan's military ruler, Ayah Khan, and the censors of Portugal, Spain and Brazil, where it was recorded in Index's own 'Index' (the core of the magazine which has grown into an incomparable catalogue – a history of censoring crimes and follies the world over) that Antonioni's film *Zabriskie Point* had been banned on the grounds of 'insulting a friendly country', although the Americans, the junta's valued friends in question, hadn't actually banned it themselves. Section two of our own Official Secrets Act also came in for a dishonourable mention, as did the Pentagon Papers, whose leaking in the *New York Times* made it impossible for Americans not to confront the nature of the war in Vietnam. And it was a message from a Greek prison cell, the end of George Mangakis's 'Letter to Europeans', that showed Index already doing the job it was designed for:

> It is true, then, that there are situations in which each of us
> represents all mankind. And it is the same with these papers: I
> have entrusted them to a poor Italian prisoner who has just been
> released and who was willing to try to smuggle them out for me.
> Through him I hope they will eventually reach you . . . I have
> raised my hand, made a sign. And so we exist. We over here in
> prison, and you out there who agree with us.

In the quarter of a century since then, Index has continued to be there for the imprisoned, censored and oppressed in most corners of the globe and across the political spectrum: for the 'disappeared' and their families in Argentina, and the resisters and victims of other fascist juntas in Latin America, as well as the banned poets of Cuba; for the Chinese student leaders who survived the Tiananmen Square massacre to serve long prison sentences, and the victims of famine and arms traders in Africa; for those afflicted by the deadly fever of ancient nationalisms in Bosnia or the implacability of religious fundamentalism, not only in its Islamic versions, but in Israel and the United States as well. And since the Wall came down, and the world began to spin so fast, there have been insidious new tyrannies to keep track of.

The distance that stretches between now and the world before 1989, less than a decade by calendar time, demonstrates as well as any of Eric Hobsbawm's arguments that historical time is different: that 1989 was indeed the end of the short, violent twentieth century begun in 1914, and that already we are embarked, ill-prepared, on a new one, buffeted by strange winds that blow from beyond the millennium. And already it is clear that the work of Index will be needed just as much in this contradictory new world of clashing civilizations and a global economy, and that in some ways new times may be more difficult and testing.

Taking censorship seriously can be a seriously subversive business, as authority has always been well aware. Insist effectively on freedom of the word and the unearthly radiance of thrones and altars fades, while dictators, chiefs of staff, armaments manufacturers and media imperialists begin to look humanly vulnerable, and nothing distresses them more than that. Soon, other more stoutly defended freedoms of the day — to dine at the Ritz, to make money whatever the social or ecological cost — are blinking in the light of critical scrutiny.

That writers and scholars should insist on the primacy of this freedom is not the special pleading of a sectional interest, though politicians may find it convenient to represent it as that. For however democracy may evolve, free speech will remain the right and empowerment without which the struggle for other human rights cannot even be articulated. So while Index never forgets to begin with the word, the connection to wider human rights dilemmas is inescapable, and they have not been shirked.

In our far from brave new world, however, an old argument in censorship debates is revived. It might be caricatured as being between the wild surmise of the subversives and the strict constructionism of classical liberals seeking to address issues of freedom solely through legal process. Stuart Hampshire's twentieth anniversary reflections set out the argument with all its new difficulties, as the increasingly fluid moral relativism of the West (or North) comes up against the fixed ethical constructions of the East (or South). The metaphysical basis of the hostility between liberal atheists or agnostics and religious fundamentalists means not only that it is likely to be more durable than the Cold War's divisions, but that it 'may even represent an opposition within human nature which is permanent and which cannot be expected to disappear'. Since, as reaction to the *fatwa* against Salman Rushdie showed so disconcertingly, this split, even in its most dramatized form, between Western liberal materialism and Islam's fundamentalist counter-reformation, now runs through the middle of countries and not just between them, Hampshire's argument that disputes between the sides can only be usefully addressed through procedural justice, with opposing views stated and reviewed, might seem to have a universal validity. *Index* would then be on safe ground, free of imputations of Western cultural imperialism (or 'being political'), by stressing 'the justice of just and fair procedures, as distinct from substantial questions of justice'.

This, after all, was very like the stance of Pavel Litvinov and his fellow human rights activists: what the Kremlin found disconcerting was their proposal not of political confrontation, but simply that Soviet legal authorities should not violate their own laws or the international obligations they had entered into, such as the Helsinki agreements.

But there are other lessons for new times to be learned from the Cold War's pathologies. One might be that the kind of responsive interest Western intellectuals once took in the struggles of independent writers in the old Soviet empire should be transferred to the problem of Islamic writers and thinkers whose work presents a less reductive or 'Old Testament' view of the teachings of their religion. Another might be drawn from a fine polemic, too long to include here, in which Václav Havel made the point that the kind of totalitarianism with which he was all too familiar could not abide stories because it couldn't know how they would end, its very *raison d'être* being that it knew all the answers. That essay appeared perhaps eighteen months before Havel's own story changed so miraculously, though I came across it only this winter. A week later I was reading the warning of no less a capitalist than George Soros that *laissez-faire* capitalism was beginning to show signs of the particular hubris of totalitarianism with its strident insistence that the market had all the answers: becoming, in short, another closed-circuit ideology to which there was no alternative – 'an ideology', as Soros puts it, 'hostile to the open society'. (Havel had a nice retort ready for 'end of history' triumphalism, too: 'If ideology destroys history by explaining it away completely, history destroys ideology by unfolding in a way other than that prescribed by ideology.')

The consequences for storytellers fictional and factual are hardly so drastic as those that faced Havel and his friends, but they are steadily eroding our freedoms. 'Liberty is ill in Britain . . . the very concept . . . is being challenged and corroded by the Thatcher government,' Ronald Dworkin was writing in 1988, only a month or two later than Havel, reviewing legislative changes involving human rights restrictions of the kind still being brought forward in 1997, though latterly not always without corrective amendments won through dogged parliamentary and extra-parliamentary criticism; as John Mortimer reminded us in that same issue, 'the price of freedom is perpetual fussing'.

There are other straws in the wind which *Index* has not omitted to notice: for example, that concentration of press ownership is generating a dismal, synthetic-populist *Gleichschaltung* of tone, range and content; and that all but one or two of Britain's best-known publishing houses are now owned and controlled by American conglomerates. Then, as inescapable as environmental pollution, there is the pollution of thought and language through the spread of deceitful euphemisms, derived in part from the new management cant – 'downsizing' and all its ugly sisters – partly from the malevolent dialects used, together with reporting controls, to obscure or 'sanitize' what happens in wars, dialects elaborated in theatres stretching from Vietnam to the Gulf, but clearly kin to Nazi usages developed to cover the realities of the Holocaust. Add to this the extension of 'confusion marketing' into American and thus inevitably into British politics, so that announcements of opaque and minimalist policies from parties hamstrung by the 'no alternative' ideology are introduced by increasingly desperate-sounding mantras – 'It is perfectly clear . . . I want to make it perfectly clear . . . We have *always* made it *absolutely* clear . . .' – and it may soon be time for writers to make an effort not unlike that which Günter Grass, Heinrich Böll and their friends in Gruppe 47 had to make amid the rubble of post war Berlin to purge the German language of accumulated poisons fatal to creative and democratic thinking.

Stuart Hampshire's prescription may be the right one in conflicts where the paramount need is to establish any ground at all between political and religious cultures on which arguments about freedom and rights might be heard, though, as the case of Salman Rushdie continues to show, there are huge difficulties. And then, theocracies or other people's tribalisms may be more or less malign or benevolent, but not many of *Index*'s writers and readers will be happy with Samuel Huntingdon's conclusion in *The Clash of Civilisations* that in future we should leave tormented populations, or minorities (or writers like Ken Saro-Wiwa?) in other cultures and continents to it, or at best to the first aid kits of politically unsupported human rights professionals, while we get on with the business of Transatlantica's business. Does such a formula satisfy even strategic, let alone moral, considerations in the case of crippled Russia, half in and half out of Europe? Might not the cause of freedom have been better and more safely served if the West had sent fewer ideological economists and more money and practical expertise? Or to put it another way, can anyone read Irena Maryniak's account of the hundreds of thousands of abandoned children adrift in the anarchic new freedom-to-make-money atmosphere of Russia and eastern Europe, without feeling that 'substantial questions of justice' have to be raised in considering the nature of what happened to those societies?

For dealing with such questions, and with the shadowy but growing threats to freedom in the more or less liberal democracies and their less than liberal quasi-protectorates and oil suppliers, the more imaginative and recruiting responses of the 'subversive' model will be needed. (The media mogul and the arms trader, the agribusinessman and the polluting developer in Africa, South America or nearer home, may well be operating, expensively advised, just within the letter of the law; and if that becomes too cramping, will often have the power and interest to get the law altered, or – as the new political correctness requires one to say of the most blatantly regressive measures – 'reformed'.)

But then readers will know that Index has long been shrewdly and productively engaged with these difficult debates and others like them, as witness, for example, the recent thoughtful critique by Caroline Moorehead and its editor, Ursula Owen, of the limits of human rights operations as presently conceived. Michael Ignatieff's reflections on the possibilities and impossibilities of truth and reconciliation commissions is a subtle unravelling of similar dilemmas.

To try to do justice both to the history and to the quality of its recording over a quarter of a century is a task verging on the whimsical. What one does realize, looking back through the files, is that in an age very much aware of the intractability of its problems, and for all the unending struggle to raise operating funds, Index, in its brave new colours, has never been more focused and effective. For just one measure of that achievement, consider its continuing ability to attract so many of the best contemporary writers – 'by-lines to kill for', as an envious contemporary once put it – something peculiarly satisfying in a culture trained to think that the only freedom that really matters is the freedom to make money.

GEORGE MANGAKIS

Letter to Europeans

George Mangakis, accused by the Greek junta of 'a lack of spirit of conformity with the regime', was dismissed from his chair of Penal Law in the
University of Athens in 1969, and later arrested on charges of terrorism,
imprisoned and tortured. Since the restoration of democracy he has served
as a minister in various governments. This 'Letter to Europeans' appeared
in the first issue of Index.

The dimensions of my cell are approximately 10 feet by 10 feet. You
gradually become accustomed to this space and even grow to like it,
since, in a way, it is like a lair in which you lie hidden, licking your
wounds. But in reality its object is to annihilate you. On one side of
it there is a heavy iron door, with a little round hole in the upper part.
Prisoners hate this little hole; they call it the 'stool pigeon'. It is through
this hole that the jailer's eye appears every now and then – an isolated
eye, without a face. There is also a peculiar lock, on the outside only;
it locks with a dry, double sound. That is one thing you never get used
to, no matter how much time goes by. It gives you the daily, tangible
sensation of the violence that is being done to you. Before I came here,
I didn't know that violence could be expressed so completely by the
dry sound of a double lock.

   On the other side of my cell there is a little window with bars. From
this window you can see part of the city. And yet a prisoner rarely
looks out of the window. It is too painful. The prisoner, of course, has
a picture of life outside the prison constantly in his mind. But it is dim,
colourless, like an old photograph; it is soft and shapeless. It is bearable.
So you don't dare look out of the window. Its only use is to bring you
some light. That is something I have studied very carefully. I have
learned all the possible shades of light. I can distinguish the light that
comes just before daybreak, and the light that lingers on after nightfall.

This light, with its many variations, is one of the chief joys of the prisoner. It often happens that a certain shade of light coincides with your mood, with the spiritual needs of that particular moment. Looking at the light, there have been times when I hummed a song, and times when I found it relieved pain. So much, then, for the window.

Apart from the door and the window, my cell also has a temperature. That is another fundamental element of my life here. It is unbearably cold in winter and extremely hot in summer. I find this natural, even though it brings me great discomfort. It is a sympton of the denudation of being in prison. Under such conditions, it has got to be like this; you just have to live in direct contact with the temperature of this particular world.

I live in this space, then, for endless hours of the day and night. It is like a piece of thread on which my days are strung and fall away, lifeless. This space can also be compared to a wrestling ring. Here a man struggles alone with the evil of the world.

I write these papers, and then I hide them. They let you write, but every so often they search your cell and take away your writings. They look them over, and after some time they return the ones which are considered permissible. You take them back, and suddenly you loathe them. This system is a diabolical device for annihilating your own soul. They want to make you see your thoughts through their eyes and control them yourself, from their point of view. It is like having a nail pushed into your mind, dislocating it. Against this method, which is meant to open up breaches in our defences and split our personality, there are two means of defence. First, we allow our jailers to take away some of our writings – the ones that express our views unequivocally. It is a way of provoking the jailers. We even derive a sort of childish satisfaction from thinking of the faces they'll make as they read. Then there are other papers which we prefer to hide – the ones we want to keep for ourselves.

My mind often goes back to the dead I have known and loved. In the vacuum of my cell, only concepts have substance. My cell is like a bottomless hole in the void. My most frequent visitor is my brother Yannis – he comes to me almost every day. He was killed in the war, but not in the act of killing others: he was a doctor. His regiment was afflicted with an epidemic of meningitis. He did not have time to cure himself. I have never been able to accept his death. I have simply managed, in time, to become reconciled to his absence. Now we are once again very close to each other. He has smiling, honey-coloured eyes. He stays on for hours, and we sit there and think together. It used to be the same when he was alive. Now he often makes me think that the value of charity cannot be put in question. That is one thing which cannot be put in question, especially now that I have come to know torturers, jailers, and their masters at close quarters. I know how utterly the bestiality of absolute power has degraded them. It seems that, spiritually speaking, everything stems from charity. Yannis is quite positive about that. And also courage, and love for certain concepts relevant to man, and receptivity to beauty. Everything stems from that. Sometimes Yannis gets up and takes those three paces forward, then backward, on my behalf. Then I can see his strong, graceful body. In the old days he used to like sailing. Now, as he paces across my cell, he brings the sea and the wind into my flat, barren cell. As he lifts his arm, he even gives the cell a perspective in depth. The kind of depth we keep looking for, he and I. Then he begins to think to the sound of music. He always loved music. And so my cell gradually fills with music. And I sail through the hours of the night in a sea of music. Those are my most serene nights, the ones suffused with a certain intimation of the meaning of the world. Yannis still remains a human being. If he is dead, then I am dead too. I believe we are both still alive.

There are moments when I sit in my cell thinking of what would be the best way to summarize my motives, those that made me end up in this cell and those that make me endure it. These motives are certainly not a belief in a single truth – not because we no longer have any truths to believe in but because, in our world, we do not experience these truths as absolute certainties. We are no longer as simple as that: we seek something more profound than certainty, something more substantial, something that is naturally, spontaneously simple. I think, then, that the totality of my motives in this connection could best be epitomized as hope – in other words, the most fragile, but also the most spontaneous and tenacious form of human thought. A deeply-rooted, indestructible hope, then, carved out the path that was to lead me, unrepentant, to this barren desert, and it is the same hope that makes me capable of enduring it, like those small, tormented desert plants which contain, inexplicably, two tiny drops of sap – drawn, I am sure, from their own substance. My hope is the equivalent of those two drops of sap. However, the intensity of my hope is equal to my difficulty in putting it into words. I might say, perhaps, that this hope concerns our humanity, which cannot be annihilated no matter how much it is persecuted on all sides; this is why there can be no purpose as serious, as noble, as to commit ourselves to its safeguard, even if we must inevitably suffer for it.

Yet I don't think that by saying this I am expressing myself as concretely as I would wish. This hope takes shape only in certain attitudes. During the past months, through all the prisons I've known, I have often come across these attitudes. When I was held at the police-station jails – those places of utter human degradation – I remember a girl who was locked in a cell next to mine. She had been there for five months. She hadn't seen the light of day once throughout that period. She had been accused of helping her fiancé to do Resistance work. At regular intervals, they would summon her for questioning and would try to make her disown him, using cunning persuasion or brutal intimidation alternately. If she disowned her fiancé, she would be set free. She refused unflinchingly, to the very end, even though she knew that her fiancé was dying of cancer and she would probably never see him again. He died on the day of her trial. She was a pale, frail girl, with a kind of nobility about her. Every evening she used to sing in her cell in a soft, low voice. She would sing till dawn about her love, in her sad voice. The girl's attitude is my hope. And so is the attitude of the doctor whom they tried to involve in our case. There was no evidence against him. If he had adopted a noncommittal attitude at the court-martial he would certainly have been acquitted. But he was made of different mettle. When his turn came to take the stand at the trial, he got up and spoke about liberty. He defended liberty, even though he had a wife and children to support. He was sentenced to seven years in prison. This doctor's attitude is my hope. I have lived through a number of similar experiences. What I would like to say here is quite simply this: in the attitude of people like that doctor and that girl, the dominant feeling is a spontaneous knowledge that the most important thing in life is to keep one's humanity. Because life does not belong to the barbarians, even when absolute authority does belong to them. Life belongs to human beings, life goes forward because of them. This is the source of my hope.

I live with a number of ideas that I love. They fill my days and nights. To the treacherous uniformity of my stagnant hours I oppose this dialogue with my ideas. Now I have come to know them better and to understand them better, I have actually experienced their significance. When I was being questioned, I discovered the essence of human dignity, in both its deepest and its simplest sense. When I was court martialled I hungered for justice, and when I was imprisoned I thirsted for humanity. The brutal oppression which is now stifling my country has taught me a great deal, among other things the value of refusing to submit. As I sit in my cell thinking about these things, I am filled with a strange power – a power which has nothing in common with the power of my jailers. It is not expressed in a loud, insolent voice. It is the power of endurance – the power that is born of a sense of being right. That is how I face the relentless attack of empty days which has been launched against me. Each time, I repulse the attack at its very start. I begin my day by uttering the word 'freedom'. This usually happens at daybreak. I emerge from sleep, always feeling bitterly surprised to find myself in prison, as on the first day. Then I utter my beloved word, before the sense of being in prison has time to overpower me. This single word works like magic. And then I am reconciled to the new, empty day stretching ahead of me.

I think of my companions. The political prisoners I have come across in my various prisons. The ones who resisted and are now pacing across their cells, taking those three little jerky steps forward, then backward. They are all made of the same stuff, even though they may be very different persons in other respects. They all possess a very rare sensitivity of conscience. A truly unbelievable sensitivity. It becomes manifest in tiny details, as well as on big occasions. When they speak, they exercise the utmost delicacy with regard to the other person's feelings. They are always at your side with a glass of water, before you have time to ask for it. I want to give an example of this extraordinary sensitivity. Some days ago, one of us was about to be released. He was in the prison hospital. He could have left directly from there, but he delayed his departure for a week, so as to come and say good-bye to us. Seven days of voluntary prison just to say good-bye to his friends. That is what I mean. These people, then, have truly taken upon themselves the entire predicament of our times. They are consciously carrying the burden of our people's trampled honour. And in so doing they feel close to all those who are persecuted on earth. Through a fundamental unity they grasp the meaning of all that is happening in the world today. It is the unity of man's yearning to be free of oppression, no matter in what form. Whoever resists oppression is a brother to them, no matter who or where he is, scattered in the innumerable prisons of my own and other countries.

I often ask myself what it was exactly that touched our consciences in such a way as to give us all an imperatively personal motive for opposing the dictatorship and enlisting in the Resistance, putting aside all other personal obligations and pursuits. One does not enlist in the Resistance – in that mortally dangerous confrontation with the all-powerful persecution mechanism of a dictatorship, where the chances of being caught are far greater than the chances of getting away with it, where arrest will result in the most unbearable and long-term suffering – one doesn't get involved in all this without some very strong personal motive. So strong, in fact, that it must literally affect the very roots of one's being – since it makes one decide to risk falling into the clutches of the most appalling arbitrariness and barbarism, being reduced from a human being to an object, a mere receptacle of suffering, jeopardizing all the achievements and dreams of a lifetime and plunging loved ones into the most terrible agonies and deprivations.

I keep thinking, then, that this motive can be no other than the deep humiliation which the dictatorship represents for you, both as an individual and as a member of the people to whom you belong. When a dictatorship is imposed on your country, the very first thing you feel, the very first day, is humiliation. You are being deprived of the right to consider yourself worthy of responsibility for your own life and destiny. This feeling of humiliation grows day by day as a result of the oppressors' unceasing effort to force your mind to accept all the vulgarity which makes up the abortive mental world of dictators. You feel as if your reason and your human status were being deeply insulted every day. And then comes the attempt to impose on you, by fear, acceptance of their various barbarous actions – both those that you hear about and those that you actually see them commit against your fellow human beings. You begin to live with the daily humiliation of fear, and you begin to loathe yourself. And then, deeply wounded in your conscience as a citizen, you begin to feel a solidarity with the people to whom you belong. With a unique immediacy, you feel indivisibly bound to them and jointly responsible for their future fate. Thanks to this process of identification, you acquire an extraordinary historical acuity of vision, such as you had never known before, and you can see with total clarity that humiliated nations are inevitably led either to a lethal decadence, a moral and spiritual withering, or to a passion for revenge, which results in bloodshed and upheaval. A humiliated people either take their revenge or die a moral and spiritual death. Once you realize, then, the inevitability of your people's destruction, one way or another, your personal humiliation is turned into a sense of responsibility, and you don't simply join the Resistance, you become deeply committed to the Resistance. In other words, you situate the meaning of your existence in this strangest, this most dangerous and unselfish of all struggles which is called Resistance. From that point onward, may God have mercy on you.

Morally speaking, the Resistance is the purest of all struggles. As a rule, you join it only to follow the dictates of your conscience; it affords no other satisfaction except the justification of your conscience. Not only is there no benefit to be expected from this struggle but, on the contrary, you are endangering, or rather you are exposing to a near certain catastrophe, whatever you may have achieved until now with your labours, and you enter a way of life that is full of anxiety and peril. You cannot expect immediate praise, because you have to act secretly, in darkness and silence; nor can you expect future praise, because under a dictatorship the future is always uncertain and confused. There is only your conscience to justify you, as you see it mirrored at times in the eyes of one of your companions. Yet this justification counts more than anything else. You are privileged to experience certain moments in which you feel that you too express the dignity of the human species. This is the deepest justification a man may feel for being alive. This is why the Resistance is the worthiest of all struggles: it is the most dramatic manifestation of the human conscience.

A lot of people don't understand us at all. It seems that it is difficult to understand an act that is motivated exclusively by the dictates of one's conscience, especially when the consequences of the act lead one to extreme situations. Our life is now based on values alone, not on interests. We have voluntarily placed ourselves in a position of unbearable suffering, and our main concern every day is not just to safeguard our humanity within this suffering, but to transmute this suffering into a component of our humanity. Upon our suffering we try to build a personality that excludes ordinary joys, the pursuit of happiness, and that is purely conceptual. We have become incarnated concepts. This means we do not live in the present. Besides, we have no days that we can call the present, except perhaps the days when our loved ones visit us. Then, yes, for about ten minutes, for as long as the visit lasts, we feel once again the happiness and pain that the love of another human being can bring; we rediscover in this way common human interests, the need for joy, the revulsion from suffering. But apart from those occasions, we live timelessly. We exist as a result of the justification of our conscience, and for its sake alone. Thus there is no such thing as time for us. In this sense we could reach the absolute, if it weren't for the necessity to conquer this justification every day again from the very beginning. For this incarnation of abstract concepts is by no means a static condition; we still have blood in our veins, blood that pulsates with needs and desires, hearts that insist on dreaming, memories that ruminate on past happiness. We have our personal loves, for certain particular people. That is a constant threat to us. It means we have to struggle with ourselves in order to retain our conceptual condition, to balance ourselves upon the magnetic needle of conscience in its ceaseless quivering. Because of this constant effort, we are not absolute beings. Because of this effort, we are not yet dead.

Another thing: we feel very European. This feeling does not derive primarily from political opinions, even though it does end up by becoming a fundamental political stand. It is a feeling that grows out of the immediacy and the intensity that our cultural values have acquired under dictatorship. Fortunately, these values, which have become our whole life and which help us to endure our long nights and days, are not exclusively ours. We share them with all the peoples of Europe. Or rather the European people, for Europe is one single people. Here in prison we can affirm this with complete seriousness. Suffering helps us to get down to the essence of things and to express it with perfect simplicity. We see only the deeper meaning of Europe, not the foolish borders, the petty rivalries, the unfounded fears and reservations. We see ourselves simply as one people, as a whole. It may seem strange – though only at first glance – how intensely the Greeks felt they were Europeans the very first day of the dictatorship. Our values are the values of Europe. We created them together. We felt instinctively, at the time, that nobody but a European could understand the tragedy that was taking place in our country and feel about it the way we did. And we were right.

We turned in despair to Europe, and the people of Europe did not forsake us. Now all those of us who have entered upon this ordeal, in the prisons of the dictatorship, say 'Europe' as we would say 'our country'. And we mean exactly that: this fusion, in depth, of common historical experiences, cultural values, and human solidarity which we call 'country', 'fatherland'. We clutch the bars of our narrow windows, we look at the world outside, and we think of those millions of people walking the streets, and we know that if they could see us, they would raise their hands in greeting, they would give us a sign. In those moments, with our mind's eye, we embrace the whole of Europe. It is a place which includes all our own people, all the ones who would raise their hands in greeting. The headhunters have locked us up in this narrow place in order to make us shrink, like those hideous human scalps which are their trophies. But what they haven't realized is that our country has widened; it has become a whole continent. They have isolated us so as to turn us into solitary, forsaken creatures, lost in a purely individual fate. But we now live in the immense human community of European solidarity. Their power is helpless in the face of this knowledge.

We often talk about the dignity of man. It is not an abstraction; it

33

is a thing which I have actually experienced. It exists in our very depths, like a sensitive steel spring. It has absolutely nothing to do with personal dignity. Its roots lie much deeper. Throughout the nightmare of the interrogation sessions, I lost my personal dignity; it was replaced by pure suffering. But human dignity was within me, without my knowing it. There came a moment when they touched it; the questioning had already been going on for some time. They cannot tell when this moment comes, and so they cannot plan their course accordingly. It functioned suddenly, like a hidden spring that made my scattered spiritual parts jerk upright, all of a piece. It wasn't really me who rose to my feet then, it was Everyman. The moment I began to feel this, I began to overcome the questioning ordeal. The effort was no longer only for myself. It was for all of us. Together we stood our ground.

I have experienced the fate of a victim. I have seen the torturer's face at close quarters. It was in a worse condition than my own bleeding, livid face. The torturer's face was distorted by a kind of twitching that had nothing human about it. He was in such a state of tension that he had an expression very similar to those we see on Chinese masks: I am not exaggerating. It is not an easy thing to torture people. It requires inner participation. In this situation, I turned out to be the lucky one. I was humiliated. I did not humiliate others. I was simply bearing a profoundly unhappy humanity in my aching entrails. Whereas the men who humiliate you must first humiliate the notion of humanity within themselves. Never mind if they strut around in their uniforms, swollen with the knowledge that they can control the suffering, sleeplessness, hunger, and despair of their fellow human beings, intoxicated with the power in their hands. Their intoxication is nothing other than the degradation of humanity. The ultimate degradation. They have had to pay very dearly for my torments. I wasn't the one in the worst position. I was simply a man who moaned because he was in great pain. I prefer that. At this moment I am deprived of the joy of seeing children going to school or playing in the parks. Whereas they have to look their own children in the face. It is their own humiliation that I cannot forgive the dictators.

*   *   *

One of the very few things I have been able to keep here is a picture of Erasmus. It's a newspaper clipping. I cut it out some time ago, and now I often look at it. It gives me a certain sense of peace. I suppose there must be some explanation for this. But I'm not interested in explanations. It is enough that there is this magic, this strange exaltation caused by the identification of this man with our own values, this victory over my solitude, which started centuries ago and which becomes real again as I look at his face. He is shown in profile. I like that. He is not looking at me, but he is telling me where to look. He reveals a solidarity of vision between us. In prison, this solidarity is a daily necessity, like the need for water, bread, sleep. When they search my cell they come upon Erasmus' picture, but they let me keep it. They don't understand. They've no idea how dangerous a mild, wise man can be. Sometimes I wonder about the jailer's eye, watching me through the hole in the door — where does *he* find solidarity of vision?

Our position as prisoners has many distinguishing features. One of them is that we sing, quite frequently. It may sound strange to people who don't know about prisons. But that's the way it is — and come to think of it, it is very natural. Singing is part of the unwritten instructions passed on by veteran prisoners to newly arrived ones: when the pain and anguish are too much for you, sing. We begin to sing precisely when the anguish becomes unbearable. On days that are free of anguish, we don't sing. Singing seems to melt away that crushing burden we carry, just when we think we can no longer carry it; and then it rises out of us like an invisible grey mist. We feel a kind of relief. *They* know this, and that is why in some prisons, the harshest ones, singing is forbidden. I often sing in my cell, or I whistle. Sometimes I sing to my wife. If she could hear me, she would be pleased, even though I sing false. She knows about singing in prison, she's been through it. In this place singing is a real, immediate need of the spirit. It is the daily bread of those who are struggling not to go insane. It softens up a harsh world and opens up the saving grace of new, wider vistas. As you sing, you feel you are travelling along these extended frontiers of the world. After all, we have our little trips too. I've got to say this: I'm grateful to songwriters, especially those who have composed sad songs. I like singing Mikis Theodorakis, for instance. In his old songs, it's as if he had a kind of foreknowledge of the prisons he was fated to live in. So we sing. I have never heard my jailers singing. Most of their time they are busy digesting their food.

We are shut away in our individual cells. In one respect we are the most helpless of creatures. They can do what they like with us. Just as we are sitting in our cell, they march in, they take us away, we don't know where, to some other prison, far away. If it weren't for their strange fear of us, I might say that they look upon us as objects. But this fear of theirs keeps our human status intact, even in their eyes. Now these helpless creatures think of nothing else but the fate of mankind. When we are taken out of our cells and meet our fellow prisoners, that is what we talk about. That is our sole concern. Like so many others, we know the meaning of this yearning for freedom that is pulsating throughout the world. And we can discern, more clearly than ever before, the enemies of freedom. We tremble for the fate of this great country which we call Europe. We know that hope hangs upon Europe, and that is the reason why it is constantly threatened. It is very dangerous to nourish the hopes of mankind. Why else should Greece have become enslaved? They built another bridgehead next to those of Spain and Portugal. They are afraid of Europe – that long-suffering fountainhead of ideas, that inexhaustible breeding ground whose ancient soil has never ceased to shelter the seeds of thinking. The simple citizens of Europe nurture these seeds, keeping them alive thanks to the restless, questing spirit which is so much a part of their being. The wealthy and the powerful are quite right to fear it. In this place, when we talk about 'man', we know what we mean. We mean the quality which makes him the measure of all things. That is our oldest, our wisest, our most explosive concept. It is because of this concept that they fear Europe. We know that someday, inevitably, Europe will play her role. That is why we tremble for Europe's fate today. That is why Europe is the sole concern of people like us – the most helpless of creatures.

It has all become quite clear to me. It had to be this way. From the moment my country was humiliated, debased, it was inevitable that I should go underground. It was an inexorable spiritual imperative. My whole life had been leading me to that imperative. Since childhood, I was taught to gaze upon open horizons, to love the human face, to respect human problems, to honour free attitudes. At the time of the Second World War, I was an adolescent; I lived through the Resistance; it left its moral mark on me. Only I didn't know at the time how deep that mark was. It has now become clear that it was to be the most vital inspiration force in my life. At last I can explain many things that happened to me between then and now. And so when the dictatorship came, I was already committed to the Resistance, without knowing it. I was carrying my own fate within me. Nothing happened by chance, by coincidence. Only the details were accidental. Diabolically accidental. But the general direction, the orientation, was rooted securely within me. Therefore it is not by mistake that I now find myself in prison. It is quite right that I should be here. What is horribly wrong is that this prison should exist at all.

I would like to write about a friendship I formed the autumn before last. I think it has some significance. It shows the solidarity that can be forged between unhappy creatures. I had been kept in solitary confinement for four months. I hadn't seen a soul throughout that period. Only uniforms – inquisitors and jailers. One day, I noticed three mosquitoes in my cell. They were struggling hard to resist the cold that was just beginning. In the daytime they slept on the wall. At night they would come buzzing over me. In the beginning, they exasperated me. But fortunately I soon understood. I too was struggling hard to live through the cold spell. What were they asking from me? Something unimportant. A drop of blood – it would save them. I couldn't refuse. At nightfall I would bare my arm and wait for them. After some days they got used to me and they were no longer afraid. They would come to me quite naturally, openly. This trust is something I owe them. Thanks to them, the world was no longer merely an inquisition chamber. Then one day I was transferred to another prison. I never saw my mosquitoes again. This is how you are deprived of the presence of your friends in the arbitrary world of prisons. But you go on thinking of them, often.

During the months when I was being interrogated, alone before those men with the multiple eyes of a spider – and the instincts of a spider

– one night a policeman on guard smiled at me. At that moment, the policeman was all men to me. Four months later, when the representative of the International Red Cross walked into my cell, once again I saw all men in his friendly face. When one day they finally put me in a cell with another prisoner and he began to talk to me about the thing he loved most in life – sailing and fishing boats – this man too was all men to me. It is true, then, that there are situations in which each one of us represents all mankind. And it is the same with these papers: I have entrusted them to a poor Italian prisoner who has just been released and who was willing to try to smuggle them out for me. Through him I hope they will eventually reach you. That man again is all men to me. But I think it is time I finished. I have raised my hand, made a sign. And so we exist. We over here in prison, and you out there who agree with us. So: *Freedom my love.*

Spring 1972

STEPHEN SPENDER

With concern for those not free

Stephen Spender, close friend of Auden and Christopher Isherwood, and to Isaiah Berlin 'the most genuine, least arranged human being I have ever known', gave his life to poetry, friendship and the cause of freedom, especially the writer's freedom to write and speak as the spirit moved. In the first issue of Index he described the founding of the magazine in response to an appeal from Soviet writers for help and solidarity in their struggles against injustice and censorship.

It may be that the year 1968 will prove to have been a turning-point in the development of intellectual freedom. This may be true in spite of discouraging reports since then from Russia, Czechoslovakia, Greece, Spain, Portugal, Brazil, South Africa, and certain 'new' countries in Africa, which sometimes make it seem as though we were moving into a period of reaction and repression.

In suggesting that 1968 was a turning-point, I am not thinking of the sensational events of that year of protests, demonstrations, and barricades. More significant than these were several appeals from writers, scientists and scholars in Eastern Europe to colleagues in the West. Some of these were connected with trials like those of Daniel and Sinyavsky. They were appeals against injustice to a court of world opinion. Important as these were, they were by no means unprecedented. But there were also letters written by individual intellectuals and writers to colleagues abroad. This was perhaps a new development, which has more recently been taken up by writers in Greece and in South Africa. The Russian writers seemed to take it for granted that in spite of the ideological conditioning of the society in which they live, there is nevertheless an international community of scientists, writers and scholars thinking about the same problems and applying to them the same human values. These intellectuals regard certain guarantees of freedom as essential if they are to develop their ideas fruitfully. It is as though they take it for granted that freedom of intellect and imagination transcends the 'bourgeois' or 'proletarian' social context.

Freedom, for them, consists primarily of conditions which make exchange of ideas and truthfully recorded experiences of life possible. Surprisingly, it was sometimes very young people (precisely those whom one might have expected to be most brainwashed) who wrote in this spirit. For example, there was the letter (published in *The Times* of 17 January 1970) of Alexander Daniel, the eighteen-year-old son of the Soviet writer Yuli Daniel, to Graham Greene, in which the young man described the trial of his father, who had been sent to a labour camp. Alexander Daniel's letter was a protest against procedures which would have seemed equally inhuman under any law. It was above all written in the name of decency and morality bound to no ideology, and it was written on the assumption that people can talk across frontiers of dictatorship and democracy – East and West – and address one another as human beings; ask one another questions to which answers can be given, in which questioner and answerer are not addressing one another as communist and non-communist but simply as human beings. 'What is it that I want of you Mr Greene? I don't know what you can do nor what you will want to do, neither do I know in general what can be done in this predicament.' The answer to the appeal is already implicit in these uncertain questionings. That Mr Greene should listen was the answer, and although there was nothing that he could do, to publish Alexander Daniel's letter was already a form of action.

Essentially Alexander Daniel's appeal is the same as that put out in the summer of 1968 by members of the Faculty, and by students, of Charles University, after the Russian invasion of Prague, which was published in *Le Monde*. This asked that those outside Czechoslovakia should concern themselves with the fate of their Czechoslovak colleagues, keep themselves informed, follow what was happening to them. The request conveys the idea that there are or there should be international values which are those of the university. For a moment, in the summer of 1968, Czechoslovak intellectuals seem to have been buoyed up by the hope that their academic colleagues would feel that what was happening to Charles University was also happening to Oxford and Cambridge and London, Paris and Harvard and Chicago. Indeed, qualitatively and quantitatively, it was happening to every university and in every place where there is a life of the intellect. For contemporary civilization, dependent on the minds of a few thousand people living all over the world, is a sum. And the subtraction of the numbers of those concerned with it in one country is a loss to the whole world, like the loss of some rare species, an asset to the whole world, in some particular place.

One writer – now packed away in a Russian labour camp – did have a positive idea of the ways in which colleagues in the countries of comparative freedom could help those in the lands of censorship and repression. He wrote to an English writer asking him whether it might not be possible to form an organization in England of intellectuals who made it their business to publish information about what was happening to their censored, suppressed, and sometimes imprisoned colleagues. He insisted that such an organization should not concern itself only with writers in Russia and Eastern Europe but throughout the world. He thought that an attempt could also be made to obtain and publish censored works, together with the news about the writers of them.

The Times also published a letter from Pavel Litvinov, appealing directly and openly for the sustained concern of colleagues abroad. A few of us decided to answer this appeal, in a direct and personal way, by telegram. The text of this message is worth recording: 'We, a group of friends representing no organization, support your statement, admire your courage, think of you and will help in any way possible.' This was signed by Cecil Day-Lewis, Yehudi Menuhin, W. H. Auden, Henry Moore, Stephen Spender, A. J. Ayer, Bertrand Russell, Julian Huxley, Mary McCarthy, J. B. Priestley, Jacquetta Hawkes, Paul Scofield, Igor Stravinsky, Stuart Hampshire, Maurice Bowra and Sonia Orwell.

An organization called Writers and Scholars International has now been formed whose aims have much in common with the sentiments expressed in this telegram. WSI has a council, under the chairmanship of Lord Gardiner, whose members are David Astor, Louis Blom-Cooper, Victoria Brittain, Peter Calvocoressi, Edward Crankshaw, Stuart Hampshire, Elizabeth Longford, Roland Penrose, Peter Reddaway, Mrs J. Edward Sieff, Stephen Spender and Zbynek Zeman, and the director, Michael Scammell. So far the tasks of this committee have been those

41

of a working party assembled for the purpose of launching the organization.

The main activity of WSI will be to publish a journal called *Index*, edited by Michael Scammell, which will (to quote its stated aims) 'record and analyse all forms of inroads into freedom of expression and examine the censorship situation in individual countries and in relation to various constitutions and legal codes. Examples of censored material (poetry, prose, articles) as well as the results of its findings will be published in the journal'.

Obviously there is the risk of a magazine of this kind becoming a bulletin of frustration. However, the material by writers which is censored in Eastern Europe, Greece, South Africa and other countries is among the most exciting that is being written today. Moreover, the question of censorship has become a matter of impassioned debate; and it is one which does not only concern totalitarian societies. There are problems of censorship in England, the United States, and France, for example. There is the question whether it is not right for certain works to be censored or at any rate limited to a defined readership. The problem of censorship is part of larger ones about the use and abuse of freedom.

The founders of WSI are well aware that there are other organizations doing parallel work with some of whom they are already cooperating. For example, there is Amnesty International, which, among other activities, conducts inquiries into abuses of the Declaration of Human Rights and international law, and which organizes legal aid for victims of political persecution; there is the PEN Club which has given much support to political exiles, and whose International Congresses provide models of free discussion between writers from all over the world, including those where there are dictatorships.

The role of WSI will be to study the situation of those who are silenced in their own countries and to make their circumstances known in the world community to which they spiritually belong. I think that doing this is not just an act of charity. It is a way of facilitating and extending an international consciousness, traversing political boundaries, which is already coming into being, though it is much hindered by dictatorships, censorship and acts of persecution. The world is moving in two directions: one is towards the narrowing of distances through travel, increasing interchange between scientists (who take a world view of problems such as the exploration of space, ecology, population): the other is towards the shutting down of frontiers, the ever more jealous surveillance by governments and police of individual freedom. The opposites are fear and openness; and in being concerned with the situation of those who are deprived of their freedoms one is taking the side of openness.

The writers and scholars whom one relies on to support WSI would obviously include those at universities. For the universities represent the developing international consciousness which depends so much on the free interchange of people, and of ideas. It is therefore right and normal and healthy that members of universities should be concerned with what happens wherever freedom of expression is attacked.

Naturally WSI's role in this sphere cannot be all-embracing. As an educational trust its aim will be to study those manifestations of state or governmental power that seek to frustrate or suppress the right to free expression and to educate the public on the situation in the world today. But if I were to express the feelings that led me to support this venture and my motives for acting in this way I would put it somewhat as follows.

Our need today is for organs of consciousness that could help us to know and to care about other members of the same intellectual community, much as Christians once were vigilant for other Christians in times of religious persecution. The word 'freedom' is of course an abstraction, and people today are probably weary of it. The simple point I would like to make is that at this moment, in many countries, there are writers and scholars interested in ideas, or in describing life exactly as they see it, who are sent to labour camps and prisons; or who are blackmailed by threats of what may happen to themselves or their families; or who are harassed by not being allowed to go abroad and meet like-minded people; or who are simply reduced to silence by various forms of censorship. Each reader of this article might say to himself: 'On the most elementary level of consideration, I might suffer similar deprivations; so I should alleviate their lot, which might easily be my own. More important, if a writer whose works are banned wishes to be published, and if I am in a position to help him to be published, then to refuse to give help is for me to support the censorship. If I complacently accept the idea that freedom is something that happens in some places and is prevented in others, I am implying that freedom is a matter of accident, or privilege, occurring – if I happen to have it – at the place where I live. This attitude to freedom really undermines it, for it is to support the views of those who hold freedom to be a luxury enjoyed by bourgeois individualists. Therefore if I consider myself not just in my role of lucky or unlucky person but as an instrument of consciousness, the writer or scholar deprived of freedom is also an instrument of consciousness, and through the prohibition imposed on him my freedom is also prohibited.'

The basis of the appeal made by Writers and Scholars International is that it is a beginning and that its foundation is itself in partial answer to an appeal: which is from those who are censored, banned or imprisoned to consider their case as our own.

Spring 1972

NATALYA GORBANEVSKAYA

And you, candle

Natalya Gorbanevskaya's poems appeared in *samizdat* in four collections during the 1960s which established her reputation as one of the most important
Russian poets since Akhmatova. After demonstrating in Red Square against
the invasion of Czechoslovakia in 1968 she was arrested and committed to
a psychiatric asylum in Kazan. Released in 1972, she emigrated with her
children in December 1975 to Paris, where she has lived since.

And you, candle, determined I
must be a holder for your eyes, your wax,
that in the pitch-black everlasting night
your trembling flame alone should gaze into the dark.

But the sill is a frontier to candlelight,
the curtain's swaying is your Boreas,
and where is the fire-worshipper more secure
than in November behind double windows.

I am not a flame, not a candle, but a light,
I am a fire-fly in the damp tangled
grass. The grass flows swiftly after me
and the woodland beast homes on me in silence:

the faintest of brightening fire-flies,
the brightest of failing fire-flies,
by whose light the night skies are not pierced,
yet the stars in their courses are guided.

Translated by Daniel Weissbort

Spring 1972

HEBERTO PADILLA

Poems

Heberto Padilla, once an eloquent supporter of the Cuban revolution, came increasingly under criticism during the 1960s for the questioning and sceptical tone of his poetry. Imprisoned in 1970, he and some of his colleagues made a public act of self-criticism so plainly under duress that Sartre, Moravia and other left-wing intellectuals broke with the Castro regime. He remained in Cuba until 1980, when he was allowed to emigrate to the United States.

Instructions on how to enter a new society

One: be an optimist.
Two: be discreet, correct, obedient.
(Do well at sports — all of them.)
And, most of all, move
like all the other members:
one step forward, and
one (or two) steps back:
but never stop cheering.

Out of the game

To the Greek poet Yannis Ritsos, in jail

Get rid of the poet!
He's out of place here.
Won't join in the game.
Not interested.
Won't make his message clear.
Doesn't even notice miracles.
Spends all day thinking.
Always got something to moan about.

Get him out!
Get the killjoy out.
That summertime depressive in the black glasses
under the new sun.
He always had a *penchant*
for great events and the noble catastrophes
of time without history.

What's more – he's out of date.

He only likes old Louis Armstrong.
Can only hum Pete Seeger or 'La Guantanamera'
under his breath.

But no one can get him to open his mouth (or smile)
when the show starts
and clowns hop about the stage;
when cockatoos mix fear and love
and the stage creaks, metals thunder.
and whips too
and they all jump
and bow
and step back
and smile
and their mouths gape

'Of course'
'Naturally, of course'
'OBVIOUSLY'. . .

And all dance so nicely
As they ought.

Get shot of that guy.
He's out of place.

Translated by John Butt

Summer 1972

ALEXANDER SOLZHENITSYN

'God keep me from going mad'

Alexander Solzhenitsyn's fortitude and titanic labours in documenting the scale and enormity of the Soviet prison camp system made an incomparable contribution to resistance to the Stalinist tyranny and the writing of modern history, as well as to Russian literature. It was one of the tragedies of the post-Soviet period that on his return to Russia after years in exile, his stern Slavophilism seemed out of date and irrelevant to much of the younger generation enjoying the fruits of capitalism, or grappling with the appalling social problems that came with its return. The following passage was the first ever publication in English of verse by Solzhenitsyn, and is an excerpt from a longer autobiographical poem composed in 1950-53 while he was serving a sentence in a labour camp in north Kazakhstan.

There never was, nor will be, a world of brightness!
A frozen footcloth is the scarf that binds my face.
Fights over porridge, the ganger's constant griping
And day follows day follows day, and no end to this dreary fate.
. . . .

My feeble pick strikes sparks from the frozen earth.
And the sun stares down unblinking from the sky.
But the world is here! And will be! The daily round
Suffices. But man is not to be prisoned in the day.
To write! To write now, without delay,
Not in heated wrath, but with cool and clear understanding.
The millstones of my thoughts can hardly turn,
Too rare the flicker of light in my aching soul.
Yes, tight is the circle around us tautly drawn,
But my verses will burst their bonds and freely roam
And I can guard, perhaps, beyond their reach,
In rhythmic harmony this hard-won gift of speech.

And then they can grope my body in vain –
'Here I am. All yours. Look hard. Not a line . . .
Our indestructible memory, by wonder divine,
Is beyond the reach of your butcher's hands!'

My labour of love! Year after year with me you will grow,
Year after year you will tread the prisoner's path.
The day will come when you warm not me alone,
Nor me alone embrace with a shiver of wrath,
Let the stanzas throb – but no whisper let slip,
Let them hammer away – not a twitch of the lip,
Let your eyes not gleam in another's presence
And let no-one see, let no-one see
You put pencil to paper.
From every corner I am stalked by prison –
God keep me from going mad!*

I do not write my verses for idle pleasure,
Nor from a sense of energy to burn.
Nor out of mischief, to evade their searches,
Do I carry them past my captors in my brain.
The free flow of my verse is dearly bought,
I have paid a cruel price for my poet's rights:
The barren sacrifice of all her youth
And ten cold solitary years for my wife –

The unuttered cries of children still unborn,
My mother's death, toiling in gaunt starvation,
The madness of prison cells, midnight interrogations.
Autumn's sticky red clay in an opencast mine,
The secret, slow and silent erosive force
Of winters laying bricks, of summers feeding the furnace –
Oh, if this were but the sum of the price paid for my verse!
But those others paid the price with their lives,
Immured in the silence of Solovki, drowned in thunder of waves,
Or shot without trial in Vorkuta's polar night.

* The first line of a poem by Pushkin.

Love and warmth and their executed cries
Have combined in my breast to carve
The receptive metre of this sorrowful tale,
These few poor thousand incapacious lines.
Oh, hopeless labour! Can you really pay the price?
Do you think to redeem the pledge with a single life?
For what an age has my country been so poor
In women's happy laughter, so very rich
In poets' lamentations!
Verse verse – for all that we have lost,
A drop of scented resin in the razed forest!
But this is all I live for! On its wings
I transport my feeble body through prison walls
And one day, in distant exile dim,
Biding my time, I will free my tortured memory from its thrall:
On paper, birchbark, in a blackened bottle rolled,
I will consign my tale to the forest leaves.
Or to a drift of shifting snow.

But what if beforehand they give me poisoned bread?
Or if darkness beclouds my mind at last?
Oh, let me die there! Let it not be here!
God keep me from going mad!

Translated by Michael Scammell

Summer 1972

MICHAEL SCAMMELL

Interview with Joseph Brodsky

Joseph Brodsky (1940-1996), heir to the great tradition of modernism in Russian poetry and protégé of Anna Akhmatova, was refused all recognition by Soviet officialdom, sentenced to hard labour on a charge of 'parasitism', and finally expelled from the Soviet Union in 1972. He was awarded the Nobel Prize for literature in 1987. On his way to a post at the University of Michigan, he gave this characteristically candid interview to the critic, translator and founding editor of *Index*, Michael Scammell.

Michael Scammell: Joseph, when did you start writing poetry?

Joseph Brodsky: When I was 18.

MS: Was your work ever published in the Soviet Union?

JB: Yes, when I was 26 I had two poems published in the literary almanac, *Young Leningrad*. That was in 1966.

MS: And how many poems have you had published since then in the Soviet Union?

JB: Two.

MS: When did it become clear to you that your poems were not going to be published generally in the Soviet Union and what was the effect of this realization upon you?

JB: I must say that it was never really clear to me. I always thought that they would be published one day and so this idea has had no effect on me at all – not for the last ten years or so, at any rate.

MS: Why do you think that your poems were not published while you were in the Soviet Union?

JB: It is difficult to say. Maybe because they were too aggressive to begin with and then later my name became a sort of taboo, it was a forbidden word.

MS: What sort of a taboo?

JB: Well, I was someone who had been to prison and so on and so forth.

MS: Why do you think they sent you to prison?

JB: I don't really know. In any case that seems to me, if you don't mind my saying so, a typically western approach to the problem: every event has to have a cause and every phenomenon has to have something standing behind it. It is very complex. Sometimes there is a cause, perhaps. But as to why they put me in prison, all I can do is repeat to you the items in the indictment. My own answer perhaps won't satisfy you, but it is very simple. A man who sets out to create his own independent world within himself is bound sooner or later to become a foreign body in society and then he becomes subject to all the physical laws of pressure, compression and extrusion.

MS: Why do you think that you were released so quickly?

JB: I don't know, I honestly don't know. Just as I have no idea why I was sent to prison in the first place. In general I am very confused about these things, the point is that I always tried to be — and was — a separate private person. I suppose it was just that my life somehow acquired an external political dimension. In one sense, I think, it was done to separate me from my audience. That, I am afraid, is the best answer I can find.

MS: How did trial and prison affect your work?

JB: You know, I think it was even good for me, because the two years I spent in the country were from my point of view one of the best times of my life. I did more work then than at any other time. During the day I had to do physical work, but since it was agricultural labour, it wasn't like in a factory and there were lots of periods of rest when we had nothing to do.

MS: You came out of prison in 1965. Did you return to being a private person and have you been working just on your own ever since that time?

JB: Oh no. I worked as a translator. I am a professional translator and I was a member of the Translators' Group at the Leningrad Writers' Union. That is how I earned my living.

MS: And in the meantime your poetry began to be distributed in *samizdat*?

JB: Well, yes, but the point is that *samizdat* is an extremely flexible concept. If by *samizdat* you mean the passing of manuscripts from hand to hand and the copying of them on typewriters in a systematic way, then my poems started to circulate before *samizdat* began. Someone who liked them would simply copy them and take them away to read, and then someone else would borrow them from that person. *Samizdat* came into being only about four or five years ago.

MS: But what about student *samizdat* journals such as *Phoenix* and *Syntax*? They printed your verse, didn't they?

JB: Well, yes and no. It would be stretching a point considerably to call them 'journals'. *Syntax* ran to only about 100 copies in all, and there may even have been less. It was difficult to find people to do the work in those days. In any case I don't think *Phoenix* published me. The *Syntax* did, I can remember that very well.

MS: You were put on trial in 1964 and you were one of the first people in the Soviet Union to be tried specifically as a writer. You were followed by Sinyavsky and Daniel and then, on another plane, Pasternak and Solzhenitsyn have had their difficulties. In contrast to them, however, you have never taken up a position of overt opposition and have never publicly, so far as I know, criticized the authorities, literary or otherwise, in the way that, say, even Pasternak did. What is your attitude to people who take a stand and why have you personally never done so yourself?

JB: It is all very simple, really. The point is that the person who seriously devotes himself to some sort of work – and in my case *belles lettres* – has in any case plenty of problems and difficulties that arise from the work itself, for instance doubts, fears and worries, and this in itself taxes the brain pretty powerfully. And then again I must say that any kind of civic activity simply bores me to death. While the brain is thinking in political terms and thinks of itself as getting somewhere, it is all very interesting, attractive and exciting, and everything seems fine. But when these thoughts reach their logical conclusion, that is when they result in some sort of action, then they give rise to a terrible sense of disillusionment, and then the whole thing is boring.

MS: But do you think that, say, the position that Solzhenitsyn has taken up vis-à-vis the authorities, and the literary authorities, in particular, has any sort of positive value, or do you regard it as a distraction from the writer's true work?

JB: In order to answer that question, of course, I would have to look at things from Solzhenitsyn's point of view, something I can't and don't intend to do. From my point of view, I think it would be better if he simply got on with writing his own works instead of spending time on these other activities. On the other hand, it does seem to have some sort of positive value for him and indeed a general value. But I think that for the writer who first of all concerns himself with his own work, the deeper he plunges into it, the greater will be the consequences – literary, aesthetic and of course political as well.

MS: Yes, but is this possible? What is your attitude to such writers as Okudzhava, Viktor Nekrasov, Voinovich and Maximov, who started out by not expressing any sort of open opposition but were forced by their work, or rather by the official attitude to their work, to take up more extreme positions? Is it possible at all to be a true writer in the Soviet Union without being forced into such a position?

JB: I think it is, although it is true that circumstances there do force you more or less to take up such a position. But from my point of view this is extremely unfortunate, first of all because the problems you are then forced to occupy yourself with and the position you are forced to take up by the situation – all these, that is to say any protest you make and the level of that protest, are determined by the nature, the quality and the level of what it is you are protesting against. If you are faced with an idiot and you say to him 'you are an idiot', well, maybe it is fun but it is not much else . . .

MS: Yes, of course, but let us take the examples of Voinovich and Maximov. They both wrote novels that they wanted to publish in the Soviet Union, but publication was refused. Nobody knows how these novels subsequently found their way to the West, but they did arrive there and then attempts were made to force these writers to denounce their publication over here. On the one hand they had not wished to go into open opposition to the authorities, but on the other hand they didn't want to make statements that were false and untrue. Don't you find that a difficult position for a writer to be in?

JB: Yes, it is a rotten position to be in. But if you have the courage to write something, then you have to have the courage to stick up for it.

MS: And you can find yourself in such a position against your will?

JB: Yes, you can find yourself in such a position without the least intent or desire. It is disgusting, of course, since the writer finds himself in a weird trap: he has a concept of life, he has a background and an upbringing and a point of view and his own ideas about life, all of which are what started him writing in the first place. But the situation develops in such a way that he finds himself forced to occupy himself with completely different activities. It is stupid and degrading; in my opinion it is a complete nonsense when the writer is forced to become a political activist.

MS: You said on BBC television that in your opinion nothing could be done in the West to help Soviet writers. What did you have in mind when you said that?

JB: I had a number of things in mind. In the first place you can't help a writer to write, can you? You can't help him to live, nor can you help him to die, and so on. A man has to do everything for himself. Everyone does this naturally. On top of this, literary work, like all work in the arts, is a very individual and lonely business. There is nothing you can do about this. All you can do is to help people get published. But I am not sure how helpful this is. I suppose it gives one a pleasant sensation, a sense of not being without hope: up or down, you still exist and you still haven't perished. It gives a certain psychological relief to a man living in rather uncomfortable circumstances. But here again you get all sorts of problems arising, because all forms of comfort are in a way a sort of escapism.

MS: Don't you think that it was a great help to you to have your verse published and to know that you had a public? For example, your poems were first read in the West by Russian literature specialists, students and so on, then were translated into other languages. Did this not influence your writing in the Soviet Union?

JB: In my opinion it had no effect at all. Just as it equally had no effect before it happened, that is to say there was a time when I was writing verses that few read and nobody translated – of course they also weren't very good, which is something I realize now. But still, we are not talking about whether the verses are good or bad, but about what happens to them after they are written. What interested me most of all, and still does, is the process of writing itself. Nothing influenced this, and what is more, I tried to cut myself off and get away from anything that might influence me. I can quite clearly remember my reaction to my first book, which was published in Russian in New York. I had a sensation of something completely ridiculous having happened. I couldn't grasp what had happened or what this book was exactly.

MS: Didn't this book and the support it represented help you to maintain your position of independence? Isn't it possible that otherwise you would have been accused of parasitism again?

JB: It is very difficult to form an opinion about something that didn't happen. Maybe it did help in some way, but I must confess that I doubt it very much. You see, I am not representative in any way, I cannot stand for anything or anybody except myself.

MS: But don't you think that your reputation and the knowledge of your work helped you in coming to the West?

JB: Certainly it had a rôle to play and it did influence the situation as a whole. But really the question ought to be turned around a bit: is it a good thing that I have come to the West? If it is, then it is fair to use the verb 'helped'. If not, we will have to phrase it in quite a different way.

Autumn/Winter 1972

NADINE GORDIMER

A writer's freedom

Nadine Gordimer, the 1991 Nobel laureate for novels and stories that illuminated the darkness of apartheid and the dilemmas and betrayals of South Africa's white liberal middle-class, has long been a supporter of Index and a regular contributor to its pages.

What is a writer's freedom?

To me it is his right to maintain and publish to the world a deep, intense, private view of the situation in which he finds his society. If he is to work as well as he can, he must take, and be granted, freedom from the public conformity of political interpretation, morals and tastes.

Living when we do, where we do, as we do, 'freedom' leaps to mind as a political concept exclusively – and when people think of freedom for writers they visualize at once the great mound of burnt, banned and proscribed books our civilization has piled up; a pyre to which our own country has added and is adding its contribution. The right to be left alone to write what one pleases is not an academic issue to those of us who live and work in South Africa. The private view always has been and always will be a source of fear and anger to proponents of a way of life, such as the white man's in South Africa, that does not bear looking at except in the light of a special self-justificatory doctrine.

All that the writer can do, as a writer, is to go on writing the truth *as he sees* it. That is what I mean by his 'private view' of events, whether they be the great public ones of wars and revolutions, or the individual and intimate ones of daily, personal life.

As to the fate of his books – there comes a time in the history of certain countries when the feelings of their writers are best expressed in this poem, written within the lifetime of many of us, by Bertholt Brecht:

> When the Regime ordered that books with dangerous teachings
> Should be publicly burnt and everywhere
> Oxen were forced to draw carts full of books
> To the funeral pyre,
> An exiled poet,
> One of the best,
> Discovered with fury when he studied the list
> Of the burned, that his books
> Had been forgotten. He rushed to his writing table
> On wings of anger and wrote a letter to those in power.
> Burn me, he wrote with hurrying pen, burn me!
> Do not treat me in this fashion. Don't leave me out.
> Have I not
> Always spoken the truth in my books? And now
> You treat me like a liar! I order you:
> Burn me!

Not a very good poem, even if one makes allowance for the loss in translation from the German original; nevertheless, so far as South African writers are concerned, we can understand the desperate sentiments expressed while still putting up the fight to have our books read rather than burnt.

Bannings and banishments are terrible known hazards a writer must face, and many have faced, if the writer belongs where freedom of expression, among other freedoms, is withheld, but sometimes creativity is frozen rather than destroyed. A Thomas Mann survives exile to write a Dr Faustus; a Pasternak smuggles Dr Zhivago out of a ten-year silence; a Solzhenitsyn emerges with his terrible world intact in the map of The Gulag Archipelago; nearer our home continent: a Chinua Achebe, writing from America, does not trim his prose to please a Nigerian regime under which he cannot live; a Dennis Brutus grows in reputation abroad while his poetry remains forbidden at home; and a Breyten Breytenbach, after accepting the special dispensation from racialist law which allowed him to visit his home country with a wife who is not white, no doubt has to accept the equally curious circumstance that his publisher would not publish the book he was to write about the visit, since it was sure to be banned.*

Through all these vicissitudes, real writers go on writing the truth as they see it. And they do not agree to censor themselves . . . You can burn the books, but the integrity of creative artists is not incarnate on paper any more than on canvas – it survives so long as the artist himself cannot be persuaded, cajoled or frightened into betraying it.

All this, hard though it is to live, is the part of the writer's fight for freedom the world finds easiest to understand.

There is another threat to that freedom, in any country where political freedom is withheld. It is a more insidious one, and one of which fewer people will be aware. It's a threat which comes from the very strength of the writer's opposition to repression of political freedom. That other, paradoxically wider, composite freedom – the freedom of his private view of life, may be threatened by the very awareness of what is expected of him. And often what is expected of him is conformity to an orthodoxy of opposition.

There will be those who regard him as their mouth-piece; people whose ideals, as a human being, he shares, and whose cause, as a human being, is his own. They may be those whose suffering is his own. His identification with, admiration for, and loyalty to these set up a state of conflict within him. His integrity as a human being demands the sacrifice of everything to the struggle put up on the side of free men. His integrity as a writer goes the moment he begins to write what he ought to write.

This is – whether all admit it or not – and will continue to be a particular problem for black writers in South Africa. For them, it extends even to an orthodoxy of vocabulary: the jargon of struggle, derived internationally, is right and adequate for the public platform, the news-letter, the statement from the dock; it is not adequate, it is not deep enough, wide enough, flexible enough, cutting enough, fresh enough

---

* The Afrikaans poet Breyten Breytenbach returned to South Africa under a false name in August 1975 after years of self-imposed exile in Paris. Arrested shortly after his arrival he was sentenced on 26 November to nine years' imprisonment, having pleaded guilty to 22 charges under the Terrorism and Suppression of Communism Acts.

for the vocabulary of the poet, the short story writer or the novelist.

Neither is it, as the claim will be made, 'a language of the people' in a situation where certainly it is very important that imaginative writing must not reach the elite only. The jargon of struggle lacks both the inventive pragmatism and the poetry of common speech – those qualities the writer faces the challenge to capture and explore imaginatively, expressing as they do the soul and identity of a people as no thousandth-hand 'noble evocation' of clichés ever could.

The black writer needs his freedom to assert that the idiom of Chatsworth, Dimbaza, Soweto* is no less a vehicle for the expression of pride, self-respect, suffering, anger – or anything else in the spectrum of thought and emotion – than the language of Watts or Harlem.

The fact is, even on the side of the angels, a writer has to reserve the right to tell the truth as he sees it, in his own words, without being accused of letting the side down. For as Philip Toynbee has written, 'the writer's gift to the reader is not social zest or moral improvement or love of country, but an enlargement of the reader's apprehension'.

This is the writer's unique contribution to social change. He needs to be left alone, by brothers as well as enemies, to make this gift. And he must make it even against his own inclination.

I need hardly add this does not mean he retreats to an ivory tower. The gift cannot be made from any such place. The other day, Jean-Paul Sartre gave the following definition of the writer's responsibility to his society as an intellectual, after himself having occupied such a position in France for the best part of 70 years: 'He is someone who is faithful to a political and social body but never stops contesting it. Of course, a contradiction may arise between his fidelity and his *contestation*, but that's a fruitful contradiction. If there's fidelity without *contestation*, that's no good: one is no longer a free man.'

When a writer claims these kinds of freedom for himself, he begins to understand the real magnitude of his struggle. It is not a new problem and of all the writers who have had to face it, I don't think anyone has seen it more clearly or dealt with it with such uncompromising

* Chatsworth and Soweto are respectively Indian and African ghettos. Dimbaza is the notorious 'resettlement area' for Africans which is the subject of the film *Last Grave at Dimbaza*.

honesty as the great nineteenth-century Russian, Ivan Turgenev. Turgenev had an immense reputation as a progressive writer. He was closely
connected with the progressive movement in Tzarist Russia and particularly with its more revolutionary wing headed by the critic Belinsky
and afterwards by the poet Nekrasov. With his sketches and stories,
people said that Turgenev was continuing the work Gogol had begun
of awakening the conscience of the educated classes in Russia to the
evils of a political regime based on serfdom.

But his friends, admirers and fellow progressives stopped short, in
their understanding of his genius, of the very thing that made him one
– his scrupulous reserve of the writer's freedom to reproduce truth and
the reality of life, even if this truth does not coincide with his own
sympathies.

When his greatest novel, *Fathers and Sons*, was published in 1862, he
was attacked not only by the right for pandering to the revolutionary
nihilists, but far more bitterly by the left, the younger generation
themselves, of whom his chief character in the novel, Bazarov, was
both prototype and apotheosis. The radicals and liberals, among whom
Turgenev himself belonged, lambasted him as a traitor because Bazarov
was presented with all the faults and contradictions that Turgenev saw
in his own type, in himself, so to speak, and whom he created as he
did because – in his own words – 'in the given case, life happened to
be like that'.

The attacks were renewed after the publication of another novel,
Smoke, and Turgenev decided to write a series of autobiographical remi-
niscences which would allow him to reply to his critics by explaining
his views on the art of writing, the place of the writer in society, and
what the writer's attitude to the controversial problems of his day
should be. The result was a series of unpretentious essays that make
up a remarkable testament to a writer's creed. Dealing particularly with
Bazarov and *Fathers and Sons*, he writes of his critics,

> . . . generally speaking they have not got quite the right idea of
> what is taking place in the mind of a writer or what exactly his
> joys and sorrows, his aims, successes and failures are. They do
> not, for instance, even suspect the pleasure which Gogol mentions
> and which consists of castigating oneself and one's faults in the

imaginary characters one depicts; they are quite sure that all a writer does is to 'develop his ideas' . . . Let me illustrate my meaning by a small example. I am an inveterate and incorrigible Westerner. I have never concealed it and I am not concealing it now. And yet in spite of that it has given me great pleasure to show up in the person of Panshin (a character in *A House of Gentlefolk*) all the common and vulgar sides of the Westerners: I made the Slavophil Lavretsky 'crush him utterly'. Why did I do it, I who consider the Slavophil doctrine false and futile? Because, in the given case, life, according to my ideas, *happened to be like that*, and what I wanted above all was to be sincere and truthful.

In depicting Bazarov's personality, I excluded everything artistic from the range of his sympathies, I made him express himself in harsh and unceremonious tones, not out of an absurd desire to insult the younger generation, but simply as a result of my observations of people like him . . . My personal predilections had nothing to do with it. But I expect many of my readers will be surprised if I tell them that with the exception of Bazarov's views on art, I share almost all his convictions.

And in another essay, Turgenev sums up: 'The life that surrounds him [the writer] provides him with the content of his works; he is its *concentrated reflection*; but he is as incapable of writing a panegyric as a lampoon . . . When all is said and done – that is beneath him. Only those who can do no better submit to a given theme or carry out a programme.'

These conditions about which I have been talking are the special, though common ones of writers beleaguered in the time of the bomb and the colour-bar, as they were in the time of the jack-boot and rubber truncheon, and, no doubt, back through the ages whose shameful symbols keep tally of oppression in the skeleton cupboard of our civilizations.

Other conditions, more transient, less violent, affect the freedom of a writer's mind.

What about literary fashion, for example? What about the cycle of the innovator, the imitators, the debasers, and then the bringing forth of an innovator again? A writer must not be made too conscious of literary fashion, any more than he must allow himself to be inhibited by the mandarins, if he is to get on with work that is his own. I say 'made conscious' because literary fashion is a part of his working conditions; he can make the choice of rejecting it, but he cannot choose whether it is urged upon him or not by publishers and readers, who do not let him forget he has to eat.

That rare marvel, an innovator, should be received with shock and excitement. And his impact may set off people in new directions of their own. But the next innovator rarely, I would almost say never comes from his imitators, those who create a fashion in his image. Not all worthwhile writing is an innovation, but I believe it always comes from an individual vision, privately pursued. The pursuit may stem from a tradition, but a tradition implies a choice of influence, whereas a fashion makes the influence of the moment the only one for all who are contemporary to it.

A writer needs all these kinds of freedom, built on the basic one of freedom from censorship. He does not ask for shelter from living, but for exposure to it without possibility of evasion. He is fiercely engaged with life on his own terms, and ought to be left to it, if anything is to come of the struggle. Any government, any society – any vision of a future society – that has respect for its writers must set them as free as possible to write in their own various ways, in their own choices of form and language, and according to their own discovery of truth.

Again, Turgenev expresses this best: 'Without freedom in the widest sense of the word – in relation to oneself . . . indeed, to one's people and one's history, a true artist is unthinkable; without that air, it is impossible to breathe.'

And I add my last word: in that air alone, commitment and creative freedom become one.

Summer 1976

LUDVÍK VACULÍK

A cup of coffee with my interrogator

Ludvík Vaculík, the wry Moravian novelist and essayist, more even than Dubček or Havel, was the voice of the Czechoslovak people during the Prague Spring, not least in his '2,000 Words' manifesto whose blunt infringements of the norms of Communist political correctness so unnerved the Soviet leadership. This Svejkish piece is characteristic of the mocking sketches he later produced of life during the glum post-1968 counter-reformation in Prague.

Unless you have been through it yourself, you wouldn't believe how difficult it is to avoid replying to polite questions. Not only does it go against the grain not to reply, because of one's good upbringing, but it is also difficult to keep up because it is hard on the ears. A beginner finds it next to impossible. Worst of all, it doesn't make for good relations between the parties concerned, the rift thus created being often insurmountable. Which is what I mean to write about.

Undeterred by his lack of success, Lieut-Colonel Noga began anew each morning: 'Would you please get your papers ready, Blanička.' His secretary, Blanka, took out a clean sheet of paper, carbons and flimsies, put them in her typewriter and, fingers poised above the keyboard, turned her face towards her boss. He hesitated while he thought out his question, then he asked me, 'Would you care for a cup of coffee?' I decided to accept the coffee.

Lieut-Colonel Noga is a smallish man, well built, dark of skin and hair. Originally a factory worker, his behaviour and speech indicate that he has spent many years in a different environment. His Czech is correct, but there is something about his pronunciation which hints at another Slav language. This wretched detail made me, willy nilly, adopt a kind of coquetry one tends to employ when dealing with fellow-countrymen.*

* Like Vaculík himself, the interrogator comes from Moravia.

'All right, Mr Vaculík, you insist that your conduct isn't in breach of the law. Let's just suppose you're right,' he was fond of saying. Then he would add, 'Well then, why don't you tell me about it.'

'I'm sorry, Lieut-Colonel,' I would reply, 'but I really don't feel I want to go over all that again.'

'You don't feel you want to? What kind of talk is that? Why don't you say exactly what you mean – after all, this is your protocol: "I refuse to testify!"'

Mrs Blanka looked up at me, I nodded shamefacedly, and she typed the words.

'When will you return my things to me?' I asked, pointing at the two suitcases standing beside his desk.

'Don't confuse the issue. Next question – take this down, Blanička: What is your opinion . . . of the way the Western press . . . is misusing the whole affair . . . for its slanderous campaign against Czechoslovakia?'

I dictated my reply: 'I will answer this question as soon as I have had an opportunity to read what the Western press has to say on the subject.'

'You so-and-so!' he rebuked me in mock anger, left the room and came back with a whole pile of foreign newspapers, which he slammed on the desk in front of me.

I requested Mrs Blanka to record: 'When I say I want to read foreign newspapers, I mean when I can buy them at a news stand.'

In the course of that week of interrogations I was able to put any number of such impertinences into my statement. No one objected.

One evening there were just the two of us, as Mrs Blanka went home at four. He sat down on her stool, turned the roller in the typewriter, and said, 'Here we've been at it all day and we've got just seven pages. Not very much, is it?'

'There isn't going to be any more,' I replied.

'Oh really? There is, you know.'

'All right, tell me something about nocturnal interrogation.'

He cast an alarmed eye at his watch. 'Half past seven already! But that still doesn't make it night.'

'Either have me put in a cell or send me home. But first of all, take me to the toilet.'

'Oh no, we don't lock up witnesses. I will take you to the toilet, though. Have you got some paper?'

I hadn't any, and so he picked up two clean sheets, crumpled them obligingly and handed them to me. Then he waited outside the toilet. Seeing that we had been at it all day, those two sheets were scarcely sufficient.

Already on the second day it was clear to me that it was more of a siege than an interrogation. Once I had repeated my initial refusal, there was really nothing else for us to do. My Lieut-Colonel was in the habit of leaving the room for long periods at a time. As for Mrs Blanka, she found me a dreadful bore. On the first few days she tried to win me over.

'Why don't you want to testify? No one is punished for expressing his opinions. You ought to hear how we complain about the office canteen!'

'Yes, but just imagine that one day the canteen manager is given powers to have you all locked up.'

'Oh, but that's absurd!'

'Isn't it. And then imagine it happening on a nationwide scale.'

She shook her head at this, smiling like one who is amazed at a child's foolishness. Then she said, 'Here the law is being respected, you know. For instance, the prisoners have a right to exercise, and look!' She beckoned me to the window.

She was speaking the gospel truth: down there in the courtyard, in deep, concrete pens, I could see the prisoners, dressed in brown, circling round, talking and laughing.

Every lunchtime Lieut-Colonel Noga escorted me to a little waiting-room, furnished something like a club. There I would be given frank-furters. On my way I would encounter Václav Havel or Professor Patočka. Most of all, however, I bumped into Dr Jiří Hájek. A friendly young woman always asked us, in Slovak: 'Would you like a coffee after lunch?' A pleasant interlude.

'Today,' said Dr Hájek, 'I gave them a little lecture on why I thought the demand for Czechoslovakia's neutrality in August sixty-eight was a mistake.'

I was surprised. 'Do you mean to say you were *against* neutrality?'

It was his turn to be surprised. 'So you also thought I advocated it?'

'Everyone thinks so,' I told him. 'Why, only yesterday they were saying as much on TV.'

'But it simply isn't true,' he said, and with all the patience of thin men who wear thick lensed glasses gave me a little lecture on why he thought the demand for Czechoslovakia's neutrality in August sixty-eight had been a mistake.

Once Mrs Blanka had to leave us in order to have her flu injection, and the Lieut-Colonel and I were left on our own. He paced up and down the office, his hands behind his back, and I knew he was about to say something.

'Now the girl's gone, I'll tell you something man to man.' I pricked up my ears. 'Modern medicine, that is, psychology and sexology . . .' a few more paces, 'are agreed in the view . . .' a few more paces, 'that where a man and a woman are concerned . . .' he stopped abruptly in front of me, 'anything goes.'

'Mm,' I thought cautiously. He gave me a smile and wagged a good-humoured finger at me. 'But you, you really deserve a thrashing.'

In these circumstances it is best to keep quiet and try to divine what the man is leading up to. I am afraid I failed to divine it.

He took two red apples from his briefcase and gave me one. I asked what sort it was, and he told me, but I have since forgotten it. What interested me was that the apples came from a tree that was only five years old and he had several kilos of them. And I was touched by his giving me one. So I told him what sort of apple-trees I had out at Dobřichovice. 'If I have to come back here again,' I said, 'and if I'm allowed to go there on Sunday, I'll bring you some.'

'Why shouldn't you be allowed?' he asked.

Next day, instead of my briefcase I took a big shopping bag and filled it with everything I had heard a detainee ought to have.

'You've brought a different bag,' he said at once.

'That's right. Today I either leave here a free citizen who doesn't get hauled in every day, or you must allocate me a cell.'

He was taken aback. 'Why, has anything happened?'

'I'll tell you what's happened. Here you are politeness itself, and out there in the street brutalities are taking place. Do you know what's happened to the Kohouts?'*

'I've heard something . . .'

'And so you can keep your politeness. And let me tell you something I haven't told you before: when they brought me in for the first time, Martinovsky told me I was under arrest, took away my house keys and said they were going to carry out a search. What can you tell me about that?'

'He said you were under arrest and took your keys?'

'That's right.'

'Well, I wouldn't consider that proper.'

'In that case, give me back my things.'

He sat down behind his desk, saying nothing and with an annoyed expression on his face. Mrs Blanka looked shattered. Then Lieut-Colonel Noga said:

'Do you want coffee?'

'No, I don't,' I replied.

I no longer remember what we put down in my statement that morning. At noon he wanted to take me to lunch as usual. I refused. He inclined his head to one side dispiritedly and said, 'You are really angry, aren't you? But why are you angry with me? Have I not shown good faith?'

'No, you haven't. If you had, you would at least have returned my manuscript.'

His brow furrowed, he dashed out of the office, returned and threw a file in black cardboard covers on the desk. 'There! But now you will go to lunch?'

A crisp winter afternoon was advancing behind the bars from the White Mountain towards the darkness. My Lieut-Colonel was standing by the window, his hands behind his back. From the courtyard came the sound of women's voices as female prisoners took their exercise.

'Look, Mr Vaculík,' he said with a smile I could not see from where I was sitting, 'I know you'll put all this into one of your articles . . .'

* The playwright, Pavel Kohout, and his wife were manhandled by police when picked up for questioning in connection with Charter 77.

'I expect so, if I'm given half a chance.'

He was silent for a while. Then:

'And you'll call it: "A Cup of Coffee with the Interrogator."'

I almost fell off the chair. It was no use – they knew everything.

The next day – it was a Friday – I had a pleasant surprise: they returned 53 volumes of 'Padlock Publications'.* I couldn't get them all into the suitcase. Lieut-Colonel Noga brought me a box, himself packed the books into it, tied it up and even made a little loop for me to carry it by.

'There, I've wrapped them up for you so nicely that I almost regret it.'

On Sunday I went to Dobřichovice for the apples. And that evening, when I was beginning to think they wouldn't come and they did arrive with yet another summons, I prepared a paper bag with samples of four different sorts of apple . . .

But on Monday, what a change! Well, so be it.

'Sit down,' he said coldly. Mrs Blanka had her typewriter all ready and she, too, looked as if she didn't know me. My Lieut-Colonel thought for a bit and then said, 'Have you changed your attitude over the weekend?'

I haven't, I thought, but you have. 'No,' I said out loud.

'And do you know how the workers are reacting?'

'Yes. I do.'

'What if I were to put you in a car and take you to a factory and ask you to defend what you have written in front of the workers?'

'First of all I'd ask them if they had actually read what we have written.'

He got up and hurried out of the room.

Now he's going to find me some workers, I thought.

He returned to his desk.

'Want some coffee?' he asked.

I didn't feel like coffee. 'Yes,' I replied.

Again he dashed out, maybe just to order the coffee, but he was gone for a suspiciously long time. Everything suddenly seemed suspicious to

---

* Padlock Publications (*Edice Petlice*) was the name given to a large number of banned books which circulated in former Czechoslovakia in manuscript form.

me, including the fact that they had returned those books. Mrs Blanka sat in silence. From the courtyard came the sound of men's voices, occasional laughter. I listened hard, trying to discern if Jiří Lederer was perhaps laughing down there now, or František Pavlíček or Václav Havel.*

No, I said to myself in sudden resolve. Chickenshit!

He came back, sat down at his desk and snapped at me: 'Do you know Jiří Lederer?'

'Yes.'

'Did you give him your articles to send abroad?'

'Look, Lieutenant-Colonel, let's be clear about this: you've been on about these articles of mine for two years now. Are they criminal? If not, it can't be a criminal offence to send them abroad either. I'm telling you this off the record. For the protocol, all I'm willing to say is: I refuse to testify.'

Lunch. Jiří Hájek was already there when I arrived. We ate our frankfurters. 'Would you like a coffee?' Jiří Hájek thanked her and said, 'You're looking after us so well that we'll grow fat in here and then won't be able to get out between the bars, and you'll say it's all our own fault.'

The girl laughed. 'Oh dear me, no!'

In the lift, as the Lieut-Colonel escorted me towards the exit, I still debated with myself about those apples in the paper bag. But I stuck to my resolve: No. Chickenshit! Perhaps it was hard of me, but it was just.

(Copy to Lieut-Colonel Noga)

Translated by George Theiner

July/August 1977

---

* Jiří Lederer, a journalist, and the playwrights František Pavlíček and Václav Havel (together with stage director Ota Ornest) were arrested in January 1977. Havel, as well as Dr Jiří Hájek and the late Professor Jan Patočka, acted as a spokesman for the Charter. Professor Patočka died on 13 March, following police interrogation, while Dr Hájek, who was Minister of Foreign Affairs at the time of the 1968 invasion, was put under constant surveillance.

EDUARDO GALEANO

Cemetery of words

Eduardo Galeano is Uruguay's leading writer, author of the epic three-volume historical narrative of the Americas, *Memory of Fire*. He has now returned to his native country after years of voluntary exile in Argentina and Spain.

1   The system that programmes the computer that alarms the banker who alerts the ambassador who dines with the general who summons the president who informs the minister who threatens the managing director who humiliates the manager who shouts at the boss who harasses the white-collar worker who despises the manual worker who ill-treats his wife who hits the child who kicks the dog.

2   In Uruguay, the inquisitors have updated themselves. Strange mixture of the Middle Ages and the capitalist concept of business. The military don't burn books any more: they sell them to the paper manufacturers. The paper companies shred them, pulp them and put them back into the market for consumption. It's not true that Marx, Freud or Piaget are unavailable to the public. In the form of books they're not. But they are in the form of serviettes.

3   Argentina has been turned into a slaughterhouse. Technique for disappearances: there are no prisoners whose release anyone can demand nor martyrs to keep watch over. The death penalty was incorporated into the Penal Code in mid-1976, but people are killed every day without trial or sentence. In the majority of instances, there is no corpse. The dictatorships of Chile and Uruguay have not been slow to imitate this highly successful procedure. A single death by firing-squad can provoke a world-wide scandal: with the thousands of disappeared people there is always the convenience of uncertainty. Family and friends go through the dangerous and futile search from prison to

71

prison and barracks to barracks, while the bodies rot in woods and rubbish tips. Men are swallowed by the earth, the government washes its hands: there are no crimes to report or explanations to be given. Each dead person dies several times. In the end, all that's left is a fog of horror and uncertainty in one's soul.

4 The machine teaches that whoever is against it is an enemy of the country. To denounce injustice is a crime against the fatherland.

I am the country, says the machine. This concentration camp is the country: this heap of rotting waste, this great wasteland empty of men.

Anyone who believes his country is a home for everyone is thrown out of the home.

5 The only thing that's free are prices. In our part of the world, Adam Smith needs Mussolini. Freedom of investment, freedom of prices, freedom of exchange: the greater the freedom for business, the more people are imprisoned. Who has heard of wealth being innocent? When there's a crisis, don't liberals become conservatives, conservatives fascists? Who do the murderers of people and countries work for?

A Minister of Finance said in Uruguay: 'Inequality in the distribution of earnings is what creates savings.' But he also admitted that the fact of torture horrified him. How can inequality be preserved except by the weapon of the electrode? The Right likes generalizations. Generalizations absolve it.

6 The torturer is a functionary. The dictator is a functionary. They are armed bureaucrats and they lose their job if they don't do it efficiently. There is no more to it than that. They are not extraordinary monsters. We are not going to give them that distinction.

7 The machine harasses the youth; it jails, it tortures, it kills. They are the living proof of its importance. It throws them out: it sells them as human flesh, cheap labour for foreign countries.

The sterile machine hates everything that grows and moves. It's able only to multiply prisons and cemeteries. It can only produce prisoners and corpses, spies and policemen, beggars and exiles.

Being young is a crime. Reality commits it every day at dawn; so does history, re-born every morning.

That is why reality and history are prohibited.

8 In Uruguay a new prison opens every month. That's what the economists call the Development Plan.

But what about the invisible cages? In what official report or opposition document do the prisoners of fear figure? Fear of losing one's job, fear of not finding one; fear of speaking, fear of hearing, fear of reading. In the country of silence, a brightness in the eyes can send one to a concentration camp. A functionary doesn't have to be sacked: it's sufficient to let him know that he can be removed without notice and that he'll never get another job. Censorship triumphs when every citizen becomes the implacable censor of his own words and actions.

Dictatorship makes its prisons from barracks, police stations, abandoned carriages, disused ships. And what it does with everyone's house, isn't that the same thing?

9 Of every hundred children born alive in Chile, eight die. Accident or murder? The criminals have the keys of the prisons.

Food is more expensive in Chile than in the USA. The minimum wage is ten times lower. Taxi-drivers in Santiago don't buy dollars from tourists any more: they offer girls who'll make love in exchange for a meal.

The consumption of shoes in Uruguay has gone down five times in the last twenty years. In the last seven years, the consumption of milk in Montevideo has gone down by half.

How many are the prisoners of need? Is a man who's condemned to spend his life searching for work and food free? How many have their destiny branded on their faces from the day they enter the world and cry for the first time? How many are denied salt and sun?

10 The list of torturings, murders and disappearances does not exhaust the crimes of a dictatorship. The machine trains you to egoism and lies. Solidarity is a crime. Victory for the machine: people are afraid of speaking, of looking at each other. No-one is to meet anyone else. When someone meets your eyes and doesn't look away, you think: 'He's going to get me.' The manager says to the employee who was his friend: 'I had to report you. They asked for lists. I had to give a name. Forgive me, if you can.'

Why doesn't murder of the soul by poisoning figure in the chronicle of violence?

11 Half a million Uruguayans out of the country. A million Para-guayans, half a million Chileans. The ships sail full of young people escaping from prison, death or hunger. To be alive is dangerous; to think, a sin; to eat, a miracle.

But how many exiles are there inside the frontiers of their own countries? Where are the statistics that take count of those who are condemned to resignation and silence? Does not hope commit worse crimes than people do?

Dictatorship is infamy become habit, a machine that makes you deaf and dumb, incapable of listening, unable to speak, and blind to what is forbidden to be seen.

The first death as a result of torture unleashed – in Brazil in 1964 – a national scandal. The tenth death by torture was barely reported in the press. The fiftieth was accepted as 'normal'.

The machine teaches people to accept horror in the same way that one gets used to the cold in winter.

12 I search for the enemy voice that gave me orders to be miserable.

Sometimes I have the feeling that joy is a crime of high treason, and that I'm guilty of the privilege of still being alive and free.

That's when it does me good to remember what was said by the local political leader Huillca: 'They came here. They smashed up even the stones. They wanted to wipe us out. But they haven't managed it, because we're still alive and that's what matters.'

And I think that Huillca was right. To be alive: a small victory. To be alive, which means capable of joy, despite the crimes and the separations, so that exile can testify to the possibility of a different kind of country.

The task in front of us is to create a real fatherland, and we won't build that with bricks made of shit. Would we be of any use when we return if we came back broken?

Joy needs more courage than suffering. Suffering is after all something we have got used to.

13 Extermination plan: strip the land of grass, root up the last living plant, cover the earth with salt. After that, erase the memory of grass. To colonize consciousness, suppress it; to suppress it, empty it of past.

Wipe out any sign that there was anything in this land other than silence, prisons and graves.

Remembering is prohibited.

There are customs regulations for words, incinerators for words, cemeteries for words.

Squads of prisoners are sent out at night to cover with white paint the words of protest which in other times covered the walls of the city.

The rain's persistent washing begins to dissolve the white paint. And there appear, gradually, the stubborn words.

Translated by William Rowe

March/April 1978

ARTHUR MILLER

The sin of power

Arthur Miller is America's most celebrated playwright of the second half of the century. His first three plays – *All My Sons* (1947), *Death of a Salesman* (1949), *The Crucible* (1953) – constitute a devastating commentary on the driven American way of life, the last named linking the Salem witch-hunting of 1692 with the hysteria of the McCarthy era. (Miller refused to give names when summoned before the House Un-American Activities Committee in 1956, and for five years was refused a passport.) This piece from 1978 expresses the hope that 'despite everything . . . a healthy scepticism toward the powerful has at last become second nature to the great mass of people.'

It is always necessary to ask how old a writer is who is reporting his impressions of a social phenomenon. Like the varying depth of a lens, the mind bends the light passing through it quite differently according to its age. When I first experienced Prague in the late sixties, the Russians had only just entered with their armies; writers (almost all of them self-proclaimed Marxists if not Party members) were still unsure of their fate under the new occupation, and when some thirty or forty of them gathered in the office of *Listy* to 'interview' me, I could smell the apprehension among them. And indeed, many would soon be fleeing abroad, some would be jailed, and others would never again be permitted to publish in their native language. Incredibly, that was almost a decade ago.

But since the first major blow to the equanimity of my mind was the victory of Nazism, first in Germany and later in the rest of Europe, the images I have of repression are inevitably cast in Fascist forms. In those times the Communist was always the tortured victim, and the Red Army stood as the hope of man, the deliverer. So to put it quite simply, although correctly, I think, the occupation of Czechoslovakia was the physical proof that Marxism was but one more self-delusionary attempt to avoid facing the real nature of power, the primitive corruption by power of those who possess it. In a word, Marxism has turned out to be a form of sentimentalism toward human nature, and this has its funny side. After all, it was initially a probe into the most painful wounds of the capitalist presumptions, it was scientific and analytical. What the Russians have done in Czechoslovakia is, in effect, to prove in a Western cultural environment that what they have called Socialism simply cannot tolerate even the most nominal independent scrutiny, let alone an opposition. The critical intelligence itself is not to be borne and in the birthplace of Kafka and of the absurd in its subtlest expression absurdity emanates from the Russian occupation like some sort of gas which makes one both laugh and cry. Shortly after returning home from my first visit to Prague mentioned above, I happened to meet a Soviet political scientist at a high-level conference where he was a participant representing his country and I was invited to speak at one session to present my views of the impediments to better cultural relations between the two nations. Still depressed by my Czech experience, I naturally brought up the invasion of the country as a likely cause for American distrust of the Soviets, as well as the United States aggression in Viet Nam from the same détente viewpoint.

That had been in the morning; in the evening at a party for all the conference participants, half of them Americans, I found myself facing this above-mentioned Soviet whose anger was unconcealed. 'It is amazing,' he said, 'that you – especially you as a Jew – should attack our action in Czechoslovakia.'

Normally quite alert to almost any reverberations of the Jewish presence in the political life of our time, I found myself in a state of unaccustomed and total confusion at this remark, and I asked the man to explain the connection. 'But obviously,' he said (and his face had gone quite red and he was quite furious now) 'we have gone in there to protect them from the West German Fascists.'

I admit that I was struck dumb. Imagine! – The marching of all the Warsaw Pact armies in order to protect the few Jews left in Czechoslovakia! It is rare that one really comes face to face with such fantasy so profoundly believed by a person of intelligence. In the face of this kind of expression all culture seems to crack and collapse; there is no longer a frame of reference.

In fact, the closest thing to it that I could recall were my not infrequent arguments with intelligent supporters or apologists for our Viet Namese invasion. But at this point the analogy ends, for it was always possible during the Viet Nam war for Americans opposed to it to make their views heard, and, indeed, it was the widespread opposition to the war which finally made it impossible for President Johnson to continue in office. It certainly was not a simple matter to oppose the war in any significant way, and the civilian casualties of protest were by no means few, and some – like the students at the Kent State College protest – paid with their lives. But what one might call the unofficial underground reality, the version of morals and national interest held by those not in power, was ultimately expressed and able to prevail sufficiently to alter high policy. Even so it was the longest war ever fought by Americans.

Any discussion of the American rationales regarding Viet Nam must finally confront something which is uncongenial to both Marxist and anti-Marxist viewpoints, and it is the inevitable pressure, by those holding political power, to distort and falsify the structures of reality. The Marxist, by philosophical conviction, and the bourgeois American politician, by practical witness, both believe at bottom that reality is quite simply the arena into which determined men can enter and reshape just about every kind of relationship in it. The conception of an objective reality which is the summing up of all historical circumstances, as well as the idea of human beings as containers or vessels by which that historical experience defends itself and expresses itself through common sense and unconscious drives, are notions which at best are merely temporary nuisances, incidental obstructions to the wished-for remodelling of human nature and the improvements of society which power exists in order to set in place.

The sin of Power is to not only distort reality but to convince people that the false is true, and that what is happening is only an invention of enemies. Obviously, the Soviets and their friends in Czechoslovakia are by no means the only ones guilty of this sin, but in other places, especially in the West, it is possible yet for witnesses to reality to come forth and testify to the truth. In Czechoslovakia the whole field is pre-empted by the Power itself.

Thus a great many people outside, and among them a great many artists, have felt a deep connection with Czechoslovakia – but precisely because there has been a fear in the West over many generations that the simple right to reply to Power is a tenuous thing and is always on the verge of being snipped like a nerve. I have, myself, sat at dinner with a Czech writer and his family in his own home and looked out and seen police sitting in their cars down below, in effect warning my friend that our 'meeting' was being observed. I have seen reports in Czech newspapers that a certain writer had emigrated to the West and was no longer willing to live in his own country, when the very same man was sitting across a living room coffee table from me. And I have also been lied about in America by both private and public liars, by the press and the government, but a road – sometimes merely a narrow path – always remained open before my mind, the belief that I might sensibly attempt to influence people to see what was real and so at least to resist the victory of untruth.

I know what it is to be denied the right to travel outside my country, having been denied my passport for some five years by our Department of State. And I know a little about the inviting temptation to simply get out at any cost, to quit my country in disgust and disillusion, as no small number of people did in the McCarthy fifties and as a long line of Czechs and Slovaks have in these recent years. I also know the empty feeling in the belly at the prospect of trying to learn another nation's secret language, its gestures and body communications without which a writer is only half-seeing and half-hearing. More important, I know the conflict between recognizing the indifference of the people and finally conceding that the salt has indeed lost its savour and that the only sensible attitude toward any people is cynicism.

So that those who have chosen to remain as writers on their native soil despite remorseless pressure to emigrate are, perhaps no less than their oppressors, rather strange and anachronistic figures in this time. After all, it is by no means a heroic epoch now; we in the West as well as in the East understand perfectly well that the political and military spheres – where 'heroics' were called for in the past, are now merely expressions of the unmerciful industrial-technological base. As for the very notion of patriotism, it falters before the perfectly obvious interdependence of the nations, as well as the universal prospect of mass obliteration by the atom bomb, the instrument which has doomed us, so to speak, to this lengthy peace between the great powers. That a group of intellectuals should persist in creating a national literature on their own ground is out of tune with our adaptational proficiency which has flowed from these developments. It is hard anymore to remember whether one is living in Rome or New York, London or Strasbourg, so homogenized has Western life become. The persistence of these people may be an inspiration to some but a nuisance to others, and not only inside the oppressing apparatus but in the West as well. For these so-called dissidents are apparently upholding values at a time when the first order of business would seem to be the accretion of capital for technological investment.

It need hardly be said that by no means everybody in the West is in favour of human rights, and Western support for Eastern dissidents has more hypocritical self-satisfaction in it than one wants to think too much about. Nevertheless, if one has learned anything at all in the past forty or so years, it is that to struggle for these rights − (and without them the accretion of capital is simply the construction of a more modern prison) − one has to struggle for them wherever the need arises.

That this struggle *also* has to take place in Socialist systems suggests to me that the fundamental procedure which is creating violations of these rights transcends social systems − a thought anathematic to Marxists but possibly true nevertheless. What may be in place now is precisely a need to erect a new capital structure, be it in Latin America or the Far East or underdeveloped parts of Europe, and just as in the nineteenth century in America and England, it is a process which always breeds injustice and the flaunting of human spiritual demands because it essentially is the sweating of increasing amounts of production and wealth from a labour force surrounded, in effect, by police.

The complaining or reforming voice in that era was not exactly encouraged in the United States or England; by corrupting the press and buying whole legislatures, capitalists effectively controlled their opposition, and the struggle of the trade union movement was often waged against firing rifles.

There is of course a difference now, many differences. At least they are supposed to be differences, particularly, that the armed force is in the hands of a state calling itself Socialist and progressive and scientific, no less pridefully than the nineteenth century capitalisms boasted by their Christian ideology and their devotion to the human dimension of political life as announced by the American Bill of Rights and the French Revolution. But the real difference now is the incomparably deeper and more widespread conviction that man's fate is not 'realistically' that of the regimented slave. It may be that despite everything, and totally unannounced and unheralded, a healthy scepticism toward the powerful has at last become second nature to the great mass of people almost everywhere. It may be that history, now, is on the side of those who hopelessly hope and cling to their native ground to claim it for their language and ideals.

The oddest request I ever heard in Czechoslovakia – or anywhere else – was to do what I could to help writers publish their works – but not in French, German or English, the normal desire of sequestered writers cut off from the outside. No, these Czech writers were desperate to see their works – in Czech! Somehow this speaks of something far more profound than 'dissidence' or any political quantification. There is something like love in it, and in this sense it is a prophetic yearning and demand.

May/June 1978

JUAN GELMAN

Distractions

Juan Gelman, the Argentinian poet and journalist, was forced into exile for twelve years when the military took power in 1975. His son and daughter-in-law (then seven months pregnant), taken as the police were looking for the writer himself, were among the *desaparecidos*, those who 'disappeared' for ever in the country's dirty civil war. Gelman now lives in Mexico City.

admiring the bird's flight
the distraction is such i forget the
doubts deficiencies ignominies of its
efforts on trying to fly/of course

the bird will hardly speak
of all this/not out of pride or dumbness but
because that's how flying is/you criticize
yourself all the time/you falter

again and again/you go back
over what you've flown to fly it again/you sweep aside
doubts deficiencies ignominies with a ruthlessness
quite incredible in a bird/i mean

that's how revolution is/you criticize yourself all the time/
    you falter
again and again/you go back
over what you've begun to begin it again/you sweep aside

doubts deficiencies ignominies with
a ruthlessness quite incredible in a bird/you fly

like the faces of the earth or the
wretched of the earth or the sun

Translated by Jo Labanyi

September/October 1978

JULIO CORTÁZAR

Apocalypse at Solentiname

Julio Cortázar, Argentina's leading novelist and critic, died in 1984 after years of exile in France and the USA. Most of his novels were translated into the major languages. He was also a fine short story writer, and one of the best modern critics of the short story.

Always the same, the Ticos, a bit on the quiet side but full of surprises, you get off in San Juan de Costa Rica and there waiting for you are Carmen Naranjo and Samuel Rovinski and Sergio Ramirez (who's from Nicaragua and not a Tico but where's the difference when you get down to it, it's all the same, what's the difference between me being Argentinian, though to be polite I suppose I should say Tinian, and the other Nicas or Ticos). It was blinding hot and to make matters worse everything began right away, a press conference with all the usual, why don't you live in your own country, why was the film of Blow-Up so different from your story, do you think a writer ought to be politically committed? The way things are going I reckon the very last interview I give will be at the gates of Hell and I bet they'll be the very same questions, and if by some chance or other it's *chez* St Peter it'll be no different, don't you think that down below you wrote too obscurely for the masses?

Afterwards the Europe Hotel and that special shower which crowns a journey with a long soliloquy of soap and silence. Except that at 7 o'clock when it was time to take a walk around San José to see if it was as straightforward and neat as I'd heard, a hand grasped my jacket and at the other end of it was Ernesto Cardenal* and then what a

---

* Nicaraguan poet and priest, who founded the community at Solentiname in 1967. After he went into exile in 1977, the Nicaraguan army destroyed the community.

welcome, poet, how good that you're here after our meeting in Rome, after so many meetings on paper over the years. I'm always surprised, I'm always moved to think that someone like Ernesto should come to see me and to seek me out, you'll say I'm dripping with false modesty but go right ahead and say it friend, the jackal may howl but the bus moves on, I'll always be an amateur, someone who admires certain people an incredible amount from below, and then one day discovers they feel the same about him, things like that are beyond me, we'd better go on to the next line.

The next line turned out to be that Ernesto had heard I was coming to Costa Rica and had flown in from his island because the little bird who'd brought him the news had also told him that the Ricans were planning to take me to Solentiname, and the idea of coming to fetch me himself proved irresistible, so two days later Sergio and Oscar and Ernesto and myself crammed into an all too easily crammable Piper Aztec biplane, a name like that will forever be a mystery to me, but which flew anyway amidst hiccups and ominous gurglings while the blond pilot kept the thing going with a selection of calypsos and seemed utterly unconcerned at my idea that the Aztec was in fact taking us straight to his sacrificial pyramid. Which, as you can see, wasn't the case, we got out in Los Chiles and from there an equally rickety jeep took us to the home of the poet José Coronel Urteche (whose work more people could do with reading), where we rested and talked of a variety of mutual poet friends, of Roque Dalton and Gertrude Stein and Carlos Martinez Rivas until Luis Coronel arrived and we set off for Nicaragua first in his jeep and then in his launch at nerve-racking speed. Beforehand though, we took some souvenir snapshots with one of those cameras that on the spot produce a piece of sky-blue paper which gradually and miraculously begins slowly to fill with images, first of all disturbing ghost-shapes and then little by little a nose, a curly head of hair, Ernesto's smile and his Nazarene head-band, Doña Maria and Don José standing out clearly against the veranda. There was nothing at all odd about this for them because of course they were used to the camera, but I wasn't, for me to see emerging from nothing, from that little square of blue nothingness those faces and smiles of farewell filled me with amazement and I told them so. I remember asking Oscar what would happen if once after some family photo the blue scrap of paper suddenly began to fill with Napoleon on horseback, and Don José's great roar of laughter: he'd been listening to everything as usual; in the jeep, off we head for the lake.

Night had already fallen by the time we reached Solentiname, Teresa and William and an American poet were there waiting for us, along with the other members of the community; we went to bed almost immediately, but not before I'd seen the paintings in a corner, Ernesto was talking with his friends and handing out the food and presents he'd brought in a bag from San José, somebody was sleeping in a hammock and I saw the paintings in a corner, began to look at them. I can't remember who it was explained they'd been done by the local people, this one was by Vincente, this one's by Ramona, some signed, others not, yet all of them incredibly beautiful, once again the primeval vision of the world, the pure gaze of someone describing his surroundings in a song of praise: dwarf cows in meadows of poppies, a sugar cabin that people were pouring out of like ants, a green-eyed horse against a backdrop of swamps, a baptism in a church with no faith in perspective that climbs and falls all over itself, a lake full of little boats like shoes, and in the background a huge laughing fish with turquoise lips. Then Ernesto came over to explain that selling the paintings helped them to get by, in the morning he'd show me some things in wood and stone the peasants had made, as well as his own sculptures; we were all gradually dropping off to sleep, but I kept on staring at the paintings stacked in the corner, pulling out the great canvas playing-cards with their cows and their flowers and a mother with her two children, one white and the other red, nestling in her lap, beneath a sky so bursting with stars that the only remaining cloud had been shoved into a corner, pressed right up against the frame, on the point of creeping off the canvas out of sheer fright.

The next day was Sunday and 11 o'clock Mass, the Solentiname Mass where the country labourers with Ernesto and any visiting friends join in commenting on a chapter from the Gospels, which that particular day was Jesus' arrest in the garden, a theme the people of Solentiname treated as if it dealt with them personally, with the threat hanging over them at night or in broad daylight, their life of constant uncertainty not just on the islands or on the mainland and in all of Nicaragua but also in nearly the whole of Latin America, life surrounded by fear and death, life in Guatemala and life in El Salvador, life in Argentina and Bolivia, life in Chile and Santo Domingo, life in Paraguay, life in Brazil and in Colombia.

After that the time came to think of going back, and it was then that the paintings crossed my mind again, I went to the community room and started to look at them in the delirious brilliance of mid-day, their colours even brighter, the acrylics or oils vying with each other from horses and sunflowers and picnics in meadows and symmetrical palm trees. I remembered I had a colour film in my camera and went out on to the veranda with as many paintings as I could carry; Sergio came and helped me to hold them up in a good light, and I went through photographing them one by one, positioning myself so that each canvas completely filled the viewer. As luck would have it, there were exactly the same number of paintings as I had shots left, so I could take them all without leaving any out, when Ernesto came to announce the launch was waiting. I told him what I'd done and he laughed, painting-snatcher, image-smuggler. Yes, I said, I'm carting them all off, and back home I'll show them on my screen and they'll be far bigger and brighter than yours, tough shit to you.

I returned to San José, passed through Havana where I had a few things to see to, then back to Paris full of tired nostalgia, Claudine waiting for me silently at Orly, back to a life of wrist-watches and *merci monsieur bonjour madame*, committees, cinemas, red wine and Claudine, Mozart quartets and Claudine. In the heap of things the toady suitcase spewed out over bed and carpet, magazines, newspaper cuttings, handkerchiefs and books by Centro-American poets, the tubes of grey plastic with the rolls of film, so many things in the space of two months, the sequence in the Lenin school of Havana, the streets of Trinidad, the outlines of the volcano Irazu and its tiny dish of steaming green water in which Samuel, myself and Sarita had imagined ducks already roasted floating around wreathed in sulphurous fumes. Claudine took the films to be developed, one afternoon when I was in the Latin Quarter I remembered them and since I had the receipt in my pocket went to pick them up: eight of them altogether, I immediately thought of the Solentiname paintings and when I got home I opened all the boxes and glimpsed at the first slide in each, I seemed to remember that before taking the paintings I'd been photographing Ernesto's Mass, some kids playing among palm-trees just like the ones in the paintings, kids and trees and cows against a background of harsh blue sky and lake only a shade greener, or perhaps it was the other way round, I couldn't say exactly. I put the box with the kids and the Mass into the carrier, I knew that after them all the rest of the roll showed the paintings.

It was getting dark and I was on my own, Claudine would be coming after work to listen to some music and to stay with me; I set up the screen and a rum with a lot of ice, the carrier ready and the long-distance control; there was no need to draw the curtains, the compliant night was at hand to light the lamps and the aroma of the rum; it was good to think it was all going to be offered to me again, bit by bit, after the Solentiname paintings I'd go through the boxes with the photos from Cuba, but just why the paintings first, why that professional vice, art before life, and why not then said the other one to him in their eternal unrelenting bitter fraternal dialogue, why not look at the Solentiname paintings first, they're just as much life, it's all one and the same.

First the photos of the Mass – which weren't much good because I'd got the exposure wrong, the kids on the other hand were playing in perfect light with gleaming white teeth. I pressed the button reluctantly, I'd have liked to spend a long moment gazing at each photo sticky with memories, that tiny fragile world of Solentiname hemmed round by water and officialdom, just like the youth I stared at blankly was hemmed in, I'd pressed the button and there he was, perfectly clear in the middle distance with a wide, smooth face that seemed filled with incredulous surprise as his body crumpled forward, a neat hole in his forehead, the officer's revolver still tracing the path of the bullet, the others standing by with their machine-guns, a jumbled background of houses and trees.

Whatever we like to think, these things always seem to arrive so far ahead of us and to leave us so far behind; I said to myself dumbfoundedly that the shop must have made a mistake, that they'd given me someone else's photos, but then what about the Mass, the children playing in the fields, then how? Without my wanting it to, my hand pressed the button and it was noon in a vast nitrate mine with a couple of rusty corrugated-iron shacks, a bunch of people to the left staring at the bodies lying face upwards, arms flung open against a bare grey sky; looking hard you could just make out in the distance the backs of a uniformed group moving off, their jeep waiting at the top of a hill.

I know I went on; the only possibility in the face of all that craziness was to go on pressing the button, seeing the corner of Corrientes and San Martin and the black car from which four men were aiming guns at the pavement where someone in a white shirt and tennis shoes was running, two women trying to shelter behind a parked lorry, somebody across the street looking on in horrified disbelief, lifting a hand to his chin as though to touch himself and feel he was still alive, then all at once an almost completely darkened room, a bleary light from a barred window high up, a table with a naked girl lying on her back, her hair reaching down to the floor, the shadow of a back pushing a wire between her open legs, the faces of two men talking to each other, a blue tie and a green pullover. I never understood whether I went on pressing the button or not, I saw a clearing in the jungle, a thatched cabin with some trees in the foreground, up against the nearest trunk a skinny youth, his face turned to the left where a confused group of five or six men close together pointed their rifles and pistols at him; he had a long face, with a lock of hair falling across the dark skin of his forehead, and was staring at them, one of his hands half-raised, the other probably in his trouser pocket, as if he were taking his time to tell them something, almost disdainfully, and even though the photo was blurred I felt and knew and saw that it was Roque Dalton, so then yes I did press the button, as if that could save him from the infamy of such a death and I managed to catch sight of a car exploding in the centre of a city which might have been Buenos Aires or São Paulo, I carried on pressing and pressing between flashes of bloody faces and bits of bodies and women and children racing down hill-sides in Bolivia or Guatemala, suddenly the screen flooded with mercury and with nothing and with Claudine too, coming in silently and throwing her shadow across the screen before bending over to kiss me on the top of my head and ask me if they were nice, if I was happy with the photos, if I wanted to show her them.

I took the slide carrier out and set it back at the beginning, we never know how or why we do certain things when we've crossed a boundary we were equally unaware of. Without looking at her, because she would not have understood or simply been terrified by whatever my face was in that moment, without explaining anything to her because from my throat down to my toe-nails was just one huge knot, I got up and gently settled her in the armchair and I suppose I said something about going to get her a drink and for her to look, for her to see for herself while I went to get her a drink. In the bathroom I think I threw up, or just cried and then threw up or did nothing but stayed sitting on the edge of the bath letting time go by until I was capable of going to the kitchen to fix Claudine her favourite drink, fill it with ice and then take in the silence, realize that Claudine wasn't screaming, hadn't come running with questions, only silence and occasionally the sugary bolero drifting through the wall from the next-door flat. I don't know how long it took me to get from the kitchen to the lounge, to see the back of the screen just as she reached the end and the room filled with the reflection of the instant mercury, then fell back into semi-darkness, Claudine switching off the projector and flopping back into the armchair to take her glass and smile slowly at me, happy, cat-like, contented.

'They came out really well, that one with the laughing fish and the mother with the two children and the cows in the field; wait, and there was that other one with the baptism in the church, tell me who painted them, the signatures aren't clear.'

Sitting on the floor without looking at her, I reached for my drink and gulped it down. I wasn't going to say anything to her, what was there to say now, but I remember vaguely thinking of asking her something really crazy, asking if at some point she hadn't seen a photo of Napoleon on horseback. I didn't, of course.

Translated by Nick Caistor

January/February 1979

JORGE MUSTO

Pale browns and yellows

Jorge Musto was an actor and director with the experimental theatre group El Galpón and a writer for the influential Montevideo cultural review *Marcha* before it was closed down by the Uruguayan military regime in 1973. Detained in solitary confinement and tortured by the army in 1972, he was released under restrictive conditions and eventually managed to leave the country secretly and escape to Paris.

At first he felt a possibly inexplicable pride. After all, there was no reason to believe that just to hear his tiny country mentioned involved any particular merit or virtue on his part. But his pride grew imperceptibly with each fresh newspaper editorial, with every TV news, or with any informal chat where someone was quick to supply the correct geographical details to avoid being taken for a foreigner only recently acquainted with what was going on in the country; grew still stronger when another person boasted some bit of knowledge about football, social reforms of the twenties, beaches, or even of a painter long since dead and unjustly forgotten. No, it was no merit of his. But the most thoroughly documented articles appeared in the specialist reviews, and journalists fought to get exclusive interviews with a representative of the most die-hard traditionalists or with the most notorious resistance figures. Not to mention the two novels of political fiction trading on the recent history and name of his tiny country. Nor the four occasions he queued to see the film about it, and the slightly morbid pleasure he got from feeling anonymous in the midst of hundreds of foreigners, absorbed in a story which involved him so directly.

Pride and something more. Because in this strange country which had welcomed him, good luck seemed to follow his every footstep, day and night. For example, he soon had the use of a free furnished flat which its owner, away on a trip or something, had insisted he take

in preference to other equally generous offers. He even had to buy a
diary to avoid over-booking himself with dinners, meetings, cocktail
parties, all sorts of invitations which came flooding in with each phone
call. Of course there was always an offer to drive him there, to spare
him the inconvenience of the metro, or the risks of getting lost in the
unknown city. Different places and faces, but always the same sympathy
for him, the same concern not to contradict his opinions, to listen to
his views on what would happen next – views he made up out of a
sense of basic politeness, in response to everyone's insistence. And also
about that time Brigitte appeared, obviously intent on hearing her own
patient and exclusive version of his story. Which she obtained without
much effort.

Everything around him was arranged for him to be protected and
admired. On the rare occasion when he found himself with people
who had not been warned, he told them where he was from. Then
everything went smoothly.

This lasted for some time. He dismissed the first seemingly harmless
warnings. After all, it was a relief not to have to check in his diary all
the time, to try to find a gap between eight and nine, not to have to
repeat the story of the airport or the embassy over and over, a relief
to use a Saturday evening to discover the city for himself, not to have
to invent a new excuse every day to fend off Jean-Claude's unequivocal
advances. So the two get-togethers that were called off meant he could
at last visit the zoo, and have a good long drink of maté staring out of
the window in silence. But he was rather put out when for the fourth
time in as many days it was Brigitte's mother who answered the phone,
with exactly the same evasive phrase but in a steadily more distant
voice, and he began to worry a little. Above all because he took it
personally as over the last few weeks the news from his country had
gradually been relegated to the inside pages of the papers, to ever more
obscure corners. The same thing on the TV. And his attempt to substitute Nicole for Brigitte had met with a sarcastic rebuff.

He wasn't prepared for what happened with the flat though. He
spent the three days' notice they gave him looking for a room to rent
which wasn't too sordid. The new arrivals in the flat came while he
was still packing. A young couple, with decidedly Asiatic features.

All this gave him pause to feed an emotion which he likened to nostalgia. He went to see the film for a fifth time, but met posters of towering Infernos, and a queue of spectators who would have remained sublimely indifferent to the loss of his anonymity.

A few days later, as a joke, or perhaps just because he felt that to see the coat-of-arms and the name on the brass plate would give him some sort of confidence, he set out to find the consulate. He looked for the address in his diary, but when he got there he could see nothing outside to identify the place. The porter, who had only been there a few months, suggested that possibly there might in fact have been a consulate there once, on one of the top floors.

Careful scrutiny of the papers only made it worse. A vague sense of hope led him to read the news from all the countries around his own, but the stories always stopped at the borders. The streets of the city had become places where he might bump into someone he knew, or himself be recognized. He wandered about for hours on end.

Although he had put up with the geographical ignorance of various public employees in recent weeks, events at the post office completely horrified him. He waited in the queue as usual, and when the clerk, after carefully checking the tariffs for each country, suggested there must be some mistake, he swallowed his humiliation and tried to convince him that he had already written several times to his family at that address. He even told the man the exact price of the stamps, and put the money on the counter. The clerk at first shook his head, but faced with growing signs of impatience from others waiting, he took the money with a weary, disbelieving air and stamped the letter. That afternoon he spent a long while seated in a café thinking it over, then decided to buy the atlas. He bought a big, recently published one. When he got back to his room he spread it open on the floor.

His foreboding was confirmed. To make quite sure he got out a magnifying-glass to peer at the blurred area where his little country should by rights have been. He could see colours, a hazy patch of pale browns and yellows, like the reluctance of the sea as it pulls away from the shore.

Translated by Alicia and Nick Caistor

April 1981

PRAMOEDYA ANANTA TOER

Manuscripts banned and destroyed

Pramoedya Ananta Toer wrote several of the novels which have made him Indonesia's most famous and most banned writer during his various spells of incarceration. From 1965 to 1980 he was detained on Buru Island, and as this undaunted account of his troubles was going to press late in 1980, *Index* learned that 10,000 copies of his novels had been publicly burned. In 1996 he was again brought in for questioning in connection with the July Jakarta riots.

The imposition of bans on literary works in colonial and totalitarian countries is but a reflection of the jealousy of those in power. These people are deified so inhumanly that they sometimes forget the most human pulsations beating in other people's hearts. Indonesia has lived through a long period of colonialism and a short period of totalitarianism, and so bans on literary works represent one aspect of its historical experience.

In 1935, I saw an official of the colonial power confiscate books written by my own father. One morning, a few days later, hundreds of beautifully-printed books – the works of someone living in our town – floated on waters swirling under a bridge. He was afraid of having to confront those in power, and preferred to surrender his writings to the river. This took place in colonial days, in a small town, and it was not reported in the press. I don't know whether similar things happened in other towns up and down the country. But we did hear about a journalist and writer, Mas Marso Kartodikromo, who was in and out of prison because of his writings, and the press did indeed report this. His books were banned by the colonial power. We read them in secret . . .

The first time manuscripts of mine were destroyed was in 1947, by Dutch marines. Earlier, the Dutch colonial army confiscated diaries I had been keeping since 1938. It was a time of revolution in Indonesia, a time when lives were at stake and no-one bemoaned the loss or destruction of manuscripts. Fortunately, a few of these writings had been published a couple of months earlier. But most of what I lost then has not been recovered to this day. They were notes about the armed struggle in East Jakarta, written in the form of a novel – documentation of the Indonesian revolution.

It was in 1960 that a work of mine was banned for the first time. *The Overseas Chinese in Indonesia* was an account which I had written very quickly, rejecting Presidential Regulation No. 10, the aim of which was to prevent Chinese traders from making a living in the villages. The aim of this book was to speak up in favour of a national economic system, and against the replacement of personnel in the commercial sector. I heard about the ban while I was abroad, and when I returned home, I was summoned for an explanation by Peperti [Supreme War Command – Indonesia was then in a 'state of siege and war' – Tr.]. My interrogator was Sudharmono, a graduate of the Military Law Academy, and I was not allowed to go home but kept in a military prison in Jakarta. Another interrogator who said he was a graduate from Al-Azhar, Egypt, accused me of 'selling the Indonesian state to the Chinese People's Republic' with that book. There was no arrest warrant. This can probably be described as a case of 'kidnapping'. Two months passed at the military prison, then I was taken to Sudharmono again. The charge: I wanted to escape. As additional punishment, I was transferred to Cipinang Prison. I was put into a block in the front of the prison. Most of the men in this block, secured with double doors, were prisoners who had gone mad. It was also the block for convicted prisoners who were being punished for misdemeanours . . .

The time I spent behind double doors in Cipinang Prison is among the most bitter of all my experiences. There was a lavatory in my tiny cell which led directly to a drain under the floor. The walls of the cell were covered with flies from the lavatory. The sounds coming from the cells of the people who had gone mad were quite unbearable.

My family was never told anything about me during this period of detention. My wife was in the final stages of pregnancy, and it was in this condition that she had to go round, looking everywhere for me;

she finally tracked me down at the military prison. A few weeks later, she gave birth. By announcing our baby's birth in the press she was able to inform people about my arrest. On the basis of this, Radio Australia broadcast a report that the Indonesian government had for the first time taken action against a communist. Yet, right up to the end of this period of detention, lasting almost a year, there was no sign that a trial would take place. I was thus convicted without trial, without a chance to defend myself, and without a court of law proving that I had committed any crime.

That was my first experience of detention after Indonesia became independent, and under a government of my own nation . . .

The fact that to this very day, all my works are still banned is but a small illustration of the condition of a formerly colonized nation, a social-historical product that must look strange to those nations that have enjoyed Western democracy for seven or eight generations. This is quite illogical. And it was precisely for the sake of creative freedom that I had to pay so dearly, with the loss of my own freedom for more than 14 years plus the loss of rights and possessions for which, to this very day, no-one is willing to accept responsibility.

A few basic points need to be stressed: that Indonesia, only a few decades old, is still searching for the most appropriate form for itself, that democracy was not a lawful legacy from colonialism, and that each and every artist is challenged to create his own conditions for creative freedom; so, until such time as the law is capable of protecting personal property and understands too that creations are the personal property of their creators, it is up to each writer and artist to safeguard his or her own works. Each possession faces the risk of being damaged or lost, of being stolen, seized or destroyed. All this depends on the cultural level of a nation and the laws that have been brought into existence for it.

During my period of detention in Buru, I was given a miserable-looking chicken that produced hardly any eggs. I hatched the few eggs it produced and cared for the chicks with what energy I had left after a day's forced labour, feeding them with a share of my own meagre food rations. A few months later, I was not only able to keep myself alive with these eggs but I was also able to acquire a typewriter. Although I then started writing with what energy still remained, I had foreseen the possibility that my writings would be seized, and this is indeed what happened.

After these seizures, I began to write 'orally'. I had never imagined that I would one day become a troubador. I have never ceased to be amazed that this could have happened because I am basically incapable of arranging my thoughts properly while I speak . . .

Only two months after I returned to my family in Jakarta, a naval captain, Heri Herriono, came to seize all the manuscripts I had saved, and he hasn't yet returned any of them to me. Thank goodness, Indonesia has saved some of them with the generous help of some people . . .

At the end of May 1981, Indonesia's attorney-general banned two Buru works [Bumi Manusia and Anak Semua Banga]. This came as no surprise to me, having seen how those in power had confiscated the books of my own father, how a book of mine had been banned in 1960, having seen the acts of vandalism against my works in 1965-66 as well as the seizure of my manuscripts at the end of 1979 and then again in 1980. But those in power are not always the ones who control justice and truth although it is true that they can control the courts. Those in power do indeed have the right to impose bans. Those without power can only call out their appeals whether or not they go hoarse doing so, whether or not they achieve anything. At the very least, some progress has been achieved in Indonesia in the way the ban was imposed, which is quite encouraging. In previous cases, bans were imposed simply by being written down on a sheet of paper on the instructions of superiors, then being typed out by reliable secretaries. This time it was not so simple. Before the ban was imposed, people in several provincial capitals and in other smaller places had to be mobilized to discredit me personally and to discredit my works. This process of discrediting me lasted for no less than two months. Many square metres of column space in newspapers and magazines with a combined circulation of half a million copies were used, many hours were spent in meetings in many different places and at considerable expense, all in order to be able to issue this ban. And another equally interesting illustration is that after the ban had been issued, two people from Surabaya who had participated in this campaign of vilification were mentioned in press reports in August: Muhamad Nur, former governor of East Java, was appointed a member of the Supreme Advisory Council, and Soenarto Timoer was awarded the art prize for literature.

Tiny though this may be, I regard it as a sign of progress for democracy, not democracy inherited as the lawful legacy from colonialism but democracy resulting from our own efforts. Another step in the right direction can be added to this first one if we include the statements, published as well as unpublished, before and after the ban, disagreeing with the bans, and also positive responses including some from individuals in positions of power, written as well as verbal.

These two tiny signs of progress give reason to hope that in Indonesia, my own motherland, publication of my works will encounter fewer and fewer obstacles, maybe tomorrow or the day after. If this doesn't happen, it will mean that these two small steps forward will not have increased in number. And this means that even more sweat will have to be shed.

Translated by Carmel Budiardjo

December 1981

IVAN KLÍMA

Variation on an eternal theme

Ivan Klíma spent several years of his childhood with others of his Prague Jewish family in the Terezin concentration camp, which was also used as a transit camp for Jews en route for Auschwitz. The experience of that time haunts many of his plays, novels and short stories which were banned in the 1970s and 1980s because of his association, together with other writers who worked with the magazine Literarni listy, with the politics of the Prague Spring. One of his more recent books, My Golden Trades, won the 1993 George Theiner Prize (named in honour of the Czech-born critic and translator who edited Index from 1983-88).

A man can be free (or not) externally or internally. He can be free as far as his external circumstances are concerned, and yet unfree inside, or vice versa. We are far more likely to be talking about *external* freedom (or unfreedom), and yet there is usually very little we can do to influence this. But it is easier, and less painful, to judge the world around us than to pass judgment on ourselves. It is easier to claim that external circumstances prevented me from expressing myself as I would have wished, from developing my talents, or speaking my mind for the benefit of mankind than it is to admit that it was I myself who failed to do these things merely because I was incapable of freeing my own spirit from its bonds. And it is of course easier to take pride in a freedom I have obtained without any effort on my part than to pause and think how well I was able to use it, what I actually did with it.

I was born in Prague in the midst of a great economic crisis. In those days my birthplace was considered to be a city in which people were able to live as free men and women, that is, they were able to think and speak without hindrance. Yet, at that very time, the hitherto latent disease of our continent was already at work, eroding those freedoms. I was eight when Prague was occupied, when even listening to a foreign broadcasting station was punishable by death. Since then I have seen many books thrown out of libraries, many trials at which writers and journalists were condemned, having been found guilty of possessing a somewhat different idea of the world and of freedom than their judges. At an age when my contemporaries in other parts of the world were fascinated by the opposite sex and by sex and love itself, I was fascinated by the idea of external freedom, without which it seemed to me one could not live honourably, satisfactorily or fully.

My speech at the Writers' Congress in 1967 had as its theme the external conditions of free literary work and the harmfulness of censorship – and this, naturally, brought me into direct conflict with the powers-that-were. And it was really at that time that my present fate as a writer first began, a writer who is not allowed to publish in his own country, whose books may not be sold, and whose manuscripts are confiscated by the police when they search his house.

There is no place on this earth where a man might be totally free. Nor can I imagine a force that would be capable of permanently depriving people of all freedom. Contemporary society cannot exist in complete freedom, nor can it exist in complete unfreedom.

Excessive external freedom which one happens to be born with, which is simply given to one without any effort on one's own part, no doubt has the same effect as any other excess: it tends to make us soft and leads to further excesses.

A lack of external freedom which one happens to be born with and which one can do nothing to change has the same effect as a shortage of anything else. It forces us to turn in upon ourselves. Just as the hungry man dreams about food and satiety appears to him to be the highest form of bliss, the man who is not free dreams of freedom, thinking that if only he could achieve it and obtain his proper rights, everything else would be at his fingertips. But it can happen that a man will only start thinking about what freedom means to him once he has lost it, and it can also happen that a man will unexpectedly gain external freedom; it is then that he discovers that this external freedom is no more than an opportunity, which may well show him his own emptiness, his unpreparedness for the free life he had been dreaming of.

It is generally accepted that an author cannot write in conditions of external unfreedom. Many times in this last decade I have been asked by visitors from abroad how I was able to bear my fate, how I could exist as a writer since I was not allowed to publish. These people have probably never asked themselves how did a writer exist who, while free to publish as and what he liked, actually had nothing to say, or for one reason or another desisted from saying it.

And so, as I have said, it is his inner freedom that really counts where an artist is concerned. He can live and work surrounded by brutality, he can live and work even though deprived of his rights. After all, the great Russian literature of the nineteenth century was created in one of the most unfree empires the world has ever known. Dostoyevsky was sentenced to death, and he lived in prisons and in exile. Solzhenitsyn conceived his works – at least in his mind – while serving time in the labour camps of Siberia. Many great works have only come to be published after the death of their author. But no worthwhile work can be created by someone who lacks internal freedom.

What do I mean by internal freedom?

In one of his greatest novels, Karel Čapek tells the story of a railway employee who, just before his death, looks back on his 'Ordinary Life'. Suddenly he finds it full of missed opportunities, of other – sometimes better, nobler, more worthwhile, or again worse, pettier, less meaning-ful – lives. He had not lived any of them, the opportunities passed him by or they did not strike him as such at the time, or he saw them but backed away for lack of courage. 'He feared the voice that might have spoken to him.' Čapek here does not assess the validity of his hero's choices, rather he is interested in the fact that we all live only one of our many possible lives, and this is something common to us all – anyone else may seize the opportunity that was mine.

I would say that it is the man who knows how to choose, to detect his very own opportunity at every decisive turn in his life, who is truly internally free; he is not afraid of that voice, should it ever speak to him.

I start from the assumption that man is not a mere 'naked ape', not just one of the animal species living purely by their instincts but a being who has understood the reality of his own death and desires to overcome it, to continue when he has ceased to exist, to survive his earthly existence (whether we think of this as the posthumous existence of his soul or of his work, his *oeuvre*). It then seems to me that the way one lives may bring one closer to, or on the contrary alienate one from, this fundamental meaning of man's existence.

The internal freedom of each and every one of us will doubtless reveal itself in the way in which we are capable of discovering and maintaining this most fundamental aim of life, the way we again and again endeavour to keep faith with it, not allowing any external influence or pressure to divert us from it – whether this pressure takes the form of fashion, trend, convention, ideology, success, police terror, or the corrupting effect of fame and wealth.

I believe that in the course of the last few years I have learned to give up a great deal of what contemporary man considers to be a natural and even indispensable part of his everyday existence. By this I do not mean owning a passport, telephone, or the possibility to choose employment best suited to his abilities and training, nor am I thinking of the possibility to borrow in the library or to buy a book of one's own choosing – I have in mind the entire way of life as it is lived by artists and journalists in the cultured world: a life consisting of a variety of minor joys and worries such as the meetings of editorial and arts committees, lecture tours, the applause or otherwise of one's audience, study trips, letters from one's readers, press interviews, discussions with publishers, the experience brought by the success or failure of one's work, prizes, awards or other forms of public approval. At first it seemed to me that my life had been impoverished, yet as time went by I began to realize that, if anything, I had been freed from what I could call external ballast. The more I was deprived of things I had earlier cherished, the freer I felt; I was gradually becoming less vulnerable and more independent.

That is not to say that the road to freedom necessarily leads via some kind of asceticism. Nor would I claim that one has to come into conflict with the powers-that-be in order to gain internal freedom. No, all I am trying to say is that these two categories – external freedom, which allows one to accept all the joys and privileges (but also disadvantages) of modern life, and genuine internal freedom – have very little to do with one another.

Deprived of one's freedom of expression a man can easily lapse into despair, accept this unfreedom as his inevitable fate, fall silent and give up his soul to darkness – on the other hand, he can see this as a challenge. He may then discover that his earlier, more public, existence had been a form of escape from his own self, that while he was always ready to hold up a mirror to the world at large, he himself avoided looking in it or looked into a less harsh and critical one. And so today I believe that it is less important for a writer to worry about his freedom of expression than about what it is he wants to express. Or to put it another way: that he should at all times endeavour to express himself as a dignified, incorruptible and free human being.

Translated by George Theiner

December 1981

TOM STOPPARD

Open letter to President Husák

Tom Stoppard, best known for his plays *Rosencrantz and Guildenstern are Dead* (1967), *Jumpers* (1972) and *Travesties* (1974), was born in Czechoslovakia and came to England as a young child. A champion of Czech writers in their struggles with censors and secret policemen, he translated Václav Havel's play *Largo Desolato*, and shortly before *Index* published this ironic appeal to Dubček's usurper Gustav Husák, whom Havel would replace as President in 1989, he wrote the play *Dogg's Hamlet, Cahoot's Macbeth* for the exiled Czech playwright Pavel Kohout. He is a Patron of *Index*.

Dear President Husák,

I'm having a little trouble getting a visa to visit the CSSR and I wonder if you can help. It would be best of all if you helped me to get the visa, but it would be helpful if, failing that, you could tell me why I cannot have one. I spent a few enjoyable days in Prague some four years ago (my first return to your country since I emigrated in my mother's arms in 1938) and I have been looking forward to a return visit.

The first time I presented myself at the Czechoslovak consulate in London and filled in the appropriate form I was impressed by the ease and efficiency with which a visa was granted. When I tried again a couple of years later I was impressed only by the politeness of the gentleman who came to the counter to say, 'I am sorry, Mr Stoppard, but it is not desirable that you should receive a visa.'

Disarmed by this politeness I didn't like to embarrass him by asking him for any reason. Perhaps he would have replied that after my previous visit I had abused his country's hospitality by writing and speaking sympathetically about the Chartists. It did not seem to be the moment to start a philosophical discussion about human rights

in general and Charter 77's objective in particular, namely the implementation of Czechoslovakia's admirable constitution. Instead, I
retired from the field. Earlier this year I decided to have another go.
My application for a visa was again refused without comment.

I should say that I think it is reasonable for any country to close
its door against any person whom it would prefer to remain outside.
I feel the same way about my house. Anybody who shows up at this
address and criticizes my way of life and my moral values will not
be asked back. I don't think that my behaviour in your house was
particularly anti-social. Indeed, set against the virulence of the critics
of government we shelter under our own roof, I would have
thought that my conduct was genteel: a number of earnest
discussions over cups of coffee, followed by an article of a few
thousand words written in a tone which would have been far too
mild to appeal to many of the newspapers and magazines which find
themselves in weekly disagreement with the government over here.
Be that as it may, I'm pretty sure that I have no 'human right' to
enter your country if you don't want me to. So this letter is not to
register a complaint, merely a disappointment. You have made your
point: a visitor whose only anti-social intentions are to give token
and pathetic moral support by drinking coffee and conversing with a
handful of Chartists is not welcome.

Ought I to have left matters there? I had a sense of frustration.
The occupational prejudice of playwrights is that things only move
forward through dialogue. I also retain my faith, which may be an
occupational naivety, in progress through reason and reasonable discussion. So on 21 July 1981, I committed the naive act of writing to
Dr Němec, Minister of Justice for the Czechoslovak Republic, asking
for an interview. Perhaps my visa application form, reduced to essential facts, carried with it an implication that I wished to run around
Prague making all kinds of mischief. I suggested to Dr Němec that if
someone could intercede on my behalf in this matter of a visa I
would come to Prague, if necessary merely for one day, just to use
up an hour of his time. I'll make no secret of the fact that at the
back of my mind was the thought that in October my friend Václav
Havel would be reaching the halfway point of his jail sentence and
by Czech law, as I understand it, he would be eligible for parole.

Frankly, Havel's prison sentence has been a great nuisance to me. Every week or so I have to ask myself what I can do to help him instead of being able to get on with my life and my work, so it would be a great relief if, after the failure of letters and telegrams, a personal word from the Minister himself settled the matter one way or another.

After five weeks without a response, I sent a telegram asking whether my letter had arrived. That was on 27 August. Seven weeks have passed. I rather think that I have now shot my bolt as regards achieving a return visit to Czechoslovakia.

And yet I am still troubled by a sense of incompleteness. Nothing that can be written or spoken is as ambiguous as silence, and I am troubled by this silence. I return to my work and to my life but at the back of my mind I ask myself whether this silence indicates a contemptuous indifference, a shiftiness, a tiny unease or a bureaucratic prudence. Perhaps it is not the endless silence which follows the last line of a dialogue, but merely a pause, a very long pause. I would still like to return to Prague, and this desire has become an end in itself, independent of any reason for going. Whether I go purely as a tourist for another look at the castle, whether I go to shake the hands of a few people who have fallen from grace and to reaffirm, uselessly, that they have not been entirely forgotten and ignored, or whether I go to have my bourgeois moral scruples corrected by someone in authority, the idea of going back, and the sense of frustration, remain with me. I have had no luck with official channels. Perhaps I'll have more luck with a sideways attempt: herewith, therefore, my final application for a visa to visit the Czechoslovak Socialist Republic.

Tom Stoppard

December 1981

106

MICHAEL TIPPETT

A convenient illusion

Sir Michael Tippett, a supporter of civil liberties throughout his long and richly productive life as a composer, was imprisoned for three months as a conscientious objector in 1943, while he was director of music at Morley College, and just two years after producing the oratorio *A Child of Our Time*, written in memory of young victims of Nazism. This article was written for Index's special issue on music and censorship in 1981. Like Yehudi Menuhin (see page 110) he is a Patron of Index.

Censorship always happens on the other side of the fence: within other cultures, political systems, religious communities or whatever – never in our own. That, of course, is an illusion. But it is a convenient one which, consciously or unconsciously, we seem always to maintain. I think we have to be on guard against it, otherwise we merely deceive ourselves and condemn from a position of manifest self-righteousness.

Let me now give an example of censorship that may surprise some people. They may even feel that the word 'censorship' is too strong in this context, though that is certainly an accurate description of it.

In 1942 the BBC published the following four-point statement of policy with regard to certain types of music and performances:

1. To exclude any form of anaemic or debilitated vocal performance by male singers.
2. To exclude any insincere and over-sentimental style of performance by women singers.
3. To exclude numbers which are slushy in sentiment or contain innuendo or other matter considered to be offensive from the point of view of good taste and of religious or Allied susceptibilities.
4. To exclude numbers, with or without lyrics, which are based on tunes from standard classical works.

The unspoken censorship in point 1 was the BBC's ban on crooners, which provoked a lot of debate and argument in the press and else-where. It was partly attributable to pressures not to broadcast anything that would jeopardize the moral fibre of the nation during wartime.

Crooning has long since become an acceptable Establishment enter-tainment on radio and elsewhere. But other forms of singing and music-making have still been censored by the BBC under point 3: songs by Billie Holiday, the Beatles, the Sex Pistols, and others. The BBC had its underground resistance, of course: the Third Programme fulfilled that function partly: and early on, a famous example was the reading of Nevill Coghill's translation of Chaucer's *Canterbury Tales* (including all the bits that were undoubtedly 'offensive from the point of view of good taste') in a series of Third Programme broadcasts.

I am sure that the BBC's policy statement of 1942 has long been superseded: indeed, it might even appear comic nowadays. But point 3 will continue to apply. It can be regarded as part and parcel of the censorship that can be found in all periods and cultures. Plato would have found the BBC's entire music policy statement acceptable, for he too deprecated the notion that music was intended merely to create cheerful and agreeable emotions. He insisted that, in his State, it was the paramount duty of the legislature to suppress all music of an effemi-nate and debasing character and to encourage only that which was pure and dignified.

Music has always been affected by the needs of religious and political propaganda. The reforms brought in by the Council of Trent in the sixteenth century were deliberately designed to ensure that in perform-ances of church music the religious music was right in the forefront. The motives underlying such reforms and the methods for putting them into effect were hardly dissimilar from those of Zhdanov and others in Soviet Russia trying to use music to support an optimistic socialist ideology.

Music continues to be approved or disapproved according to its impact on particular cultural or religious sensibilities. Beethoven's fate in Maoist and post-Maoist China is a ludicrous story. In Israel there is a continual debate as to whether the music of Wagner and Strauss should be played in public concerts and broadcast on the radio. At present both composers are, to my knowledge, banned – though presumably recordings of them, playable in the home, are not. At one stage, it was apparently impossible for my own oratorio, *A Child of Our Time*, to be performed in Israel because it contained the name *Jesus*. That, I'm glad to say, no longer applies.

Censorship exists, then, in all societies, be they communist, fascist, democratic or whatever. In its worst manifestations, it is part of a complex of restraints on personal liberty. Discovering the whole truth about it entails de-schooling society, not just expressing abhorrence or condemning those on the opposite side from ourselves. For my part, I can only salute those who manage to break through: people like Shostakovich who, in his music, often used officially acceptable 'programmes' as a kind of 'front' or alibi, whilst communicating to the world – inside and outside Russia – both the distress and the courage of countless individuals; people like Nadezhda Mandelstam who memorized all her husband's poetry to keep it alive. From such people we constantly get signals, which tell us that the individual has somehow the fortitude to survive.

I received one such signal when I read a line by a young Polish poet, Jacek Bierezin, whose censored work was published in *Index on Censorship* 2/1975. It said, 'cherish men but do not choose nations'. I am sure that a lot of censored music, all over the world, would say just that, if it were allowed to be performed.

February 1983

YEHUDI MENUHIN

Why should music be censorable?

Yehudi Menuhin, the virtuoso violinist, conductor and musical educator, was largely responsible for developing cultural exchange programmes between America and the Soviet Union in the inhospitable Cold War years and for bringing Indian music and musicians to the West. Here he provocatively prescribes the establishment of 'zones of silence', giving freedom from the sound of muzak and other '"music" injurious to the ear, soul and sensibility'.

I could circle the thorny centre of the argument, but I shall plunge into the brambles. There is a case to be made for restricting certain types of musical activity – as there is for regulating other potent human drives.

(a) In an ideal world it should be possible to protect people from 'music' injurious to the ear, soul and sensibility.
(b) Such music, or muzak, is the deadening refrain piped into lifts, arcades, restaurants and aircraft to a captive audience who must be abused in this fashion without consultation.
(c) I would dearly like to see (and hear) some system for regulating these unwelcome broadcasts by restricting the financial gain of those operators who exploit both music and the hapless consumers of their product.

Why can there not be zones of silence prescribed, as now exist near hospitals, where one is free of man-made, mechanical, recorded or amplified noise, or those degenerate soundwaves which pass for music?

Today we regulate drugs, food, films – and think it right to do so. Why can there not exist similar proscriptions on the infliction of ersatz music, which is no less open to abuse?

There are of course certain types of real music which are censored

– and this is in itself a token of its power. This has been recognized by governments and philosophers since the time of Plato. Music in some regimes has charms only when it conforms to the propaganda of the day; in these regimes it is not art but power which is music to the ears. I remember in Russia in 1945 hearing an oratorio, for that is what it was, in praise of Lenin. Again, in China, until recently, music and musicians suffered considerably under the Gang of Four.

Commercial interests and tyrants: both attempt the censorship of music, the former by harnessing its potency for financial gain, the latter for the consolidation of their own power.

February 1983

ANKA KOWALSKA

Madness

Anka Kowalska, a leading Polish poet, was one of the hundreds of intellectuals detained during General Jaruszelski's pleasure after the proclamation
of martial law in Poland in December 1981. She was a founder, with Jacek
Kuron, of the Workers' Defence Committee, KOR, one of the taproots of
Solidarity, and was actively involved in the production of the country's
formidable output of samizdat writing during the 1980s.

In the camp for women the prison authorities, in accordance with the
Internment Decree, removed every scribbled note; most often this
was done during searches preceding our transfer to another detention
centre. From 13 December 1981 I kept a sort of diary. In order to
overcome a sudden but long-lasting inability to concentrate, I spent
several weeks trying to reconstruct 'Reason of State', my last poem.*
Both my diary and the as yet imperfect version of 'Reason of State'
were taken from me during a thorough search preceding my transfer
from Goldapto to Darłówek. Frequent searches in Darłówek made it
impossible for me to retain any notes with literary pretensions; in any
event, I was being shunted about so frequently that I thought that
tomorrow, the day after, or today, I would have to tear up with my
own hands whatever I might have written once I had managed to
overcome the creative cramp caused by continued overcrowding and
lack of privacy. What could be saved had to be jotted on scraps of
flimsy paper the size of postage stamps; here the austerity of the poetic
form helped.

Anka Kowalska

* Published in Index 6/1981.

Madness

How brave our young soldiers
how prettily they warm their hands at fires
which light up my country far and wide
how proudly my tanks turn their guns
toward my enemies in my towns and villages

How numerous are the patrols
in the handsome camouflage of my citizens' militia
how vigilantly they examine the identity of trams buses trains
suitcases bags files pockets and identity cards

How bravely detachments of my armed boys
hidden behind Mars-like masks and shields
conquer week by week
my mines my steelworks my docks

How full are the cellars of my orders
what hubbub in my prisons and detention camps
how skippingly
from one corner of my country to the other
Tsarist sleigh transports carry the slaves from place to place

How effectively my summary my military courts
pronounce sentence after sentence
how eager is my Seym
how firmly is peace bolstered up by my decrees

How creative is the silence of the police curfew
what salutary ideas and solutions come to me then
how interesting is the television news

How properly winter has passed
how orderly is spring forecast
how deeply convinced I am that summer will come in its
   own time
how fittingly will I design autumn

How inevitable is the change of hate into love
achieved by the descent of my security services
one December night Saturday through Sunday

How directly
how effectively
in such beautiful spectacles
how irreversibly I enter history

Translated by Adam Czerniawski

April 1983

SALMAN RUSHDIE

Last chance?

Salman Rushdie, whose novels and stories demonstrate the actuality of world literature, has also become the emblematic literary victim of the politics of the post-communist world, rather as Havel, Sinyavsky, Brodsky and their kind were of the order that preceded it. At the gathering at which he was awarded 'the Booker of Bookers' to mark the twenty-fifth anniversary of the prize he had won with his novel *Midnight's Children* in 1981, he expressed his intense – and visible – relief at being among people who were treating him simply as a writer once more.

My first memories of censorship are cinematic: screen kisses brutalized by prudish scissors which chopped out the moments of actual contact. (Briefly, before comprehension dawned, I wondered if that were all there was to kissing, the languorous approach and then the sudden turkey-jerk away.) The effect was usually somewhat comic, and censorship still retains, in contemporary Pakistan, a strong element of comedy. When the Pakistani censors found that the movie El Cid ended with a dead Charlton Heston leading the Christians to victory over live Muslims, they nearly banned it until they had the idea of simply cutting out the entire climax, so that the film as screened showed El Cid mortally wounded, El Cid dying nobly, and then it ended. Muslims 1, Christians 0.

The comedy is sometimes black. The burning of the film *Kissa Kursi Ka* ('Tale of a Chair') during Mrs Gandhi's Emergency rule in India is notorious; and, in Pakistan, a reader's letter to the *Pakistan Times*, in support of the decision to ban the film *Gandhi* because of its unflattering portrayal of M. A. Jinnah, criticized certain 'liberal elements' for having dared to suggest that the film should be released so that Pakistanis could make up their own minds about it. If they were less broad-minded, the letter-writer suggested, these persons would be better citizens of Pakistan.

My first direct encounter with censorship took place in 1968, when I was 21, fresh out of Cambridge and full of the radical fervour of that famous year. I returned to Karachi where a small magazine commissioned me to write a piece about my impressions on returning home. I remember very little about this piece (mercifully, memory is a censor, too), except that it was not at all political. It tended, I think, to linger melodramatically on images of dying horses with flies settling on their eyeballs. You can imagine the sort of thing. Anyway, I submitted my piece, and a couple of weeks later was told by the magazine's editor that the Press Council, the national censors, had banned it completely. Now it so happened that I had an uncle on the Press Council, and in a very unradical, string-pulling mood I thought I'd just go and see him and everything would be sorted out. He looked tired when I confronted him. 'Publication,' he said immovably, 'would not be in your best interests.' I never found out why.

Next I persuaded Karachi TV to let me produce and act in Edward Albee's *The Zoo Story*, which they liked because it was 45 minutes long, had a cast of two and required only a park bench for a set. I then had to go through a series of astonishing censorship conferences. The character I played had a long monologue in which he described his landlady's dog's repeated attacks on him. In an attempt to befriend the dog, he bought it half a dozen hamburgers. The dog refused the hamburgers and attacked him again. 'I was offended,' I was supposed to say. 'It was six perfectly good hamburgers with not enough pork in them to make it disgusting.' 'Pork,' a TV executive told me solemnly, 'is a four-letter word.' He had said the same thing about 'sex', and 'homosexual', but this time I argued back. The text, I pleaded, was saying the right thing about pork. Pork, in Albee's view, made hamburgers so disgusting that even dogs refused them. This was superb anti-pork propaganda. It must stay. 'You don't see,' the executive told me, wearing the same tired expression as my uncle had, 'the word pork may not be spoken on Pakistan television.' And that was that. I also had to cut the line about God being a coloured queen who wears a kimono and plucks his eyebrows.

The point I'm making is not that censorship is a source of amusement, which it usually isn't, but that – in Pakistan, at any rate – it is everywhere, inescapable, permitting no appeal. In India the authorities control the media that matter – radio and television – and allow some leeway to the press, comforted by their knowledge of the country's low literacy level. In Pakistan they go further. Not only do they control the press, but the journalists too. At the recent conference of the Non-Aligned Movement in New Delhi the Pakistan press corps was notable for its fearfulness. Each member was worried that one of the other guys might inform on him when they returned – for drinking, for instance, or consorting too closely with Hindus, or performing other unpatriotic acts. Indian journalists were deeply depressed by the sight of their opposite numbers behaving like scared rabbits one moment and quislings the next.

What are the effects of total censorship? Obviously, the absence of information and the presence of lies. During Mr Bhutto's campaign of genocide in Baluchistan, the news media remained silent. Officially, Baluchistan was at peace. Those who died, died unofficial deaths. It must have comforted them to know that the State's truth declared them all to be alive. Another example: you will not find the involvement of Pakistan's military rulers with the booming heroin industry much discussed in the country's news media. Yet this is what underlies General Zia's concern for the lot of the Afghan refugees. It is Afghan free enterprise that runs the Pakistan heroin business, and they have had the good sense to make sure that they make the army rich as well as themselves. How fortunate that the Quran does not mention anything about the ethics of heroin pushing.

But the worst, most insidious effect of censorship is that, in the end, it can deaden the imagination of the people. Where there is no debate, it is hard to go on remembering, every day, that there is a suppressed side to every argument. It becomes almost impossible to conceive of what the suppressed things might be. It becomes easy to think that what has been suppressed was valueless anyway, or so dangerous that it needed to be suppressed. And then the victory of the censor is total. The anti-*Gandhi* letter-writer who recommended narrow-mindedness as a national virtue is one such casualty of censorship; he loves Big Brother – or *Burra Bhai*, perhaps.

It seems, now, that General Zia's days are numbered. I do not believe that the present disturbances are the end, but they are the beginning of the end, because they show that the people have lost their fear of his brutal régime, and if the people cease to be afraid, he is done for. But Pakistan's big test will come after the end of dictatorship, after the restoration of civilian rule and free elections, whenever that is, in one year or two or five; because if leaders do not then emerge who are willing to lift censorship, to permit dissent, to believe and to demonstrate that opposition is the bedrock of democracy, then, I am afraid, the last chance will have been lost. For the moment, however, one can hope.

December 1983

FATHER JERZY POPIEŁUSZKO

In memoriam

Father Jerzy Popiełuszko, the young Polish priest who ministered to the Warsaw steel workers and regularly attended the trials of opponents of the Jaruszelski regime, made the church of St Stanislaw Kostka, famous for the ardour of its crowded monthly 'Mass for the Homeland', a place of practical and spiritual comfort for prisoners' families and a centre of the 'Workers' University'. He was murdered by renegade security policemen on 19 October 1984 and his body thrown in a reservoir – after which the church became a national shrine, its Masses attended by thousands, overflowing into the nearby parks and streets.

Father Popiełuszko's kidnap 'by unknown perpetrators' was first announced on Warsaw television on 20 October 1984. On 21 October Warsaw radio and television broadcast descriptions of three men, described as the 'presumed' kidnappers. The descriptions were based on information provided by Popiełuszko's driver, Waldemar Chrostowski. On 27 October, the Polish Interior Minister, General Kiszczak, appeared on television and spoke for 20 minutes. He stated 'with the greatest sorrow' that those involved in the kidnapping were three officers of his Ministry. The one who organized the abduction was Captain Grzegorz Piotrowski, head of a section at one of the departments of the Ministry; his accomplices were Lieutenant Waldemar Chmielewski and Lieutenant Leszek Pekala, both working in the same section of the Ministry under Piotrowski. On 30 October Polish television broadcast a statement from the Ministry of Interior saying that the body of Father Popiełuszko had been found in the waters of the reservoir in Wloclawek.

Father Jerzy Popiełuszko, born in 1947, was an outspoken supporter of Solidarity, and his abduction and killing was the ultimate step following a number of cases of harassment in recent years.

The following excerpts from a homily delivered by him during the

Mass for the Homeland at St Stanislaw Kostka's Church in Warsaw on
25 October 1983:

I would like us today to turn our thoughts to the word Culture. I
am aware that it is a theme as mighty as a river, but I would like
at least to touch upon some of the problems connected with this
word.

The Holy Father, John Paul II, speaking to the young during his
first pilgrimage to his homeland said, that '. . . Culture is the
expression of Man. Culture is the confirmation of Humanity. Man
creates Culture and through Culture he creates himself . . . Culture
is the common Good of the Nation . . .'

Polish culture is the good on which the spiritual well-being of
the Poles depends. Thanks to our culture the nation has remained
itself despite the loss of independence over many years.

Only a spiritually free and truth-loving nation can survive and
create the future . . . Therefore let us take care of our free spirit
and do not let ourselves be enslaved by fear and intimidation.

All attempts to constrain the freedom of the human spirit work
against culture. Professional artists became deeply aware of this
under the influence of the workers' patriotic movement in August
1980. Actors, journalists, writers, painters, sculptors, they all
realized it. Their conscience was awakened, as was the conscience
of the whole nation which had been asleep for many years. The
year 1980 was hard, but showed the great virtues of our nation:
consideration, caution, competence and cooperation.

The social, professional, economic, cultural and political
conscience was awakened. The artists started to speak out
unconstrained. They decided to serve the truth.

But wherever a lie is officially nursed, there is no room for
truth, which contradicts and unmasks lies. Therefore the war
started once again – against truth and the freedom of expression,
against freedom and the greatness of ideas spoken out loudly,
influenced by awakened conscience. Every remark about human
rights is now labelled a hostile activity.

Lately, the artists who create our culture have become an
example to us. Especially actors, who after 13 December 1981

showed unprecedented fortitude, courage and sacrifice. [They boy-cotted the official mass media.]

The progress of culture is not helped by monstrous censorship, which bans all truthful and courageous words, sentences, articles or ideas. It censors what was written by pens soaked in truth. And after all, words, in order to be alive, have to be truthful.

Translated by Andrew Short

February 1985

DARIO FO

'When they beat us, we suffer'

Dario Fo, Italian playwright (*Accidental Death of an Anarchist; Can't Pay, Won't Pay*) and founder of the theatre group La Commune, has been attacked verbally and physically for his radicalism. For four years he and his wife were denied entry to the USA under the notorious 1952 McCarran-Walter Act, but in 1984, after pressure by free speech organizations and other writers of international standing, he was allowed to travel to New York for the American première of *Accidental Death of an Anarchist*.

In Italy, censorship today exists only for young people under eighteen or fourteen. It took a long time and a great deal of struggle to get rid of the more general censorship that survived from the days of fascism. Where the youngsters are concerned censorship comes into force every time a taboo topic rears its head – violence, obscene language, and so on – but the truth is that at bottom it is always of a political nature.

I wrote a play called *Fabulazzo osceno* ('Obscene Fabulazzo'), which had scenes of sexual intercourse in which sex was openly discussed. The play followed the French classics of the eleventh and twelfth centuries, including Boccaccio and others. It wasn't concerned with political issues, and so they passed it, and it was even judged suitable for young audiences. The following year Franca and I put on a show called *Coppia aperta* ('Open Couple'), about a husband and wife and issues such as sexism, virility, the right of men to go out with other women whereas women are considered prostitutes if they go out with other men, and so on. There was also a monologue for Franca playing the mother, speaking about the problem of civil rights and how people were to defend themselves against laws such as the one for the *pentiti* (penitents), which obliges prisoners to wait for five, seven, eight years before coming to trial; one can spend a lifetime in jail without ever being tried. All these things were censored.

The show was not passed for people under eighteen. We fought against the ruling, Franca collected signatures among the audience, there were articles in the press both by reporters and critics, and in the end they gave in and lifted the censorship. This was our most recent experience, it happened this year, 1984.

There exists another kind of censorship, to do with prizes, grants, opportunities to tour. This, of course, does not interfere with the text of your play, but it is understood that if certain cuts aren't made or if certain topics are included, it will be difficult to obtain the grant. It is a kind of blackmail which governs the selection of texts.

As for our banning from the USA, we applied to go there to perform, and twice we have had invitations to visit the country. On the first occasion – and this is grotesque – the tour was organized by the Italian Ministry of Arts; but the Foreign and the Home Office intervened, urging the US government not to allow us in. And the American government had its own doubts whether it ought to let us have a visa. Why? Because we had for years been making satires about the USA, about the war in Vietnam, Chile, the ethnic minorities. We naturally accused the US of responsibility for the coup d'état in Greece, for example, when the Colonels came to power.

Most recently, we were invited to take part in a Shakespeare festival in 1983. The refusal of the US authorities to let us in led to enormous protests by American intellectuals, and I must also say that the Italian press behaved well in this matter. The whole thing is absurd – my books are published over there and my plays performed, and the same applies to the other authors who are not allowed to visit the USA, but I'm banned from entering the country. It really is difficult to understand how someone like me can make America tremble merely by what I say. It is grotesque, a leftover from McCarthyism.

At home in Italy, we have been attacked several times in the theatre because the police insisted on entering premises which were private clubs. It was, in fact, an association they attacked. They claimed it couldn't possibly be an association with 80,000 people. What kind of club was it? It's a club with 80,000 people. The law permits this, there is no numerical limit, an association can have fifty million people. One always tends to think of a club as something belonging to an élite, but we had this thing with 80,000 people in Milan, 30,000 in Bologna, 40,000 in Turin – there were eighty groups with a total of some half a million people. All over Italy.

They went so far as to arrest me. They arrested me at Sassari and took me to jail. Franca was kidnapped, she was seized, we don't know who exactly was behind this, but yet again it had to do with the police. She was beaten up, they were very violent. They kept her in a van for two or three hours, and they disfigured her, slashed her face and breast. It is all part of the violence.

They also planted bombs and blew up half a theatre. Another time, at Salerno, they burned down the theatre, shortly before Franca arrived. That was seven years ago this December.

There are other small groups in Italy which have suffered similar harassment, but none with such continuity, only sporadically. I can truly say that our group has been in the vanguard both of the struggle and then of the oppression which followed as a consequence.

During our recent visit to Argentina someone threw a teargas bomb while we were playing. It was the fascists, who resented the political topics in our work, or perhaps because we criticized the Pope. Whatever their motive, they threw a bomb at us. And every night they turned up to protest and demonstrate against us. They broke all the windows in the ten-storey theatre, the San Martin, the biggest in Buenos Aires. It has an enormous window which they destroyed completely by throwing stones while the police just stood by, watching.

One thing I would like to say is that we don't want to complain. When they beat us, we suffer, we feel tense, even frightened. In Argentina it would have been quite easy for them to shoot us. Many theatres have been burned down there, actors and directors have been killed, their houses burned, they have 'disappeared'. There was a danger that some crazy person might shoot us, in the same way as they threw that bomb. They gave us to understand that they were ready to do anything. In Italy, too, we could not travel around with impunity, and when we wanted to rent a house, we found that people were unwilling to let it to us because they were afraid someone would plant a bomb in it. That is why, on many occasions, we couldn't sleep at home, having to hide and go to the houses of friends instead because of death threats against us. But it's useless to complain. We have to live with the situation as it is and carry on working.

February 1985

IVAN KRAUS

A simple solution

Ivan Kraus left Prague in 1968 to work as a scriptwriter for Radio Free
Europe and the BBC. Since 1990 six of his books have been published in
Prague to critical acclaim. His sketch *The Censor*, published in *Index* in 1976,
was made into a short film narrated by Anthony Hopkins.

Dear Mr Ceausescu,

I have for some time now been following your political career
with great admiration because I know that you alone decide what is
and what isn't good for Romania. This in an age when in many
countries politicians still waste a lot of time by indulging in lengthy
and fruitless debates in parliaments and legislative assemblies. I'm
therefore convinced it is no exaggeration to say that there is no
statesman in the world today who would show so personal an
interest in his citizens as you do.

I have just learned about your latest measures from the daily press.
Having ascertained that the Romanians eat too much and that, as a
result, a full third of the population suffers from diseases due to
obesity, you have proposed a diet consisting of ten eggs, ten
dekagrams of butter and a kilogram of meat per citizen per month.

You have also decreed that room temperatures should not exceed
15 degrees Celsius, being well aware that citizens of a socialist state
must not be too delicate.

Your order that lifts should only operate from the third floor up
will likewise help to improve the physical fitness of your people, just
as the decision not to use refrigerators in winter and to switch the
TV off at 10 pm every night, except on special occasions such as the
days when the nation is celebrating a birthday – yours, your wife's,
or that of some other member of your family.

It is to be regretted that some of your citizens seem not to understand the wisdom of these measures you have decided to take, so
that it is necessary for the police to step in and keep a watchful eye
to make sure that people don't overheat their homes, use their
fridges in winter, or consume too much energy on illumination,
cooking, ironing, or watching TV. It is only the irresponsible
attitude of a few individuals that makes it necessary to resort to
blocking up their points.

I, however, am an optimist and believe that before too long everyone will realize that they can only hope to see a brighter tomorrow
if today they switch the lights off early. It is no secret that you and
all your family have to work very hard. Your son Nicu is Minister
for Youth, your brothers Ion and Ilie are in charge of the Ministries
of Planning and Defence respectively, another brother, Nicolae, heads
the Ministry of the Interior. Moreover, your wife is your First
Deputy.

It is well known that altogether 50 members of your family have
to devote all their time, energy and talents to the job of running
Romania, with its 22 million inhabitants. That makes it almost half a
million citizens per member of your family, and that is a record that
cannot be equalled anywhere in the world today. Not even Flick in
West Germany, Heineken in Holland, Grundig or Ford can measure
up to you in effectiveness. Duvalier achieves only minimal output
with his employees, Idi Amin has gone bankrupt, and Khomeini has
too many shareholders and still cannot make a go of it.

I mention all this only because I think that your latest idea – to
register all typewriters in the country – requires a little more
elaboration. Allow me therefore to discuss this interesting measure
and to make a few suggestions as to how it could be improved.

First of all, it is absolutely essential also to register chalks, pens,
crayons, pencils, brushes, as well as ink, varnishes and sprays
(insofar as these are obtainable in your country), and other material
such as paper, note-pads and exercise-books. And talking about
paper, you mustn't forget wrapping and toilet paper. Also all kinds
of material used to cut out, stick on or otherwise position letters of
the alphabet. I am referring to newspapers, sacks, textiles, scissors,
glues, drawing pins, needles, pins and nails.

However, people can use other means too to express anti-State or otherwise harmful sentiments. By means of the Morse-code, for example, which can be transmitted with the aid of light. For that reason I would recommend the registration of lamps, chandeliers, torches, bulbs, batteries, spotlights, lanterns, fireworks, as well as mirrors.

More primitive methods such as smoke signals can also be used to convey anti-State slogans, for which reason I would restrict the sale of matches, candles, lighters, as well as cigars and cigarettes.

Furthermore, you must not forget all the objects that can be used to transmit sound signals. No citizen should thus be in a position to obtain without permit bells, whistles, and musical instruments (percussion, wind and string – for short distances). The number of musical instruments owned by all orchestras and ensembles should be checked without delay, and reliable musicians issued with music passports.

All this, however, is still not enough.

People wishing to express some anti-State thought can be extremely ingenious, as I discovered in Prague in 1968, when the arrival of Soviet troops gave rise to what I might call a festival of anti-State creativity.

The lesson we learned then was that citizens can make use of empty tins, dustbins, boxes, barrels, as well as tyres and building materials such as bricks, breeze blocks, beams and planks. Tools to be found in any storeroom must also be included in this category: pliers, picks, hoes, shovels, drills, scythes, even sickles.

Furniture, too, can come in handy. All you need is a few tables, chairs, hat-stands, benches or wardrobes and you can put together a slogan.

Nor should farmers and farm labourers be left out. They can achieve the same result with the aid of sugarbeet, potatoes, marrows, any kind of vegetable and also all larger – i.e. legible – species of fruit. Even the smaller fruits, such as redcurrants, blueberries and raspberries, can be made use of for writing, if not on walls, then certainly on tables.

Similarly, pots and pans, saucepans, lids, plates, in short all kitchen utensils, crockery and even cutlery offer similar possibilities.

And, alas, we cannot exclude medicine bottles and pills, including vitamins, while foodstuffs too can be misused. Sausages, salamis, hams, loaves of bread, rolls, butter, yoghurt, ice-cream, beer and other bottles – all this is potential communication material, just as various personal items such as lipsticks, compacts, make-up kits, purses, watches, and chewing gum.

Finally, I must draw your attention to yet another object – the book. Or rather books. I know that these are carefully censored before they ever get to the bookshops, libraries, schools or scientific institutes. But it is not their content which concerns me here.

The very shape of a book makes it an ideal tool for the compiling of words or whole sentences, so that all an inventive anti-State person needs, for instance, is a pile of your own, ideologically absolutely innocuous autobiographies, or some other officially sanctioned works, from which to compose an unsuitable slogan.

I am well aware that any systematic measures to prevent the spreading of anti-State ideas in the way I have outlined above would be extremely costly.

I realize that it would require the appointment of special censors in every office, factory, institute and co-operative. They would also have to be sent to other sectors, such as the railways, road transport, and district and regional administration, and above all every street and house. Not to mention the armed forces and the police.

If I take into account the cost of the reporting and systematic registration of all individual objects, to which has to be added the expense incurred in setting up and operating the central censorship offices and control commissions, it occurs to me – as I sit here typing on what is as yet a free, unregistered typewriter – that there would be a far simpler and cheaper solution, which I take the liberty of offering for your consideration.

I suggest that we solve the problem rationally and simply by *abolishing the alphabet*.

That is the only way we can achieve socialism quickly and without risk.

Translated by George Theiner

August 1985

IRINA RATUSHINSKAYA

Two poems

Irina Ratushinskaya was arrested in 1982 and sentenced to seven years' hard labour after being convicted of writing articles and documents of an 'anti-Soviet' nature and the 'manufacture and dissemination' of her poetry. After a period of 're-education' at the KGB prison in Saransk, she was released in 1986 and settled in Britain. Among her recent collections of poems are Grey Is the Colour of Hope (1989) and The Odessans (1992).

Stars suddenly rain down, and the heavens are filled with cold
The moon is wavering – hold on, don't loosen your grip!
Close your eyes – out there, beyond your weary vision
A skater inscribes his rings, precise as compasses.
Shades vanish in the black-and-white engraving of winter
Grim, beggared phrases rumble with a verb.
Five steps to the window, four from wall to wall
And an eye winks absurdly, framed in the iron door
Monotonous, sly, the interrogation drags by
The young escort has a soldier's artless crudity . . .
Oh what peace – to wander through winter in silence
Not letting a single 'no' pass sore, cracked lips
The pendulum of snow has failed: what week is this?
But my eyes have dimmed on the page and my head is burning.
Through the heat and the chill I shall stagger my way to April!
I'm on my way. And God's hand is on my shoulder.

Translated by Sally Laird

And we remain —
In place on dreadful chessboard squares —
All of us prisoners.
Our coffee
Smells like burned letters
And post offices
Smell like opened letters.
City blocks are deaf —
And there's no-one there to shout:
'Don't!' And the chiselled faces
On façades have their eyes shut.
And every night
Birds are flying away from the city.
And blindly
Our dawns drench with light.
Wait!
Is it just a dream? Could it be?
But in the morning
Newspapers hit the street.

Translated by Pamela White Hadas and Ilya Nykin

October 1985

NUNCA MÁS

File 2819

File 2819 is just one piece of testimony from Nunca Más (Never Again), the report of the Argentinian Commission on Disappeared People presented to President Alfonsin in 1984. This documented in searing detail the systematic sequence of the policy of extermination of the opposition – abduction, torture, murder and concealment of the bodies – carried out by members of the armed forces in the time of the three military juntas which ruled Argentina from 1976 to 1982. Faber and Faber in association with Index published the first English translation of Nunca Más in 1986.

Life in the detention camps

In Campo de Mayo, where I was taken on 28 April 1977, the treatment consisted of keeping the prisoner hooded throughout his stay, sitting, without talking or moving, in large blocks which had previously been used as stables. Perhaps this phrase does not express clearly enough what that actually meant, because you might think that when I say, 'sitting, hooded, all the time', it is just a figure of speech. But that is not the case: we prisoners were made to sit on the floor with nothing to lean against from the moment we got up at six in the morning until eight in the evening when we went to bed. We spent fourteen hours a day in that position. And when I say 'without talking or moving', I mean exactly that. We couldn't utter a word, or even turn our heads. On one occasion, a companion ceased to be included on the interrogators' list and was forgotten. Six months went by, and they only realized what had happened because one of the guards thought it strange that the prisoner was never wanted for anything and was always in the same condition, without being 'transferred'. He told the interrogators, who decided to 'transfer' him that week, as he was no longer of any interest to them. This man had been sitting there, hooded, without speaking or moving, for six months, awaiting death. We would sit like this, padlocked to a chain which could be either individual or collective. The individual type was a kind of shackle put on the feet; the collective type consisted of one chain about 30 metres long, long enough to be attached at either end to opposite walls in the block. Prisoners were chained to it every metre and a half, as circumstances required, so that they were all linked together. This system was permanent.

March 1986

VÁCLAV HAVEL

My temptation

Václav Havel was already established as a fine playwright before 1968, with
The Garden Party (1963) and *The Memorandum* (1965), a mordant send-up of
Party pomp-speak and mystification. After the Soviet invasion of Czechoslo-
vakia he became the focus of opposition with the founding of Charter 77.
He was bugged, censored, banned and imprisoned from 1979-83. (*The
Mistake*, written on his release, was first published in English in *Index*.) He
led Civic Forum in the toppling of the Communist regime, replacing Gustáv
Husák as President of Czechoslovakia in January 1990. In this interview
with Karel Hvížďala, he discussed two of his later plays, *Largo Desolato* (1984)
and *The Temptation* (1985).

I always used to spend a long time on my plays, something like two
or three years, with each of them undergoing a great deal of rewriting.
I never found it easy to write, and I would produce a number of
versions before I finished the final draft. I suffered a lot in the process,
and not infrequently gave way to utter hopelessness. You can see from
all this that I am hardly a 'spontaneous' type of author. And then
suddenly something quite extraordinary happened: in July 1984 I wrote
Largo Desolato in a mere four days, and in October 1985 *Temptation* in ten
days. Obviously, something had changed. Not that I want to exaggerate
this, and I certainly don't intend to draw heaven knows what far-
reaching conclusions from this change in my working rhythm. It seems
to me that it was due mainly to outside influences. After I returned
from prison, my nerves were in a bad state for a long time, I suffered
from depression, nothing seemed to please me, everything seemed to
me to be a duty, while at the same time I carried out my duties – real
or imagined – with a kind of stubborn doggedness. An Austrian critic
once wrote about one of my plays that it had risen from the very
bottom of my despair and that it represented an attempt to save myself.
I actually sneered at this at the time, ridiculing his idea of how a play

comes into being. Now, I think I owe him an apology: maybe that speedy writing of mine after I came out of jail really *was* an act of self-preservation, an attempt to shake my despair, a safety valve I needed to make life bearable.

Another thing, perhaps even more important: one of the expressions of the various obsessive neuroses which I suffered from at that time (or perhaps still do) is one that is well known to every dissident: you live in fear for your manuscript. Until such a time as the text which means so much to you is safely stowed somewhere, or distributed in several copies among other people, you live in a state of constant suspense and uncertainty – and as the years go by, surprisingly enough, this does not get easier but, on the contrary, the fear tends to grow into a pathological obsession. And if, at first, all you feared was a police search of your house or person, so that you hid your manuscript with friends every night, in time this fear becomes far more universal – you begin to worry that they'll lock you up tomorrow, that you'll fall ill or die, that something indefinite is going to happen to you (and the more indefinite the danger you fear, the more advanced is your disease), all this making it impossible for your work to see the light of day. As that work grows in size, your suspense grows in keeping with it – what if someone will trip you just as you are approaching the tape? You can't imagine how I always looked forward to the time when I would have no work in progress! And prison only served to increase these fears. It really seems to me that in my case this played a very important role: I wrote these two plays in a state of increasing fever-ishness and impatience, you might almost say in a trance. That is not to say they are unfinished – I would never let anything out of my hands if I did not consider it complete. All it means is that I was possessed by a little demon, which forced me to get done as quickly as possible. Once the play is finished and in a safe place, they can do with me as they will; I am happy and feel that once again I have triumphed over the whole world. But as long as the papers are spread over my desk in an almost illegible manuscript, I tremble with appre-hension. Not only for the play, you understand, but for myself, that is, for that piece of my identity which would be torn from me were I to lose the manuscript.

To come to *Largo Desolato* – it has frequently happened in the past that

I used and 'misused' a motif derived from my immediate surroundings, thus earning the reproaches of those who – rightly or wrongly – felt I was writing about them. Every time this happened, I of course felt bad about it, but it never occurred to me to leave out that particular motif or avoid something like that happening the next time. You see, I know I have no right to do that: when the drama *demands* something. I have no choice but to respect its will, I must not censor it. That would be to sin against the very essence of my calling: it is the author's job not only to organize existence according to his own lights – he must at the same time serve it as a medium. Only if he does that, can his work amount to more than its creator and aim further than he himself can see. And so – however unwittingly – I must have hurt quite a few people. In *Largo Desolato* all these victims of mine could rightly see an instrument of God's justice, which wreaked vengeance on me on their behalf. With this play, I damaged *myself* for a change; many people, including foreign critics, have found the chief protagonist, Dr Kopřiva – an intellectual whose mind is in turmoil – to be me, and they pity me for being in such a state. However, I cannot possibly make an exception in my own case and censor the topics and motifs which persecute and inspire me. That is to say, I knew in advance what I was in for, but I had no conceivable right to try and avoid it. The play really does owe its inspiration to my own personal experience more than any of my earlier plays, which goes also for its main, basic theme: the turmoil Kopřiva finds himself in does indeed reflect a part of my own, in a certain sense it is a caricature of something in myself, of my despairing state of mind after I came out of prison. Nevertheless, it isn't an autobiographical play in the sense that it would be if it was about me and *only* about me. It is meant above all as a more universally applicable allegory, so to speak, about mankind in general. It is thus not all that important to discover to what extent it was inspired by my own experience – what is important is whether it tells people anything about their own human condition. Anyway, if I really were as badly off as Dr Kopřiva, I could hardly write about it, much less write about it with ironic detachment – and so the very existence of the play refutes the suspicion that it is an autobiography of its author.

Now, as far as *Temptation* is concerned, as far as I know, nobody has sought to find me in *that* play. Yet, it has likewise been inspired by my personal experience, indeed more profoundly and more painfully so than *Largo Desolato*. The plays I wrote in the sixties tried to describe the social situation and the position of ordinary people crushed by the events of their time; the plays were, as it's called today, about 'structures' and about the fate of people within them. There was, in those days, no sign in my plays of the man who has been rejected by the establishment and who at the same time is trying to voice his opposition to it – there was no sign then of any 'dissidents'. Understandably enough, for whether we like it or not, we invariably reflect conditions as we experience them. And I was then, in a way, part of the establishment – even though I gave it a special slant by looking at it from the outside. I had no experience of 'dissidence', which I was to gain later, in the seventies. And of course, when I was then cast out and found myself in the position of a 'dissident', I naturally began to analyse it and write about it – again, among other things, by taking an outsider's view of it! This gave rise to the series of one-act plays about the banned writer Vaněk, and led in the end to *Largo Desolato*. In that play I tried to discover what happens when the personification of dissent finds itself right at the bottom. Then, after this play, it seemed to me I had nowhere to go in that particular direction. And so I suddenly felt the urge to start anew from a completely different angle, to abandon this entire field of 'dissident experience', which has in any case given rise to suspicions, however unjustified in some respects, of excessive exclusivity. In short, I no longer wished to base my play so transparently on my personal experience, to be told yet again that dissidents are only able to write about themselves and their predicament. I decided therefore to go back to writing about 'structures', as if I were still part of them, deliberately returning to the atmosphere of my early plays. I was curious to see how this would work today.

All this, naturally, had its own, deeper roots. Ever since 1977, when I landed in jail the first time, I was vaguely haunted by the theme of Dr Faust. Although I was only imprisoned for a relatively short time on that first occasion, for various reasons I found it extremely hard to bear. I didn't know what was happening outside, all I could see was the hysterical witchhunt against Charter 77. I was deceived by my interrogators, and even by my own counsel. I fell victim to curious, almost psychotic moods. It seemed to me that, as one of the initiators of the Charter, I had brought terrible misfortune on a large number of people. I of course was trying to shoulder an excessive responsibility, as if the others had not known what they were letting themselves in for, as if it was all just my fault. And it was in this unhealthy state of mind, towards the end of that first period of imprisonment, that I realized that they were preparing a trap for me: they intended politically to misuse something I had said in one of my appeals against my detention, something that I had said in all innocence, but which was now to be distorted and twisted in order to discredit me. I could not see how I was to prevent this, how to defend myself against it. Those were nasty moments, and at the same time I encountered a number of strange coincidences. Suddenly, instead of the usual reading-matter such as the Soviet novel *Far from Moscow*, Goethe's *Faust* arrived in my cell, followed shortly afterwards by Thomas Mann's. I had strange dreams and strange ideas. I felt I was being – quite physically – tempted by the Devil, that I was in his clutches. I realized that I had somehow got tangled up with him. The fact that something I had written, something I had really thought and that was true, could be misused in this way brought it home to me yet again that the truth is not only that which one thinks, but also under what circumstances, to whom, why and how one says it. And that became one of the themes of my latest play, *Temptation*. It was then, in prison, that I conceived the idea of doing my own version of the Faust theme. As time went on, I returned to this again and again, but every time I threw away what I had written because I did not like it. And then, last October, I had an idea – and I started to play around with it, to draw, as is my custom, sketches of the individual scenes, until I actually sat down to write, and completed the play in ten days. That is how *Temptation* came about. Perhaps it will be the starting-point of a new stage in my writing – quite a few people believe it's the best of all my plays, but I cannot be a judge of that. Maybe, on the other hand, it is simply a recapitulation of everything that went before, a kind of personal revival in the form of a résumé. I don't know, I just can't tell.

November/December 1986

ARIEL DORFMAN

Trademark territory

Ariel Dorfman, born in Chile in 1942, was exiled in 1972 and allowed to
return in 1985, though he has since been the target of death threats for his
outspoken writing, and in 1987 was for a time denied re-entry after a
visit to the United States. His best-known study of the legacy of guilt and
suppression from the years of junta rule following the coup which overthrew Salvador Allende's government is *Death and the Maiden*, first published
in *Index*, before it was made into a powerful film by Roman Polanski.

*. . . and then the door bursts open as if driven by a gust of wind and he comes in,
embracing her and tossing the kids in the air and laughing, happy for the first time
in eight months, feeling like the man of the house again, the one who brings home
the bacon, the breadwinner, and, well, old girl, I got a job, they hired me, they hired
me and tomorrow I have a training course all day, then on Thursday I'm on my
own, I'll be a salesman, selling the latest things, so she should go to Don Fernando's
store and ask him to trust us one more time, to tell him I have a contract now, that
it's a sure thing, I'll earn a 10% commission on sales and those appliances sell like
hot-cakes, and we need some noodles, a few onions, flour, eggs, a little milk for the
kids . . .*

Congratulations. You've been chosen from among fifty thousand appli-
cants to fill one of eight vacancies as doorbell salesman. As you will
see as this course proceeds, we're dealing with a very special bell,
patented and sold only by Health and Home, our company, a bell
which screens visitors to the home. Now, a small demonstration. Do
we have a volunteer? Thank you. Let's bring that warm finger closer,
that sweaty palm, this way, yes, that's it, you're going to press the
product in question with the obvious intention of ultimately getting
into that home. The bell responds to this pressure in one of two different
ways. The first and normal response is for the bell to sound, so that

139

the residents of the house can be advised of the presence of a friend
and thus welcome him. The second response – and this is the characteristic that distinguishes our product from all others on the market – is
for the bell to reject the request of the caller. It does so by means of
a slight electrical reaction, like this, just like this, thank you, Mr Salesman, for graciously lending us your finger for this demonstration, you
can return to your seat now, there's no permanent damage to the
brain, just a slight spasm of the skin, but we've already administered
a corrective for this unfortunate individual. Please write down in your
notes that that electrical charge is authorized by the Interior Ministry
and supervised by the Ministry of Energy and Commerce, and is purely
pedagogical in nature. It is administered only if the bell perceives
excessive timidity in the finger that touches it. In which case it will
automatically block the entry of any young man with only slightly
frayed collar and tie who might come forward to offer his services,
whether to wash windows, walk the dog, rake the leaves, whatever the
case may be, madam, sir, miss, at your service. The mechanism is
equipped with a magical nose that will immediately pick up from that
hand any sign of excessive, albeit disguised, hunger, will sniff out any
foot odour at that early hour of the day. The caller has smelly feet!
What greater proof do you need to confirm that those limbs have
already covered many city blocks in search of a few crumbs of bread,
weighed down by empty bottles for babies whose hunger is never
satisfied, that those feet have already paraded their poverty in front of
downtown shops, dreaming in front of the windows, that they've
dragged themselves to and from ever more distant towns, because they
can no longer afford the bus fare. The bell is infallible; in accordance
with scientific laws, it has determined that this same young man will
today bother not only this home but many others as well. Which, as
stated clearly in Article 84 of the new labour code – be sure to memorize
that paragraph!! – gives you the right to penalize the beggar, petitioner,
jobseeker and good-for-nothing who turns up to annoy the mistress
of the house in the middle of her morning chores, just when she's
writing the day's menu for the cook and going over the chauffeur's
accounts. That's what the bell is for, to keep everything in its proper
place, meting out tiny, almost painless jolts, educational buzzes. It's
now nine in the morning and someone will surely appear with the

same old song and dance: would you have some old clothes, ma'am? Some floors that need waxing? Perhaps your children need some tutoring in mathematics, or English, or botany or maybe trigonometry? Let's understand that we're often dealing with very well-spoken people, in fact, even well-shod, and with a certain level of culture. No-one can affirm that they're delinquents just because they're unemployed. But any excessive excitement flowing from the finger-tips, any annoying hoarseness tickling the throat, is enough to activate the bell implacably. It knows how to separate the wheat from the chaff, it knows family friends like the back of its hand and the door is opened automatically to people of trust, even before they get there, it welcomes them with triumphal music of Lully. This product has pedigree. It knows that at ten in the morning homeowners do not want their view sullied by all that unavoidable misery that must walk the streets if the country is to progress and move forward.

So your morning exercises and your Japanese flower petal sauna won't be interrupted by the downstairs maid, coming and going with useless and unfailingly boring messages the reply to which must inevitably be negative. You have to save those lips; it's not good to waste your vocal cords with useless repetitions. Let's not have an impertinent bell ringing in the middle of the morning, just when little Richie is playing in the pool and about to swim his first stroke and the instamatic camera goes click. Let the bell answer for the lady of the house while she tastes the Coquilles Saint Jacques and puts them back in the oven to frolic while she awaits the arrival of the gentleman of the house. Don't forget these examples, because they constitute true psychological motivations for buying the product; they show that you respect your patrons' lives and customs. Remember that our product is trained to sense that undeniable aura of defensiveness which the poor wear like a cloak, when they appear to sell forks, shawls, spoons, chairs, and all of it at the precise hour that the family is sitting down for lunch. The X-ray and infra-red mechanisms in the bell are sensitized to distinguish the worn article of clothing, the frayed elbow, the tie that just doesn't match the socks, the spectacles that are held together by a rubber band. At this point, nonetheless, you have to allay certain doubts of the young people of the house. This mechanism can in no way, you will say, block the entry of those who are wearing worn-out jeans or those who

141

have multi-coloured patches on their lovely garb. Perish the thought! The Bell is aware of the latest advances in fashion, it has real swing, not to mention punch. It's easy to prove that it's a prototype for fanatical ecologists, master conserver of energy in these times of petroleum crises, it has an internal thermostat that limits and regulates the level of its charge capacity. It's true it could literally fry the unsuspecting caller. It does, in fact, raise the charge level for the most persistent. Its magnetic memory recognizes the repeat offender, the one who shows up again months later to ring the same bell to sell the same soup bowl or the same unsurpassable set of mock china. A double dose, one for being unworthy to touch that button even once, and the second for being an idiot on top of it, so that this little scorching will be the last one and it won't have to be increased yet more, the third and final time, when the solicitor is electrocuted. That's the way people learn: that fingerprint missing from the offending forefinger will be a reminder and a guide for the rest of his life. Be careful. For those purchasers who may be upset by violence, now is the time to insist that it's not a matter of isolating the family from the stir of outside life either, which really should be introduced into the bosom of every home that considers itself modern. This bell, ladies and gentlemen, is capable of selecting a couple of beggars each month to whom you could donate that pair of old slippers that are no longer of any use to you, or how about a little bread, my good man, a few leftovers from our dinner two nights ago. The instrument possesses the necessary magnanimity to allow those grimy fingers, smelling of grease and soot, of weakness and suffering, to touch the august face of the Prince of Butlers, its own immaculate surface. When you offer this product, my young aspiring salesmen, you must emphasize its common sense, its protective but not isolating benefits, its charitable nature, which allows a reasonable quota of indigents to get by so that the homeowners can organize a raffle on their behalf. In these times when it's the in-thing for the housewife to sell raffle tickets to benefit the orphans at her afternoon bridge teas, we guarantee that this bell can programme regular incursions from the outside world. It therefore possesses an innate sense of the dramatic. What could be more appropriate, in the middle of the most heated after-dinner marital spat, than the sound of the front door bell to divert attention from the subject, to calm spirits and to allow the appearance of a starving stranger to reconcile the husband and wife. Being respectful of the family's privacy, it can also spice up life with the seething, passionate, obscure existence of those who suffer from powerful emotions and moving personal tragedies. Programmed by distinguished psychiatrists, the Bell digs into the preferences and appetites of its clients. And you, my dear aspirants, can know no less than the product you are offering: you must master that same art of stimulating those interests, of appealing to every whim of the customer's personality. The moment has come to place on the table not only the Model itself, but also extensive additional equipment, accompanied by catalogues.

This one, madam, leaves whip marks, that one, on the other hand, is called the Hemlock Model, it bites the persistent caller not on the finger but on the tongue, while this other one twists the arm of anyone who dares put on rubber gloves to avoid the electric shock. And here, sir, we have a magnificent example of the Slap in the Face Model, an amazing innovation. You have to lay out all this additional material when the lady of the house begins to hesitate, when she's looking for other benefits. That's when you have to toy with her superiority complex: we're not talking about cheap merchandise; the home is not losing a beggar, it's gaining a friend, a real son. It's a privilege to own this product, we don't offer it to just anybody. This Bell marks the dividing line between the Yes, of Course group and the Forget It group, between those who have the right to date your daughter and those who shouldn't get anywhere near her. Then, to drive it all home, you dramatize in the customer's presence various typical situations: tell the lady of the house I'm prepared to repair any plumbing problem she might have, I'm a qualified mechanic, engineer, nuclear scientist, you know, ma'am, with the present unemployment rate, tell her I have a great voice and I'll give singing lessons in exchange for a dish of beans every two weeks, ask the lady if she'd like to buy combs, goat cheese, little plastic toy cars, colonial lighting fixtures. Make the customer nervous with all those threats of possible intrusions. And at that point the Bell itself appears, like a busload of soldiers, like a gentle and silent volley of machine gun fire, the Bell sniffs and smells the air around the offending finger, and almost, only almost, we don't promise miracles, it almost doesn't need to feel the tips of the fingers on the button, it's enough for the intruder to get close to produce a reaction, it's enough for it to realize that he's coming to beg, to offer, to plead, to harass, he doesn't have any work and it's now four in the afternoon, and he hasn't eaten a mouthful all day, not even breakfast, and he has the nerve to put his finger on a Piece of Merchandise of that calibre. And nobody tricks it with good manners and gallant gestures, it isn't taken in by poems by Gabriela Mistral about children's games nor by snapshots of a deaf-mute brother who needs an operation. None of that business. Its judgments are without appeal: this guy lost his job eight months ago, this one here lost his a year ago, this other one lost his kid because he couldn't afford a doctor, this one can't even get it up in bed anymore, and this one would be willing to lick the toilet clean with his tongue for a pot of veggies, and this one has gums like mashed pasta. All the callers are well computed. It opens its tasty little needles, its sharp, drooling tongue, and burns the finger that would present itself without recommendation or letters of introduction into hearth and home. It knows how to stop those ungrateful voices in their tracks, to disconnect them so they won't be heard inside: I'm an architect, ma'am, don't you want me to build you a birdhouse; I'm a ploughman, ma'am, can't I pull the weeds in your garden; I'm a nurse, ma'am, I can give your cat a shot; none of that should molest the ears nor pollute the beds that are made for better things. That's what Mr Bell is all about, His Excellency the Threshold, His Doormanship, Sir Electricity, so show some enthusiasm, boys, the customer always likes that, so any intruder will know that you don't call at those doors with impunity. And that warm little needle pricks the over-eager finger, tears at the poppy-red fabric of the skin, terrorizes the tissues, interrupts their breathing for a few seconds, leaving their bodies feeling like the long back-bone of the ox after a hard day's work in the fields, that same sensation of painful numbness that our volunteer salesman has just experienced, the bell that produces a regular cacophony of ringing inside their heads, in the pits of their stomachs, in the passageways of the penis, in the creaking of a vertebra. Let them know they can't bother us just like that at six in the evening when the gentleman of the house is approaching the bar to choose tonight's appetisers, we can't receive anyone now, don't insist, come back next week, the year before last, we already have someone to take care of the chrysanthemums, the bell ringing inside the skin and bones of the intruder and not in the delicate epidermis of the homeowner, just a light whiplash to warn them that this sort of thing just isn't done no matter how hungry you are, judge them severely, where's your sense of dignity, man, are you some kind of whore, young woman, offering yourself like this from house to house, decent people don't go around soliciting employment from complete strangers, where are your credentials, your visiting card? The Bell fixes its searching eye on any shadow that crowds the doorway at eight in the evening, while the family is having dinner together. Our Bell who art at the door, at the windows, at the drawbridges, at the control towers, hallowed be Thy Buzz, Bell who knows how to distinguish man from beast, the wealthy from the mendicant, Bell who relieves our complexes and allows us to enjoy the video, our daily cocktail, our stereo hi-fi, Bell who answers our prayers down to the final letter and who never incurs cheap sentimentality like one of these foolish domestics who supposedly have hearts of gold but who really have lead dentures, our Lord the Bell, wise in Your sermons, Don Bell who art just, righteous and mighty, and who is not carried away by the supplications of our enemies, Bell who art gentle with the misguided, who has never left a man crippled or mute or paralysed, although our unscrupulous competitors would accuse us of every kind of infraction just to lower our sales, Bell who only frees our pathways of the drunk, the filthy, the unemployed, the widowed, the painter, whether with a wide or a narrow brush, and all those who ask God's favour or any kind of favour, or those who just ask, those who invoke your Bell in vain and you answer for us. Bell whose perfection is such that you even know when our windows really need washing, or our third floor balcony needs re-tiling, Bell who knows the law of supply and demand, and who only lets the lowest bidder pass. Learn this prayer by heart, boys, it's our company's ABC. And now, ladies and gentlemen, everyone is sleeping except the Bell, the best guardian against disagreeable dreams, impassable, guardian of decency, nightwatchman while you snore, because any nightmare that would dare appear gets electrocuted in the act, any ragamuffin that would disturb your pillow because he couldn't get through the front door is taken prisoner then and there, struck by a full, quivering and unforgettable volley, now that's a real Bell, your own private curfew, martial law made to order, that's all ready to go into action at six in the morning, prepared to scream its

145

little warning into the first palm that comes to knock unwisely at your door a little before eight, protector of your daughters' purity and of the heavy and satisfied sexes of your male progeny, of your ancestors' peaceful tombs, of all the portraits on your family tree, so now the clock has gone its full circle, twenty-four hours in the life of a Bell, every minute of full and dedicated service, there should be one in every decent home, if there were such an instrument in every well-to-do dwelling in the country, we would have no more problems of delinquency, vagrancy, our economy would be under control once and for all, there'd be an end to this plague of beggars that won't let us live in peace. Most of those criminals would end up far, far away, and as for the rest, the ones that have work, we'd put one of these bells around their necks, the way we do cows, to keep them from screwing things up in the future, and there we'd have them, under wraps, in the circumvolutions of the brain, then we could really mass-produce the product, gentlemen, then the sales would be enormous, for export.

Do you have all the pamphlets? Are the instructions all clear? Are you ready and willing? Fine. Good luck to each of you, the course is over.

Translated by George R. Shivers

May 1988

JOHN MORTIMER

So where do we go for freedom?

John Mortimer, author, playwright and barrister in landmark cases involving censorship and civil liberties, is best known for his fine memoirs, *A Voyage Round My Father* (1970) and *Clinging to the Wreckage* (1982), and for the television series adapted from his *Rumpole of the Bailey* (1978). In the article which follows, he charted the waning of respect for freedom of expression during the 1980s in Britain.

The denial of information is, of course, a form of censorship. A public who knows nothing is not free to criticize or denounce injustice. However, the newly suggested Official Secrets reform goes further than preserving secrecy. It might well act as a protection for the most serious crimes, including fraud and murder, provided that such crimes are committed by a government servant in what he might conceive, however wrongheadedly, to be the exercise of his duties.

In its most recent proposals the government insists that a civil servant or journalist could be sent to prison for disclosing information which is perfectly harmless. Mr Richard Shepherd, the Conservative MP, has instanced giving particulars of an innocent victim of mistaken telephone tapping or the allocation of airline routes. It will be no defence that such disclosures could do no possible harm to anyone or, indeed, that they might result in considerable benefit to the long-suffering and frequently mystified public.

Worse still, it will be no defence for anyone accused under this draconian measure to argue that the disclosure has uncovered serious crime. Perhaps the Secret Services are planning to sink an innocent ship, as their French confrères did: perhaps they have tried to subvert a properly elected government, as Mr Peter Wright has said our Secret Service once did. None of these matters can be disclosed to the public under pain of imprisonment; so in these cases the Official Secrets proposals appear a mere licence for illegality. It might have been that merely to state these facts, in an age when free speech was still respected, would have caused Parliament and the public to turn from such a piece of legislation in disgust. Now, when freedom seems to mean only freedom to make money, it is possible that the new secrecy proposals may become law. The only hope is that sensible juries may decline to convict civil servants who reveal the crimes and misdemeanours of their superiors.

In the 'progress' of the law of blasphemy the question of 'intent' has been removed and the law has been made more restrictive and less fair. The Secrets proposals go further in removing any defence based on 'intent'. The effect will be to punish the honest man acting from honourable motives and protect the inept, the corrupt or the criminal. This is an extraordinary result from a government which habitually protests its devotion to that highly respected lady, Laura Norder.

Recent government actions quite apart from the Secrets proposals have thrown some doubt upon its alleged devotion to the blind Goddess of Justice. Not only has it pursued, past all reason and expense, in the Peter Wright case, an attempt to cover up alleged past misdeeds by state servants, it has clearly connived at alleged crime in the case of the police officers in Northern Ireland who have been said to have perverted the cause of justice and are not to be brought to trial. If ever there was a decision contrary to the interest of law and order this was surely it. 'Justice should be done', said William Watson, 'though the heavens fall', to which the government has added, 'Not if we have to give away our secrets'. The brave new world, it seems, is to be divided into two classes, government servants, who will not be prosecuted for alleged crimes, and the rest of us who certainly will be, however admirable our motives.

Perhaps the present attitudes were shown most clearly in the matter of the shootings in Gibraltar. Now it may very well be that the soldiers involved acted entirely in self-defence and should be entirely acquitted of unlawful killing, let alone murder. But even the late Lord Goddard at his most authoritarian would have let that matter be decided after due legal process and not have accepted the word of some shadowy army officer or government minister. There is to be an inquest in Gibraltar, which those who performed the killings may or may not attend. It is well known that a coroner's inquest is a most inadequate forum for attributing responsibility for a death, and many lawyers will remember the case of the late Blair Peach. [Peach was killed by a blow to the head during an anti-National Front demonstration in London in 1979; his family have only this year been paid damages by the Metropolitan Police.] So if there is to be no proper trial of what happened in Gibraltar, and this, of course, remains to be seen, why did the government get so excited by a discussion of the facts on television? If possible injustice is to be concealed by the state, what have we but the newspapers, radio and television to rely on?

This brings me to the government's plans for television. Now it may be that some of those suggesting radical change in the structure of British television are genuinely concerned about satellites and discs and other so called technological advances. However, I believe there are other motives in the desire of our rulers to break up an excellent, independent and authoritative service, fortified by certain standards, and convert it into a jumble of thirty-seven third-rate channels peddling thirty seven similar varieties of rubbish. In the new world of British television there will be endless game shows, pop programmes, situation comedies and re-runs of old movies. There won't be high quality drama and there won't, so I believe and some people in government devoutly hope, be controversy. If the status of television is lowered from that of a public service, with its long tradition of political independence, to something not much more interesting than commercial radio, it will no longer be able to challenge governments with any sort of conviction.

The BBC, funded by the television licence, can be seen as a powerful ally of free speech. A BBC with high standards sets a necessary challenge to its commercial competitors, and the commercial companies are spurred on to produce good television by the threat of having their franchises removed. It is interesting to see how the BBC, the key to good broadcasting, has been undermined and attacked because it has, from time to time, produced programmes not completely flattering to the government. First it was bullied by the then chairman of the Tory party, Norman Tebbit. Then government supporters were placed on its board. Then a committee was appointed which produced a report which was not destructive enough to meet the requirements of the powers-

149

that-be. Now new schemes are said to have been hatched. The licence fee may be abolished and the commercial television franchises sold off to the highest commercial bidder. If an institution, be it the Greater London Council or the BBC, becomes over-critical, it's not long before the demolition squads are sent in.

So where do we go for freedom, and who can we rely on to voice that dissent without which a society stagnates, however well the economy may be doing? We are left with writers and journalists no doubt, and the Church unexpectedly enough. No doubt journalists have a heavy responsibility to be forever watchful, and many discharge it admirably. But the times are not propitious. In healthier days most newspapers, certainly those which were the most readable, attacked the government of the day, whichever government it might be. Now, however, too many journalists censor themselves, and the temptation to write what they fear the proprietor or the editor may require is no doubt hard to resist. So opposition politicians are treated as objects of scorn and derision: Mr Foot, the ex-Labour leader, has a funny donkey jacket, or Mr Kinnock (the present leader) is a windbag, as though Sir Geoffrey Howe, the Foreign Secretary, or Mr John Wakeham, Leader of the House of Commons, were men of elegance and masters of oratory. Sadly, young writers who should be manning the barricades against such monstrosities as the new Secrets reform are merely muttering approval, like clubland bores. Perhaps they will read all this and say, well, we're better off than the Russians or the South Africans so what on earth is the point of complaining? In answer to this I can only go back, as I so often do, to Wordsworth.

We must be free or die, who speak the tongue
That Shakespeare spake; the faith and morals hold
Which Milton held . . .

But then Wordsworth, of course, was born before Mrs Whitehouse said her prayers.

September 1988

WOLE SOYINKA

Jihad for freedom

Wole Soyinka, Nigeria's foremost novelist, playwright, poet and critic, is an outspoken campaigner for democracy and civil liberties. In 1986 he became the first African Nobel Laureate for literature, and he is currently Woodruff Professor of Arts at Emory University, Atlanta. The following essay was written in the aftermath of the *fatwa* issued against Salman Rushdie for his novel *The Satanic Verses*.

This statement is not, of course, addressed to the Ayatollah Khomeini who, except for a handful of fanatics, is easily diagnosed as a sick and dangerous man who has long forgotten the fundamental tenets of Islam. It is useful to address oneself, at this point, only to the real Islamic faithful who, in their hearts, recognize the awful truth about their erratic Imam and the threat he poses not only to the continuing acceptance of Islam among people of all religions and faiths but to the universal brotherhood of man, no matter the differing colorations of their piety.

Will Salman Rushdie die? He shall not. But if he does, let the fanatic defenders of Khomeini's brand of Islam understand this: the work for which he is now threatened will become a household icon within even the remnant lifetime of the Ayatollah. Writers, cineastes, dramatists will disseminate its contents in every known medium and in some new ones as yet unthought of. This is the great age of communication, and its tempo cannot be halted by the Quran, the Bible, the Apocrypha, the Book of Ifa or the Bhagavad-Gita. Writers everywhere will produce pastiches of Rushdie's work, flood Iran with them by every means including parachutes. Rushdie's *Satanic Verses* will provide the text of the funeral obsequies of Ayatollah Khomeini which will be celebrated in every writers' gathering in the world, including within Iran. That long-looked for elevation of the Ayatollah Khomeini to the ranks of faithful martyrs will be marked by public sales of the fifth, maybe ten millionth copy of Salman Rushdie's *Satanic Verses*.

The world recognizes courage, and cowardice. It is easy for any leader of a nation, protected and cushioned by the entire machinery of state, to issue death warrants on a solitary writer, summoning to his aid the hundreds of thousands of mindless zealots which every religion indiscriminately produces at every phase of its existence. It is also cowardly, unmanly, and impious. But the fact that this is indeed a Head of State acting in a criminal manner places an immense burden of conscience on other Heads of State. They must know that Iran must be ostracized as long as it boasts a common criminal at its pinnacle of power. The Ayatollah's incitement to murder is criminal by any laws, secular or theocratic. Governments must know that it is their duty to expel Iranian diplomats from their territories. These embassies have been instantly turned, by Khomeini's fiat, into staging posts for the murder of an individual and of his publishers. At the very least, Iranian diplomats should be subjected to the severest curtailment of their movement. The displeasure of the civilized world with uncivilized conduct in a Head of State must be expressed by the most drastic and uncompromising means.

But we do know that it is part of the business of states to compromise. Writers and artists must therefore act, not simply talk. If Salman Rushdie dies, then his work must be unleashed upon an expanding readership by every available means. But Rushdie must not, and will not, die. And the Ayatollah must be punished for his arrogance, for his hubris, and the implicit blasphemy in his arrogation of a Supreme Will. It is the duty of all believers in freedom of expression to work for the triumph of a genuine secular revolution in Iran. That must be Ayatollah Khomeini's punishment. We must seek out the dissidents of Iran wherever they are and assist them, by every means – material and moral. We must become an active force in the overthrow of the Ayatollah's tyranny of zealotry. Intellectual association is under threat by individual bigotry. Salman Rushdie will not die; it is the Ayatollah's doctrine that must die, that must be seen to crumble against the resolve of all free people everywhere.

I must now address the Organization of Islamic Councils, directly. Let me begin by informing you that, during a visit to India last December, I caught some flak from sections of the artistic and intellectual community for commenting that I quite understood the action of the Indian government in banning Salman Rushdie's book, *The Satanic Verses*. I stated that, given India's harrowing situation of religious unrest, I probably would have done the same if I were the Prime Minister. I did not condone the ban; I merely tried to understand the horrible dilemma in which the government of India was placed. At that time, of course, the Ayatollah Khomeini had not yet intruded his own homicidal remedy; neither had you met, and taken the decision which you recently did, one which remained totally silent on the jeopardy in which Salman Rushdie's life had been placed. The situation and, indeed, the implications of the publication of this work, have changed drastically. I must let you know that, were I to be asked the same questions today on the soil of India, I would declare that it is not Salman Rushdie's work which should be banned from India, but Ayatollah Khomeini's person, voice, thoughts, sayings, photographs etc, etc. Indeed I would go further and declare that everything which is Iran should be banned as long as Ayatollah Khomeini remains accepted as a leader in Iran, everything except the voices of Iran's political and cultural dissidents and the protests of her repressed womanhood.

I should also let you know a little about some of the religious problems we have had to encounter in this nation, problems which occasionally spring, admittedly, from the suspicions of one religion towards another, but which have erupted in the most violent forms in recent times from the opposition of one sect of Muslims to another. I refer to the Maitatsine sect whose badge of piety lay in the strangulation and the slitting of throats – not even of non-Muslims as primary targets – but of 'orthodox' Muslims such as, for instance, the Ayatollah Khomeini might consider himself. To the Maitatsine, the Muslims you and I interact with daily were deemed apostates to the true faith and were massacred in an uprising that lasted months. The Nigerian state performed its duty, went as far as it could in exterminating this virus in the body politic of the nation. Our experience here therefore is such that we do not recognize the propensity for violence as the test of the true voice of the Commonwealth of Islam. To do so would be to accept that the late Maitatsine

153

was the pre-eminent Muslim of our time – at least within Nigerian borders. While we do hold that it is the Islamic world which must decide who and who are their false prophets and messengers of Allah, the majority of nations today accept that Islam, like other major world religions, speaks with many voices, and remain unimpressed by the resort to obnoxious forms of zealotry, such as a universal call to murder in the name of Islam, as proof for any one of the many claimants to worthiness of successorship to Mohammed.

There is yet another pertinent instance of our adaptation to tolerance in matters of religious contestation. One noted Islamic scholar here (very prominent, indeed a recent winner of the prestigious King Faisal International Award for Islamic scholarship) declared only last year that – and here I quote – 'Christianity is nothing'. Now, I have not read Salman Rushdie's book, but I doubt very much if there could be anything in it that equals such a blasphemous dismissal of one of the acknowledged major religions in the world. And this statement was made in a nation which is, in the estimation of many, roughly equally divided amongst Muslims and Christians and animists, with the former two constituting a floating adherent population of the 'animist' in addition to being what they publicly proclaim. Sheikh Gumi, a reputable scholar and therefore a professional colleague of Salman Rushdie, received nothing worse than the usual verbal brickbats including some savage cartooning from the Nigerian population. No price was placed on his head, no stones were thrown at his house. He has not been deprived of Nigerian citizenship, much less threatened with a withdrawal of his earthly passport. We, in this country, cannot therefore accept the privileged status which the Ayatollah's brand of Islam seeks to place upon its existence. Nor will the creative world to which millions belong accept such an impudent invitation to submit ourselves to the terminal censorship of any one religion or the other. However much the Ayatollah may now believe that he is the representative of the Divine Will upon earth, those who have access to any language that will unblock his obviously sclerotic mind must inform him that there do exist today several interlocking worlds – be they defined as national, racial, religious, cultural, technological or simply professional. It is up to the Islamic world to decide and to declare, in unambiguous terms, whether their interlocking arc of this world is as described, and wishfully controlled by Ayatollah Khomeini, or whether the Islamic world will choose to be that recently recalled by Pakistan's Prime Minister Benazir Bhutto in the following words:

> When Muslims start breaking scientific barriers, they start breaking technological barriers, then they take their place with pride and glory on the world stage. But then Islam is known in the world through dictatorship. I don't think that is the essential message of Islam. I would like to see a renaissance of Islam, but for me the renaissance of Islam is not the cutting off of arms. For me renaissance means a greater Muslim unity, a greater Muslim glory, and this unity and glory coming because our people live lives like human beings, they have good standards of nutrition, they have good standards of morality . . . they are creative and they can break the barriers of technology and science. In early Islam, if you recall, the great scientists on the world stage came from Islamic countries, the great historians came from Islamic countries. So I would like to see Muslim countries gain a place of prominence in the international world through their creativity.

The Islamic world must choose. Between this vision of Islam and the Islamic fervour that consecrates the hired killer, albeit 'authorized' by self-vaunting divine surrogates. Organizations like the OIC must declare an allegiance. In meeting to ban *The Satanic Verses* while remaining silent on the criminal activity of Ayatollah Khomeini, the Organization of Islamic Councils is saying that it cannot yet be counted upon as a partner in the desirable alliance towards creating an alternative strategy within a western dominated world. The OIC has let slip a unique opportunity; it is not too late. It must find, and quickly too, a formula for stressing its own wounded religious sensibilities – assuming that its members have even read the book! – while at the same time denouncing the even greater un-Islamic affront to the brotherhood of man in Ayatollah Khomeini's resort to an incitement to murder. The dictatorship of Khomeini, coming especially after that of Shah Pahlavi, is an indecent prolongation of the agony of a people with an enviable history of cultural and scientific achievements. Khomeini is a creature of the Darkest Ages of any society. If Egypt's political

'crime' (under Anwar Sadat) could earn expulsion from the Organization of Arab States, Iran's hideous aberration under Khomeini more
than merits expulsion from the Organization of Islamic States. For
while, as now appears in recent developments, that political 'crime'
is proving to be no more than statesmanship before its time, there
is no time in universal usage when it will ever be accepted that any
Head of State pronounce himself a common, bloodthirsty criminal in
the pursuit of the citizen of another nation over interpretations of faith.
The OIC should have the courage to declare Ayatollah Khomeini a
pariah and treat him as such.

Let us face the truth: Ayatollah Khomeini's pursuit of the scant quarry
in the form of Salman Rushdie, after a bloodying at the hands of his
implacable foe, Iraq, is a parlous arithmetic of compensation in the lust
for global relevance. This belated pursuit of theocratic authority after
a political (and military) diminution is as obvious as it is pathetic and
unworthy. The mullah should be made to understand that, unlike those
who so desperately cling to life when they should have quit the illusions
of earthly glory years ago, there are, in this world, those who do not
conceive of survival within any form of fetters, least of all from rulers
who exercise control over the brainwashed products of an imperfect
world. For every Salman Rushdie, there are a hundred thousand others.
And no one should continue any longer under the illusion that the
Crusade, or Jihad, or Holy War, or indeed any title by which we are
constantly menaced these days, as if the mere talismanic jingo is its
own fulfilment, is the exclusive preserve of any one religion. If anything,
it has become boring. Wars in passionately held causes underscore the
entire history of human development, and the 'Jihad' in the name of
freedom of expression is one of the oldest known and the most resilient.
It is older than political systems and older than any theocracy. The
Ayatollah needs to be taken back to the history school, then he might
begin to understand why this Jihad which he flaunts in the face of the
modern world is only an enfeebled descendant of the real Jihads that
have freed, not further enslaved, contemporary man, and will sustain
him against dictatorships that hide themselves under a cloak of
piety.

If Salman Rushdie is unnaturally and prematurely silenced, the creative world will launch its own Jihad. It has the will, it has the resources

and, above all, it has the imagination. The zombies and dacoits of unreason, no matter how well sheltered and evilly unleashed from embassies around the world, will not stop it, nor will a million acts of terrorism organized against the innocent. It will outlast the Ayatollah Khomeini's great grandchildren; it will, in fact, become a permanent feature of a world that has mastered the art of communication.

May/June 1989

DROR GREEN

The train of wonders

Dror Green's *Stories of the Intifada* describe life in the Occupied Territories as seen by its inhabitants. After many excuses and refusals from Israeli publishers, Green himself published the collection in Hebrew in 1989. The Arabic edition, published a year later, carries the warning 'Forbidden to be distributed, bought or sold in the Occupied Territories'. This story, 'The train of wonders', based on an incident which the author himself witnessed, caused an uproar when it first appeared in Israel because of its clear reference to the Holocaust.

The little daughter of Ra'if was afflicted by epilepsy. Though she was more beautiful than her older siblings, her face was disfigured by the illness, which had also made her mentally backward. Her beauty was of a unique kind: her body was tall and lean even though she ate rather too much, and her opaque skin was stretched taut and fragile over her bones. The girl looked like a small angel about to take off at any moment to return to the tranquil skies. Her large, dark eyes, prominent against high cheekbones, were always clouded as if she were immersed in a distant dream. But the illness marred the beauty: her tongue hung out of her mouth to her chin, giving her an ugly appearance.

Every morning, Ra'if got up early to take his daughter to the special school for children with difficulties. He tried to arrive at the bus stop particularly early so that his daughter could sit by the window and look at the ever changing views during the journey. It was the only pleasure the young girl enjoyed each day and she eagerly awaited these hours of travel.

After taking his daughter to school, Ra'if would return to the bus stop and travel to town to arrive punctually at the scaffolding factory where he had worked as a labourer ever since the soldiers had closed his grocery. David Green, the boss, knew Ra'if's story and so would turn a blind eye if Ra'if came to work late. Once, he even visited him at home when he was ill and brought him a jar of quince jam which he had made himself.

It was a clear summer morning and, as every morning, Ra'if set off early for the bus stop. When the bus came, he hurried to get on and sit his daughter beside the window. Then the two of them sat in silence, watching the tired workers standing in the bus queue, the women carrying baskets of figs to market and the elderly on their way to hospital. Slowly but surely, the old bus filled with passengers. Those who did not find a seat either sat on the back steps or hung onto the leather straps suspended from the long bar fixed to the roof.

Soon the bus set off. Because of its heavy load, the old engine rattled and the bus made its way slowly through the city exit. As every morning, the soldiers stopped the bus and were about to get on to check the passengers when the group commander caught sight of Ra'if's daughter and of her tongue drooping to her chin. The commander swelled with anger: it was his first day in this unfamiliar town and he was sure that the girl was making fun of him. When, to his alarm, Ra'if saw the soldier's anger, he quickly pulled his daughter to him and held her in his arms. But the group commander's anger did not dissipate and he ordered the bus driver to drive to the nearest police station. He himself drove behind the bus to the police station. When he arrived, he told the station commander how the girl had insulted him and asked him to detain the bus passengers in order to teach the ill-mannered locals a lesson.

So the bus stood under the searing sun, in the square outside the police station. After about an hour, the driver opened the doors of the bus and asked that the frightened passengers, who were thirsty and crammed, be allowed out into the open air. But before any of the passengers could get off, policemen surrounded the bus and shouted orders at the driver to shut the doors and the windows immediately. When the driver tried to remonstrate, one of the policemen struck him with his baton and when another policeman fired into the air, the passengers hurriedly closed the windows of the bus.

By afternoon the heat in the closed bus was so intense it was almost unbearable. Those passengers who previously had been standing and holding onto the leather straps became so weak that they tumbled in a heap on top of each other onto the floor where they lay motionless and semi-conscious. A heavy odour of sweat pervaded the bus and filled the nostrils of its occupants.

Strangely, not a sound was heard from the passengers. Only the sound of their heavy breathing from lack of oxygen filled the bus as if a huge animal were gasping its last. After so many years of occupation, the passengers knew what to expect and none of them dared revolt and disobey police orders.

One by one the passengers began to remove their sweat-soaked clothes. Any thought of convention or modesty was abandoned. All they could think about was a breath of fresh air and a glass of cold water. The children were the first to lose self-control and their wet pants gave off a stench that fogged the senses of the passengers. There was no longer any sense of shame and in no time the floor of the bus was covered in excrement.

By late afternoon when Ra'if had still not arrived at work, his boss David Green grew worried. Filled with foreboding, he got into his small car and drove to Ra'if's house. He was tired after a day's work, tired of his workers' woes when they told him about their hard lives, and he looked forward to the day he could stop working and retire.

When he reached the road block at the entrance to town, the soldiers told him about the bus that had been punished by a long wait at police headquarters. 'Why should you worry about these fellaheen [peasant farmers]?' the soldiers laughed. 'Don't bother getting involved in things like this. Go home. This is no place for you.'

But David Green drove to police headquarters. When he saw the bus, its windows steamed up by sweat and urine, he explained to the police commander that a dreadful mistake had been made here. He told the policeman about the girl's illness and about her tongue which fell to her chin. Only after repeated appeals did the policeman agree to examine his claim and allow him onto the bus.

When David Green entered the bus, he was hit by the stench of urine and excrement; at the sight of the naked people lying like corpses in terrible filth, he lost consciousness. A while later, he came round to find himself lying among the gasping bodies. He heard the sound of the railway carriages of his childhood and at the end of the carriage saw his mother and sister thrown onto the floor. At that moment, the train stopped and he saw the soldiers of the SS enter the carriage.

When the commander of the police station got onto the bus he discovered that the girl was indeed sick and that her tongue stuck out of her mouth uncontrollably. He ordered the windows opened and drinking water to be given to the passengers; then he released the bus. To his surprise he did not find David Green on the bus and informed the army commander. An investigation at his place of work revealed nothing. But when relatives of the disappeared man were found, they were astonished to hear that their relative was alive. All they knew was that the last time he had been seen was getting into the train that transported him to the extermination camp over 40 years ago. Since then nothing had been heard of him.

Translated by Shirley Eber

November/December 1990

PHILLIP KNIGHTLEY

Here is the patriotically censored news

Phillip Knightley, author of The First Casualty, a history of the war correspondent 'as Hero, Propagandist and Mythmaker', contributed this article about news manipulation by the military and politicians to a special issue of Index devoted to the Gulf War.

The war in the Gulf marks a major change in censorship. Although the Alliance gives 'military security' as its ostensible reason for the rules it has imposed on correspondents – the excuse used ever since the British invented military censorship in 1856 – there has been a covert expansion of aims. In the Gulf War, the Alliance goal is much more ambitious – to manage the news to its own advantage.

News management in the Gulf has three main purposes: to deny information to the enemy; to create and maintain support for the war; and to change public perception of the nature of war itself. Of these the third is by far the most important and the most sinister. How did we get to this alarming state of affairs?

After the failure of an Allied attack on Sevastopol in June 1855, sentiment in Britain swung about The Times and its correspondent, William Howard Russell, the pioneer of modern war reporting whose critical dispatches from the Crimea had helped bring down the government. Prince Albert called Russell 'that miserable scribbler', one MP suggested that the army should lynch him, and there were suggestions that the behaviour of The Times and Russell was little short of treason.

This made it easier for the new commander-in-chief, Sir William Codrington, to acquire government support for some sort of restraint on the press. The government favoured putting the reporters on their honour not to report anything that might endanger victory, but Codrington, whose opinion of journalists was not very high, went further.

162

On 25 February 1856, he issued a general order that must rank as the origin of military censorship. It forbade the publication of anything the authorities considered could be of value to the enemy.

Britain has been involved in no major war since then in which some degree of censorship has not been imposed. And as early as the First World War, the government had expanded the aims of censorship to include point number two from above – create and maintain support for the war.

In 1914-18, the military allowed only six correspondents to report from the front. It put them in officer's uniform, provided them with orderlies, lorries, cars, conducting officers and censors. The censors lived with them, ate with them, read their dispatches, and opened their private letters.

The correspondents drew lots to see who would cover a particular attack and then shared the report with their colleagues, an early form of the modern 'pool' arrangement. Each then submitted his story to his censor and what was left was sent by military dispatch rider to Signals where it was telephoned to the War Office and then sent by hand to the various newspaper offices.

The aims were to provide the public with colourful stories of heroism and glory so as to sustain enthusiasm for the war, to cover any mistakes the high command might make, preserve it from criticism in its conduct of the war, and to safeguard the reputations of the generals.

The correspondents went along with all this. One of them, Sir Philip Gibbs, wrote in 1923: 'We identified ourselves absolutely with the Armies in the field ... There was no need of censorship of our despatches. We were our own censors.' *The Times* approved: 'They felt that their task was to sustain the morale of the nation in mortal combat; therefore they praised victories no less highly than they deserved; in stalemates they found elements of advantage; and defeats they minimized, excused, or ignored.'

The effect of this distortion was immense. The average British citizen, now a soldier, had been accepting all along that if something was printed in the newspapers, then it was true. Now, in the biggest event of his life, he was able to check what the press said against what he knew to be the truth. He felt that he had found the press out, and as a result he lost confidence in his newspapers, a confidence to this day never entirely recovered.

By 1939, the government had come to regard the war correspondent as a part of the armed forces – 'an integral and essential part of our fighting activities on land, on the sea and in the air' – who, for the most part, again went along willingly with what the censors said. This was understandable because the war was one of national survival in which the wickedness of the enemy did not have to be invented.

But it did produce worrying after-effects – when censorship was finally lifted many correspondents were bewildered. One spoke for them all when he said: 'But where will we go now to have our stories cleared?' A Canadian, Charles Lynch, summed up: 'It's humiliating to look back at what we wrote during the war. We were a propaganda arm of our governments. At the start, the censors enforced that, but by the end we were our own censors. We were cheerleaders.'

Vietnam upset the status quo. Censorship had always been a problem in the United States because the first amendment to the Constitution guaranteed freedom of expression, and prior restraint (censorship) could only be justified in a national emergency. There was no declaration of war against Vietnam and therefore no censorship. Correspondents were free to travel where they wished and write what they liked. The military confined itself to trying to persuade them to 'get on side' and to using its political clout in Washington to influence editors.

It did not succeed. At first correspondents supported the war, but when they saw that government policy was not working they said so. Graphic television coverage brought home to Americans the nature of the war itself, its bloody brutality, and the suffering of Vietnamese civilians. That, and increasing American casualties, sapped public support for the war and the United States pulled out.

The lessons were noted. On 13 October 1970, a Royal United Service Institution seminar in London discussed television coverage of the Vietnam war. Robin Day, then the BBC commentator, told those present that war on colour television screens in American living rooms had made Americans far more anti-militarist and anti-war than anything else. 'One wonders if in future a democracy which has uninhibited television coverage in every home will ever be able to fight a war, however just?'

And the Director of Defence Operations, Plans, and Supplies at the Ministry of Defence, Brigadier F. J. Caldwell, said that if Britain ever went to war again, 'we would have to start saying to ourselves, are we going to let the television cameras loose on the battlefield?'

The answer was no. By the time the Falklands campaign had started, the Ministry of Defence (MoD) had in place its plan to manage the news. The MoD started with one major advantage – it, and only it, controlled access to the war. So no one was let loose on the battlefield unless he had first agreed, as a condition of being allowed to accompany the task force, to accept censorship at source. And, to give the correspondents an idea of their duty, they were issued with a booklet which told them that they would be expected to 'help in leading and steadying public opinion in times of national stress or crisis'.

The MoD succeeded in managing the news brilliantly – censoring, suppressing, and delaying dangerous news, releasing bad news in dribs and drabs so as to nullify its impact, and projecting its own image as the only real source of accurate information about what was happening. Those stories it suppressed until the war was over give an indication of a trend that was developing in the culture of censorship.

After the war, correspondents back from the front rushed into print with the 'untold story', incidents that the MoD had refused to pass at the time. The intriguing thing is that most of these stories would have been of no value to Argentina whatsoever. What they did was to paint too vivid a picture of the face of battle, where highly-trained groups of men were doing some very nasty things to each other on two otherwise peaceful islands in the South Atlantic.

So by the time the Gulf War had started, censorship's additional aim was to convince the public that the new technology of war had removed a lot of war's horrors from early on: the emphasis was on the 'surgical' nature of air strikes; the cancer would be removed but the living flesh around it would be left untouched. Bombs dropped with 'pinpoint accuracy' would 'take out' only military targets; there would be little or no 'collateral damage' (dead civilians). Iraq's military machine would be destroyed from the air so that there might even be no need for soldiers to kill soldiers in a ground war of attrition.

The picture that this news management has painted is of a war almost without death, a sanitized version of what has gone before. It was weeks before any bodies were shown on television, and then British television chiefs voluntarily cut the more horrific scenes. A new language was brought into being to soften the reality of war. Bombing military targets in the heart of cities was called 'denying the enemy an infrastructure'. People were 'soft targets'. Saturation bombing was 'laying down a carpet'.

The idea was to suggest that hardly any people were involved in modern warfare, only machines. This explains the emphasis at Alliance press briefings on the damage 'our' machines have caused to 'their' machines, and the reluctance of the briefing officers to discuss casualties – on either side.

So the Gulf War is an important one in the history of censorship. It marks a deliberate attempt by the authorities to alter public perception of the nature of war itself, particularly the fact that civilians die in war. The rationale, as yet unproven, is that the public will no longer support any war in which large numbers of civilians are killed, especially by Western high technology armaments. Whether the new censorship succeeds or not remains to be seen.

April/May 1991

MATTHEW D'ANCONA

LOW warspeak*

Matthew d'Ancona, deputy editor of the Sunday Telegraph and a polemicist of the libertarian right in Britain, was guest editor of Index's 1991 issue on the arms trade. This examination of warspeak (the deceitful 'sanitization' of language, using words 'to salve the conscience, to cordon off the truth, rather than communicate it') appeared in Index''s Gulf War issue.

Euphemism is the subtlest form of censorship, and the Gulf War has been a riot of euphemism. The crisis rapidly generated its own lexicon, a language with its origins in military jargon, which has mediated between the battlefield and the public and provided a form of psychological insulation from the bitter reality of war.

The staple of the new warspeak has been capitalized initials. The shimmering technology (or 'kit') of the Allied arsenal is often described in this shorthand: mention of ECM (Electronic Counter-Measures), FAE (Fuel Air Explosives – firestorm weapons), GCI (Ground Control Intercept – defensive ground radar), KH (Keyhole – a spy satellite), MBT (Main Battle Tank), and TFW (Tactical Fighter Wing) has become common coin at military briefings. This is a verbal ploy which manages simultaneously to glamorize and to sanitize the weaponry referred to.

Human beings can be capitalized, too. Casualties of the fight to shape the NWO (New World Order) are variously categorized as MIA (Missing in Action), WIA (Wounded In Action) and KIA (Killed in Action). Those in the last category are shipped home in HRPs (Human Remains Pouches – body bags) and replaced by BCRs (Battlefield Casualty Replacements). The mayhem of the KZ (Killing Zone) might also take its psychological toll in the form of CSR (Combat Stress

* LOW = Lexicon of War

Reaction – shell-shock). Iraqi troops who call it a day and defect are LCs (Line Crossers).

Acronyms are also popular: the new lexicon has introduced the civilian world to the 'ponti' (Person Of No Tactical Importance), 'tads' (Target Acquisition and Designations Sight), 'slar' (Side-Looking Airborne Radar), 'slam' (Stand-off Land-Attack Missiles), 'slipar' (Short Light Pulse Alerting Receiver), 'jaat' (Joint Air Attack Team), and 'harm' (High-speed Anti-Radiation Missile). Personnel not wearing their NCB (Nuclear, Chemical and Biological) outfits during a CW (Chemical Weapons) attack are likely to 'slud' (Salivate, Lachrymate, Urinate and Defecate). The word-play has proven infectious: filling in airtime before 'G-day' (the day land war began), ITN invited its viewers to suggest what 'Scud' might stand for. Amazingly, it transpired, it didn't stand for anything.

Never have so many synonyms for 'to kill' or 'to destroy' been assembled outside the pages of a Thesaurus: to 'degrade', to 'interdict', to 'stealth', to 'take out', to 'impact', to 'suppress', to 'eliminate', to 'decapitate', to 'de-air', to 'down' or to 'neutralize' have all been used. Khafji was said to be 'cleansed' after the removal of Iraqi troops. General Colin Powell was more up-front in his promise that when the Allied forces came up against the Iraqi army they would 'cut it off and kill it', the image of amputation echoing the equally medical idea of 'surgical bombing'.

However surgical the AAF (Allied Air Forces) have tried to be, 'circular error probability' (the circle around a target within which a weapon is likely to fall) remains a problem. Civilian casualties unlucky enough to find themselves in a 'target-rich environment' fall under the heading of 'collateral damage', which – according to BDAs (Bomb Damage Assessments), to which the Allied Command attached a 'high confidence value' – is almost invariably 'minimal'; since mid-February, the more candid 'civilian impacting' has also enjoyed a vogue at the briefing lectern. The collective noun for the aircraft doing the damage is 'package' (as in a 'package' of aeroplanes), although, confusingly, 'package' is also used to refer to a targeting campaign. Ensuring that aircraft on the same side don't crash into one another is a matter of 'deconfliction'.

In its most excessive moments, the new warspeak has seemed merely comic, impossible to take seriously. Correspondents recall the evasions of the 'Five O'Clock Follies' of the Vietnam War. And historians may be reminded of Churchill's appropriately scandalized reaction to the terms ICP (Impaired Combat Personnel – wounded soldiers) and 'body count' (the number of the dead). Yet the Gulf War's lexicon has had its own insidious force, acquiring momentum as the media adopt, in a piecemeal way, the terminology used by the military. It has been the perfect script to accompany the video game imagery of laser bombing, in a war which – until the devastation of the Baghdad air-raid shelter – has seemed somewhat remote. Rarely has it been so obvious that language is volatile stuff, that it succumbs easily to manipulation, to the sedulous distortions of propagandists and censors. In the Gulf War, words have been used to salve the conscience, to cordon off the truth, rather than to communicate it.

April/May 1991

ADEWALE MAJA-PEARCE

Suffer the little children

Adewale Maja-Pearce, until recently Index's Africa editor, is the author of
In My Father's Country (1987), How Many Miles to Babylon? (1990), and Who's
Afraid of Wole Soyinka? (1991). Here he gives his impressions of the effects
of the IMF's 'squeeze' on Zambia, and the state of tension and riot in
Lusaka.

There were riots in Lusaka the month before I arrived. The International
Monetary Fund (IMF) had forced the government to remove the sub-
sidy on mealie-meal, doubling the price of the nation's staple food,
and the city had erupted. The most serious disturbances occurred on
the university campus, but only after the para-military had been
despatched to crack a few skulls. 'When they send in those guys you
must know that the time for compromise is over,' was the way that
David, my journalist friend, put it. Now, in August 1990, the university
was closed, but the evidence of the brutality inflicted by the armed
wing of the ruling United National Independence Party (UNIP) was
everywhere to be seen in the broken doors and smashed windows.

This was the first time in 26 years of independence that such a thing
had happened in Zambia, and President Kenneth Kaunda was sufficiently
shaken to agree to a hasty referendum on multi-party democracy. A
date was set and disaffected ex-UNIP politicians crawled out of obscurity only to be shoved back again when the continent's elder statesman
had recovered from his initial trauma. It seemed that he had been too
precipitate; October was much too soon. 'The people' wouldn't be
ready to take such a momentous decision concerning the country's
political future until August next year at the earliest. And now everybody
was in doubt as to how far, precisely, they were even permitted to
discuss the issue, at least in public.

That was presumably why General Tembo (retired), the most likely of the presidential hopefuls, refused to declare in favour of democracy at the press briefing he called, even though he insisted that he intended to put himself at the disposal of the most 'progressive forces' in the country. What did he mean by progressive? He didn't want to say at this early stage but, well . . . progressive. Why had he bothered to call the briefing at all? Then somebody pointed out that the whole of Zambia didn't contain even half the number of supposed 'journalists' who were gathered in that room, and that Tembo, who had only recently been released after two years in prison, could yet find himself incarcerated again on charges of treason.

In short, nobody quite knew what was happening, including, it soon transpired, the father of the nation himself. He, too, gathered the press together, but then insisted on answering all questions, from the economy to his possible successor, with reference to the scriptures. This in itself wasn't unusual. Everybody knows the mission-educated son of a preacher to be a deeply religious man ('religious faith has played a central role in my life'), hence his 'philosophy' of Humanism, the country's official ideology since 1967.

A clear-cut definition of Humanism is difficult, largely because Kaunda's own pronouncements on the subject are vague and often contradictory. However, in *Letter To My Children*, one of his numerous publications, he himself describes it as a kind of Christianized Marxism which 'operates on the boundary between religion and politics as a channel for the best gifts of all true faith: compassion, service, and love – to be lavished on the nation's people'.

Letter To My Children is an interesting document, less for its politics (confused), than for what it tells us about the man (more confused). He himself offers it as an explanation of 'what makes me tick – my philosophy, if you like; the things I believe and why I believe them'. But not in the way he imagines. For instance:

Africans are born, I think, with an innate sense of rhythm – the beat of drums sends pulses through our systems and awakens deep emotions and strange feelings that link us to our ancestors from time immemorial.

And:

The coming of Christianity had a complex effect on [the] African world view, partly disrupting and partly enlarging it. I don't want to get bogged down in all that business, though. It is enough to say that I feel within myself the tension created by the collision of these world views which I have never completely reconciled. It is a ludicrous and indeed insulting over-simplification to claim, as some missionaries have done, that we non-western peoples are still deepdown pagan with a top dressing of Christianity.

Reading this book, it is important to remember that the writer is a Head of State, responsible for the well-being of almost eight million people. Out of respect, therefore, we might be inclined to pass over in silence the implications of the first passage, only to be confronted by the same problem in the second: that of a man with a fragile notion of his own identity, never mind the collective identity of the people over whom he is pleased to rule.

'I'm haunted', he tells us, 'by the fear that the massive power the nation has entrusted to me may . . . violate the integrity of those who are on the receiving end of such powers.' But language has betrayed him. The 'massive power' to which he refers was seized, not given, and in the same year, 1973, that he wrote these words. The condition of powerlessness is, by definition, a violation of integrity, which is why power is always taken, never freely given; but the fact that Kaunda imagines he can delude those who are on the receiving end as easily as he can delude himself, tells us what he thinks of them as surely as it explains the title of his book.

In this Kaunda is typical enough. All African leaders despise their subjects (never citizens), which is why they behave in the ways they do towards them. The only difference is one of style. Unlike his neighbour, President-for-Life Dr Hastings Kamuzu Banda – 'The Malawi system, the Malawi style is that Kamuzu says it's that, and then it's finished. Whether anyone likes it or not, that is how it's going to be here' – Kaunda professes a more circumspect, or more hypocritical, approach, one that permits him to talk about 'the right to active participation in the political life, to a measure of consent in the form of government, to *free association and free debate*' (my italics), while he turns Zambia into a one-party state and imprisons his political opponents.

Banda doesn't give a damn what his people think of him; Kaunda wants his children to reciprocate the 'compassion, service and love' that he lavishes on them:

> Every wise parent learns that though he has the physical strength
> to compel his children to obey him . . . he must refrain from
> using such power in the belief that patient example is a better
> teacher than the whip. The parent-child relationship is one
> common example of the truth that the test of mastery of power is
> the willingness to refrain from using it. It may sound paradoxical,
> but experience has taught me that such a gamble can pay off.

But now his children were rebelling, and the Great African Chief, pagan or not but with flywhisk (or – modern times – handkerchief) in hand, was stunned. And since it wasn't possible for him to imagine that he had actually been rejected by his children, he told himself instead that democracy was the name of the game.

However: 'We can't cope with democracy. This isn't the West. We're still too backward.' The speaker was a moderately successful entrepreneur in his early forties. I say moderately: he was on his way to Johannesburg to buy a secondhand car – 'a Mercedes, or perhaps a BMW, what do you think?' – before flying to South Korea and Taiwan to seal a couple of deals. This made him positively wealthy in a country where the average monthly wage was less than the new price of a bag of mealie-meal, and where owning a car, no matter its condition, was generally taken as a sign of prosperity.

The taxi driver I spoke to the following day concurred. 'Do you like politics?' I had asked, picking up his newspaper and glancing at the latest agency reports on the civil war in Liberia. 'Too much,' he said. 'What do you think of this multi-party business?' 'It's not good,' he said without hesitation. 'Just watch, when these politicians start their nonsense we're going to have trouble in this country. Better leave it as it is. One party is good for us.'

Later, when I got back to David's place, I asked him what he thought of all this. He simply shrugged and wouldn't be drawn. For a journalist, he was a man of few opinions. In fact, all he wanted to talk about for the fortnight that I stayed with him was his impending trip to a college

173

in the north of England, where he had been accepted on a one-year journalism course. He was now busy trying to raise the money. A local businessman had offered to help by providing the kwacha equivalent of David's foreign exchange allocation; the businessman, in return, would take half the sterling – £5,000 – at the official rate, which was less than half the black market rate. But the balance would only cover David's fees; he still had to find the money for board and lodging.

With all this to think about, he had little time for the multi-party debate, or so I mistakenly – and charitably – assumed. And I could see very well that food was a more pressing problem. He earned 3,000 kwacha a month – £25 – after deduction for the rent on his bungalow. On the day I met him, for instance, he was preparing to eat his first meal in 12 hours, a bowl of mealie-meal made into a kind of porridge. I insisted that we go to the nearby market, where I filled his shopping bag with everything in sight. He was shocked at my extravagance. He thought that 600 kwacha (£5) was a lot of money, and in his terms it was.

But, however poor, he still recognized that he was more fortunate than his married colleagues. 'If you go into their houses you will be shocked. Some of these senior editors don't even have a bed to sleep on.' David himself had a bed but little else: he owned just two shirts (both frayed at the collar), two pairs of trousers (one too short and the other too big around the waist) and one pair of leather shoes (but without the heels).

He did volunteer that Kaunda should have stepped down last year, when he was still quite popular, but that the people hated him now and might even kill him if he attempted to retire. But that was all he would say. Besides, what did his opinions matter? He couldn't publish them; he couldn't even publish the relatively mild criticisms in the 'letters to the editor' which arrived on his desk at the rate of two or three a week. So he concentrated on his trip to England instead, and roped me in to help. It seemed that the businessman was beginning to have doubts about the scheme. Mightn't David disappear with the money once he was abroad? Wouldn't it be safer, if more expensive, to buy his sterling on the black market? And now he was prevaricating over the letter to the bank manager which stood between David and Darlington.

'If he sees you he'll be shamed into keeping his word,' David said. I was sceptical, but I should have known better. This was his country, after all. In the event, we were kept waiting only half-an-hour. 'You saw how uncomfortable you made him? I knew it; I knew he wouldn't be able to give me any excuses.' Darlington had moved that much closer, and now he wanted me to tell him more about England. 'So it's cold up there, eh?' he said, and pretended to shiver; but even on a windy, mid-winter morning in Lusaka he couldn't conceive of real cold. England itself was just a few photos of Darlington in the flashy prospectus, and the cultured, disembodied voices of the World Service announcers that we listened to every evening.

The BBC, in fact, was his only source of information about the outside world, including events in his own continent. It happened, for instance, that there were new developments in the Liberian civil war, with the neighbouring countries about to despatch a peace-keeping force to stop the carnage. Such direct intervention in the internal affairs of another African country was a momentous development, but any hope (always hope) that Nigeria was about to assert its position as the regional heavyweight was being undermined by the country's familiar anxiety not to be seen to be pushing its weight around.

But even here David didn't seem terribly interested; and while he might have argued that the possible repercussions of the Liberian conflict for the future of Zambia were sufficiently remote for him safely to ignore, the unexpected developments in the Middle East – the Iraqi invasion and subsequent annexation of Kuwait – were of a different order altogether. Iraq was Zambia's sole supplier of crude oil, which Iraq sold at a reduced rate in return for copper, Zambia's sole, and rapidly diminishing, foreign exchange earner. Zambia simply didn't possess the necessary reserves of hard currency to buy oil on the open market. Sure enough, within 48 hours there were five-mile queues outside the petrol stations, and this was only the beginning. Another week and whatever little industry the country possessed would be forced to shut down.

I've said that David couldn't afford the luxury of political opinions, even where they concerned his own country, but this wasn't the whole story. In fact David, along with the businessman and the taxi driver, exhibited a base level of political consciousness that chimed perfectly with the President's own sentiments. If Kaunda thought of his people as children to be led by the guiding hand of the all-wise, all-powerful father — 'Every wise parent learns that though he has the physical strength to compel his children to obey him . . .' — they themselves responded in suitably infantile fashion. And if Kaunda was now hated, if his people wanted him to go, it wasn't because they had matured politically overnight and suddenly discovered the virtues of democracy, but because their father was seen to have failed them. He couldn't deliver; he couldn't even guarantee the price of a bag of mealie-meal. He was revealed as human, after all, and the people rioted. The only option left to him was to exploit whatever physical strength he still possessed in order to maintain himself in power, which was why he didn't hesitate to despatch the para-military to the university campus when even he recognized that the reciprocal love he expected from his people was unable to transcend the simple fact of hunger.

June 1991

IRENA MARYNIAK

The Lubianka's hidden treasure

An interview with Vitaly Shentalinsky

Irena Maryniak, Index's eastern Europe editor, prefaced the magazine's publication of excerpts from the Lubianka's archives in 1990 with this interview with Vitaly Shentalinsky, a representative of the Commission for the Lost Literary Legacy of the Soviet Union, founded in the mid-80s to collect lost material by writers persecuted by the Soviet authorities before *perestroika*. Shentalinsky's finds included extracts from a novel by Platonov, and letters from the Writers' Union that helped to seal Mandelstam's fate.

Irena Maryniak: How was the Commission launched and who initiated the idea?

Vitaly Shentalinsky: It began as a writers' pressure group. We knew that quantities of literature were still locked in secret government archives. During house searches, arrests or raids on editorial offices, anything apparently seditious was confiscated. When a writer was arrested, his archive usually disappeared with him. We estimate that about 2,000 writers were imprisoned; that's a conservative figure. Around 1,500 died. Hundreds vanished. Nobody knows what became of them, or where they are buried. All documentation about them was falsified. Their manuscripts are the most important evidence we have.

There were doubts and misgivings about what we could do, of course. People maintained that everything had been burnt and warned that we would never be admitted into the Lubianka.

IM: Did you have much support from the Writers' Union?

VS: No. We began independently as a group of writers who shared similar views. Our more prominent members include Bulat Okudzhava, Yury Karyakin, Viktor Astafev, Vladimir Makanin ... It took about two years before we gained access to the Lubianka archives. We met with

177

resistance, of course: a kind of elastic wall which gave a little and then sent us right back to where we had started. There are officials who have no interest in seeing the material made public. Many were involved in the cases I examine; writers frequently informed on their colleagues. Some are still living, and very comfortably too. They are scarcely enthusiastic about our work. This isn't just an academic project; it's explosive material. The KGB archives are a dossier on everybody. Anyone can be exposed. And there were many, many thousands of informers. The victims died. Those who denounced them are still with us.

In the middle of 1989 we were given access to our first case file. It was on Isaac Babel. Once the work had gathered momentum, Vitaly Korotich, editor of *Ogonyok*, invited me to contribute regularly to the magazine. We also publish in the journal *Voprosy literatury* and we're working on a three-volume collection of material from the camps entitled *The Islands of the Archipelago*. It covers Solovki, Kolyma and Vorkuta. The country was littered with these 'zones' and we only have a partial sense of what went on there. Our primary sources are in secret government archives, the Lubianka and the procurator's office. Of course, there are also personal documents and memoirs which people kept in their homes. We have been flooded with letters, memoirs, diaries, prose and poetry which people have kept hidden until now.

IM: Why is all this necessary? Haven't we read enough material from the camps? Solzhenitsyn, Shalamov, Ginzburg . . . The environment is all too familiar. Isn't it time to look in a different direction?

VS: No doubt to a Western observer it's like the theatre of the absurd. But things are less clear cut from the inside. There are many Stalinists left in the Soviet Union. It's hard to abandon your views if you have a little store of medals and a photograph reminding you of the days when you were working with the great man himself. And, suddenly, you are told that it was all a dreadful mistake. Stalinists . . . Leninists . . . there are millions of them.

People are still very ignorant. The Soviet era was deeply traumatic. We were dragged into barbarism, and when we finally emerged we found we had to learn how to live anew. Each and every one of us. To start living afresh you have to remember who you are and that you have a history. Ah yes . . . we had a Tsar once . . . and perhaps not everything he did was entirely wrong . . .

The case files I have studied are tightly interwoven with our own lives. Many of these writers are working far harder now than contemporary authors. They have a deeper effect on the consciousness of the readership. We found extracts of a novel by Platonov in the Lubianka. No one knew it was there, not even Platonov's daughter. It's a work which is highly relevant today. Even the word *perestroika* features . . .

There are fierce debates at present regarding the future of the Writers' Union. Documentation proves that it was created by Stalin. It informed against its own members. There is a letter from the General Secretary of the Union, Vladimir Stavsky, written in 1938 to the head of the OGPU, Yezhov,* calling for Mandelstam's arrest. Enclosed with the letter was a derogatory review of Mandelstam's verse by a minor writer named Pyotr Pavlenko. He was a secret observer at Mandelstam's interrogation and later reported on his 'poor performance'. That's the Writers' Union for you. It was an organ of repression. It's obsolete and should be dissolved. We must create a completely new professional centre for writers.

IM: And how does the present Writers' Union view your work?

VS: There are those who welcome it. Others profess support but do nothing to improve matters for us. Others still maintain that we have no right to meddle in something which should be the responsibility of relatives. One woman brought her father's manuscript to the Writers' Union all the way from Kharkov (Ukraine). She was told that the Commission was inundated with material and that the time had come to wind up the project. It was just as well that she didn't go straight back to the station but found me through *Ogonyok*. Her father was a friend of Shalamov's named Georgy Dimidov — an interesting short-story writer never published before. So you see what kind of obstacles we face.

IM: Have you met with any other serious difficulties?

VS: Many documents have been destroyed and it can be very hard to find your way around. If we were to publish everything without analysing it first, the falsification would be permanent. We have to try to glean the truth, and for that you have to work with a certain institution . . .

---

* N. I. Yezhov, Commissar of Internal Affairs 1936-8. Succeeded by Lavrenty Beria.

IM: You mean the KGB?

VS: Access to the Lubianka is strictly controlled. The first case I looked at, Babel, was presented to me by a KGB official who had made a selection of documents and wouldn't let me examine the file. It was tense at first. They watched me carefully. Now, a year later, I can simply phone and ask to see a particular file. I'll sit and read it in a room which may have been used to interrogate the very writer whose case I am studying.

We don't show them anything we plan to publish. That's our domain. Initially, they didn't want us to include case numbers and names of interrogators. At times they have indicated that publication is undesirable. But we have gone ahead, and they seem to swallow it. They don't object if someone else bears the responsibility. The KGB isn't staffed by cardboard figures. There are real people working there. And there is a struggle between the old guard and the young generation. A year ago a young employee of the procurator's office prepared a document on the rehabilitation of the poet Nikolai Gumilyov [shot in 1921]. It still hasn't been ratified. The position of Deputy Chief Procurator is occupied by a hard-liner who was involved in the cases of Sakharov and Solzhenitsyn. And he won't sign. We've published material on Gumilyov's case in *Ogonyok*, but he still hasn't been rehabilitated.

At the Lubianka they have a military sort of mentality. The files are marked 'strictly confidential' and sometimes they'll say: 'There's nothing secret here, but by law we don't have the right to show it to you. When the Supreme Soviet repeals the law you're most welcome to look.' And the Supreme Soviet is dragging its feet. Why? Pressure from the Party. The KGB still has more respect for the views of the Party than for the Congress of People's Deputies. Old laws paralyse us. It's the same with economics, ideology, culture . . .

IM: Old attitudes may play a part as well . . .

VS: Many people still don't believe that we have passed the point of no return. They are afraid. As a society we are still shell-shocked from the Lubianka terror. Now they're inviting us to get up and dance, and people won't. It'll take two generations to resolve. If you give a slave his freedom he'll treat it as yet another arbitrary act. He'll snatch at what was repressed within himself and make slaves of those around him. Our own left wing radicals are now using methods worthy of the

Bolsheviks: suppression, deception ... It's habitual behaviour. And people are tired. They want to live out their lives in peace. Food and possessions are the priorities. We have a hungry nation on our hands; cultural and spiritual values come second.

IM: And have there been any major cultural discoveries in your work in the Lubianka? Have you found any great pieces of literature which slipped through the *samizdat* network?

VS: A 'great' writer is a rarity after all. But I've come across some very significant ones. There are a number of manuscripts of the calibre of Evgenia Ginzburg's *Journey into the Whirlwind*. But we have only just begun. And you can't quantify literary discoveries. Anything may turn up. We have found an unknown novel by Platonov and discovered Kluyev's best poetry. For now, those two names vindicate the effort and the struggle.

August/September 1991

ANTHONY SAMPSON

From wimps to warriors

Anthony Sampson, journalist and author of *Anatomy of Britain* (1962), *The Arms Bazaar* (1977) and *The Money Lenders* (1981), contributed this piece to *Index's* special issue on the arms trade, criticising the media for failing to educate and mobilize public opinion against the selling of weaponry to poor or undemocratic states, and squandering the unique opportunity that the end of the Cold War provided for agreements on disarmament.

The arms trade has always thrived on secrecy and unaccountability. Its most successful practitioners have remained in the shadows and, if they come into the limelight, like the Saudi dealer Adnan Khashoggi, it is after they have conducted their main business. Normally, the big arms deals are only revealed to the public after the weapons have been delivered and when it is too late to stop them.

The Western media, which have often been influential in other fields of investigation, have been ineffective in breaking through this secrecy to report arms sales. And since anyone interested in controlling weapons must be concerned with using the media as a means of mobilising and channelling information – and also as a political platform for making the case for control – we need to understand why the media have been so reluctant.

Arms deals provide dramatic stories which lie at the heart of contemporary world politics and can change the balances of power. The arming of Saddam Hussein by Western countries after he had clearly emerged as a potential enemy, was a historic diplomatic blunder. Why did news of these deals, which were known to thousands of people beforehand, not reach the public until after the damage had been done?

The first problem rests with the editorial structure within the media. Traditionally, any reporting about weapons has been the preserve of defence correspondents who derive most of their information and their status from their closeness to the military. They are carefully cultivated by generals and admirals: they are flown free of charge to distant bases and trouble-spots on RAF planes. Inevitably, most of them are reluctant to offend the services which provide so many of their indispensable sources.

There is also a political problem. In Britain, the Labour Party is theoretically opposed to the arms trade; but the majority of Labour MPs are unwilling to pursue the argument in detail because arms exports help to provide jobs, many of them in northern or Scottish constituencies which are Labour strongholds. The actual numbers of defence-related jobs may be small, but the arms companies have a lobbying-power out of proportion to their size.

There is also the macho problem. This affects male politicians and journalists who are reluctant to depict themselves in a role which could be regarded as pacifist or wimpish. The great majority of campaigners against arms sales are women. They include the remarkable group who have organized the Campaign Against the Arms Trade (CAAT) in London; and such formidable academic opponents as Emma Rothschild of King's College Cambridge and Mary Kaldor of Sussex University. But the world of defence and defence journalism remains dominated by men; editors are inclined to regard protests against the arms trade as part of 'women's subjects'.

All of these factors have limited the motivation of the media to investigate arms deals; these require unusual perseverance and resources to penetrate their secrets. The government arms dealers who are responsible for most of the business, from the offices of the Defence Exports Services Organization (DESO) in London's Soho Square, are protected by the Official Secrets Act and by their own sense of patriotism. Their links with the intelligence agencies fortify them further.

There have been very few 'whistleblowers' from within the arms-sales business, chiefly because of the character of the people who go into it in the first place. And without such whistleblowers, the media need far greater resources and motivation if they are to provide their own oversight of the arms trade.

Yet it has never been so important to reveal it. The end of the Cold War provides a unique opportunity for agreements on disarmament; it also provides a nightmare of huge arsenals of surplus weaponry, scattered over the former Soviet Union and Eastern Europe, waiting to be bought by arms dealers at knock-down prices. The Middle East appears within sight of a peace agreement; the Gulf War provided a terrifying object-lesson on the dangers of arming an enemy. But the West resumed selling weapons to every major buyer except Iraq as soon as the Gulf War was over.

The major powers are now giving some support to the proposal for a register of arms transfers to be kept by the United Nations: a proposal first promoted by Mrs Gro Brundtland in Norway, supported by Eduard Shevardnadze from the former Soviet Union and now taken up by other leaders including John Major from Britain and Toshiki Kaifu from Japan. But monitoring any official register of this kind will depend on far greater public interest and much more information from unofficial sources to provide some check on the truthfulness of governments.

Within the Third World, the need for disclosure of arms exports is even more critical. The World Bank and richest donors, headed by Japan, have at last begun to link aid to developing countries to limiting their arms production and exports. This is an attempt to cut back the escalating arms race and arms selling, particularly in Asia and, above all, in China, which has become a major arms seller to the Middle East, including Iran and Iraq.

But any attempt to restrict arms spending and selling calls for much more public awareness in these countries. The case of China, a permanent member of the Security Council which depends critically on aid from Japan and the USA, is particularly significant: any agreement on an arms register and subsequent arms control depends on pressurising China. Diplomats and observers have been pessimistic about internal Chinese pressure, yet there are some indications of growing concern within China, as illustrated by the recent showing of *Major Barbara*, Bernard Shaw's play about the arms trade.

The involvement of the media, whether in the developing or the developed world, is essential to any pressure to restrict the arms trade. For arms selling still needs secrecy to protect it: the most irresponsible acts of governments, like the US Irangate conspiracy, or the European sales to Iraq, would never have been allowed if they had been submitted to Parliament or Congress. And the media, once motivated and equipped, can do much to increase disclosure and mobilize public opinion, as they have shown, for instance, in publicising 'Prisoners of Conscience' for Amnesty International.

The media, with their own traditional bias towards military sources and war reporting, are unlikely to mobilize themselves as effective monitors of arms sales without external pressure. Only a major change in the political scene, together with more effective institutions dedicated to arms control, are likely to make newspapers and television as interested in preventing wars as they are in reporting them.

November/December 1991

STUART HAMPSHIRE

Should Index be above the battle?

Stuart Hampshire, a Patron and one of the founders of Index, was Warden of Wadham College, Oxford from 1970-1984. His philosophical works include Thought and Action (1959), Morality and Conflict (1983) and Innocence and Experience (1989).

There has never been a genuine history of the world in the sense of a history of humanity as a whole. There have been broken-backed and half serious attempts, as by H. G. Wells, but there has been no possibility of such an attempt succeeding. The possibility will only become real when humanity seems finally to have formed some kind of whole, in spite of its divisions and of the diversity of its many isolated and hostile populations. This possibility in turn depends upon most, or many, of the various divisions of humanity, each with their separate histories, seeing themselves as parts of a simple whole. Then the idea of humanity having an intelligible history, and an order of development, may come alive as a matter of observation and experience, not of mere theory.

Living for centuries in their own valleys and islands, and separated by uncrossable frontiers, the divided populations may have for many centuries had little knowledge of each other, and often little interest in each other, except for the exchange of merchandize along trade routes. The Industrial Revolution and the development of world trade in the last century has gradually, and very slowly, changed these effects of geography. The situation of separated populations has much more rapidly changed in our time because of the acceleration of advances in the technology of communication. Across the globe, the contemporary history of every population and nation is accessible, through television and through real-time communications, to a majority of other populations and nations.

The spread of world-wide communications is bound to accelerate even more, as more information satellites become available. The immediate diffusion of information can now only with great difficulty be arrested. A very well-organized tyranny in a fairly remote part of the world may for a time succeed in cutting off at source the flow of information about its activities to the outside world. But it will certainly become more and more difficult to keep any Iron Curtain in place; even the remote areas of China and Tibet, scenes of tyranny, will gradually be linked to the rest of humanity through the enterprise of broadcasters and journalists. Humanity will then become capable of seeing itself as constituting a whole, and to feel a loose kind of unity, in spite of the vast diversity of its ways of life.

Index on Censorship was originally founded in response to Pavel Litvinov's account of the horror of being buried in prison, of having one's work as a writer suppressed, of disappearing into darkness, as if one had ceased to exist. The idea behind Index was to try to ensure that this and similar disappearances, the tyrant's concealments of oppression and of absolute cruelty, should always be challenged. There should be the noise of publicity outside every detention centre and concentration camp, and a published record of every tyrannical denial of free expression, whether in literature or scholarship or journalism. The writers and scholars reduced to silence would know that there was some noise of protest outside, even if the protest was not effective. They would not have disappeared into total obscurity and loneliness. Their names, and the names of their works, would remain among the names of the living.

The disintegration of the Soviet Union – one sixth of the earth's surface, we used to say in the '30s – has exposed many more relatively isolated populations to the possible light of publicity. This is a further opportunity. The goal that Index still pursues can be described as the embarrassment of tyranny, wherever it appears. Embarrassment is not the most dramatic of sentiments, and the sensations associated with it are not as violent as with shame. But while well-established tyrants, whether an individual, an ethnic group or a party, are unlikely to feel shame, they are likely to suffer political and personal embarrassment, which is a social sentiment, when they go out into the world and meet their peers – even if, like the governments of the Soviet Union and of

South Africa, they are for a long time sustained by their belief in the God-given, or history-given, righteousness of their cause. Probably economic pressures are always the strongest pressures, but public embarrassment certainly has a part to play.

Suppose we now assume that the 'glare' of publicity (the metaphor, however hackneyed, is a good one) from now onwards can be switched to any part of the world where the denial of free expression in its grosser forms still survives, or where it comes into being. Stories of the imprisonment of dissidents, and of the suppression of books and newspapers and works of art, will become very widely known through the efforts of *Index* and others. It will become more and more difficult to conceal from the rest of the world that the common decencies of humanity are in specific countries being ignored.

'The common decencies of humanity'. In considering the meaning of this phrase, and giving it some precise content, it is important that we are not deceived by the too easily acceptable rhetoric of our time. If one surveys contemporary humanity as a whole, and in all its diversity, what precisely are the common decencies universally acknowledged, even if not always observed? Perhaps there are none, or very few, if we try to be more precise about the limits of censorship and of free expression. What will be accounted shameful or embarrassing within one political morality is thought acceptable in another. The historic religions have proclaimed the distinguishing and peculiar virtues, and the peculiar paths to happiness, which are accessible to the faithful; but these virtues and those paths to salvation are not available to the faithless and to the heathen populations. Humanity is split and divided by its religions, and its separate parts have different duties and different destinies: almost everywhere there are the self-appointed elect and the scattered populations which live beyond the boundaries of God's first concerns.

Similarly, pre-industrial populations are segregated in distinct tribes and ethnic groups, and hold themselves apart in order to honour their origins and their distinctive customs and for the sake of a local glory. They refer with pride to their own canons of excellence, and they have lower expectations of what can be achieved by outsiders. Seen from within a Pale of Settlement, those beyond the Pale live in a lower level of moral requirement; their duties are less strict and their accepted practices seem more or less repugnant. To the insiders they seem to live in a coarse indifference to the finer discriminations between clean and unclean habits. They are morally and metaphysically ignorant, and what they count as success is not success in the eyes of God and of God's community on earth. Seen from outside the Pale, those living within it are seen as enslaved and distorted by their unnatural practices and fanatical moral prejudices, and they cannot ever become normal persons with the full range of natural powers and natural interests of those who live outside the Pale.

There seems to be no possibility of compromise between the two standpoints, the liberal and the authoritarian, whether Christian, Muslim or Jewish, and there is no way in which the two contrasting sets of beliefs can somehow be welded together and combined. Perhaps there will always be persons, and even whole populations, who ignore any clear formulation of the two sets of opposing beliefs and who do not recognize, or do not acknowledge, the impossibility of combining them. They have a way of life which requires that they do not raise questions about the compatibility of the beliefs about free expression which allegedly guide their actions. In fact they do not attach much importance to beliefs as such, and therefore they do not trouble themselves with any reflective evaluation of them.

Such people, Christian, Muslim or Jewish, find no difficulty in living peacefully alongside genuine believers on both sides of the line, and for practical and private purposes they are able to overlook the differences between them. But they do finally find themselves compelled to make a choice, and to recognize the incompatibilities, when any substantial political issue presents itself, that is, any issue of fairness in the allocation of resources and in the promotion by governments of essential educational and moral interests. When justice is involved in settling some conflict in such basic interests, the irreconcilable opposition of the two moral standpoints will come to the surface. The ability of men and women in different parts of the world to see humanity as having some kind of unity does not entail their willingness to see humanity as forming a harmonious whole. On the contrary, they may come to see humanity as held together by mutual awareness, but as constituting a whole of competing and contrasting parts: the competition between irreconcilable standpoints, and the consequent tension, may be the common and unifying factors all the way from New Guinea to Finland, and between conservatives and reformers.

Take as an example the decisions that have to be made about public education. The fundamentalist – whether Muslim, Christian, Jewish or of another faith – will not accept as fair the liberal agnostic's idea that resources should be available for a purely secular education alongside the religious schools: a pluralist solution. For a fundamentalist, the right education is not a matter for individual choice and for the expression of personal allegiances and convictions. The difference between good and evil in education has been authoritatively and finally revealed, and there is no justice in allowing the young, and their parents, to go to the devil in their own way, which is the proposal that liberals count as just. The deepest moral principles are invoked on both sides, and both sides will think it morally disreputable to give way and to allow the other to prevail.

There are several reasons to believe that clashes between these bitterly opposed moral standpoints will become even more frequent in the coming decades than they have been in the past. The recent elections in Algeria, with Muslim fundamentalists at the top of the poll, point one probable way to the future. Within Algeria the French-educated and deeply secular middle class will be asked to share their political and legal institutions with devout Muslim believers who wish to detach Algeria from the traditions of the French Revolution and of its liberal and free-thinking aftermath. As loyalty to the revolutionary ideals of socialism has declined, religious enthusiasm will tend to take its place. It seems altogether contrary to what is known about human nature, as it has been revealed in history, to expect that, suddenly, populations, when released from Marxist dogmatism and political enthusiasm, and will turn to a disillusioned scepticism or to liberal principles. The great inequalities of opportunity within ordinary capitalism, and the ugly effects of the scramble for wealth which it engenders, are still hateful to the unsuccessful crowds in the streets.

Even the display of wealth can be morally repugnant to men and women of a religious and puritan temperament, as in Iran and elsewhere in the Middle East. Such people naturally look for compensation in some future triumph and recompense, on one side of the grave or the other. As socialism associated itself with nationalist feeling, so also religious enthusiasm associates itself with the repudiation of foreign influences and of cosmopolitan customs. A whole new morality is institutionalized and imposed by an authoritian government: new sexual conventions, new family structures, new forms of censorship, new undemocratic procedures in government. A fundamentalist revolution involves as great a transformation of the social order as the Communist revolutions which preceded it.

It was the plan of Index from its earliest beginnings to be as impartial as is humanly possible in recording offences against human rights on both sides in the Cold War, while it lasted. All forms and every instance of censorship, of the suppression of the work of writers and scholars, was to be recorded and denounced, whether the abuse of a human right was part of the defence of capitalism against Communism or of Communism against capitalism. Censorship, imprisonment without trial, the outrages of the secret police, have been the commonplace and typical offences of Communist governments, but they have occurred also on a vast scale in South Africa, South America, in Turkey and throughout the Middle East, in Kenya and in other post-colonial African states, and, generally, wherever there have been acute religious and ethnic conflicts.

The editors of Index and the council of its associated charity, the Writers & Scholars Educational Trust (WSET), have always been aware of the danger that in many parts of the world Index would seem to represent only the ideology of the industrialized West and the liberal values which generally prevail there, or to which lip-service is paid. This was a danger, because the exposure of abuses of power in Index would have much less effect if these exposures could plausibly be said to serve the exclusive interests of one side in the Cold War. The aim of Index has been to serve an interest presumed to be universal or species-wide: the defence of a sovereign right to free expression. But is not the recognition of such a right just the very specific and defining peculiarity of Western liberalism? And why should it be presumed that this value should be given nearly equal precedence in every part of the world?

Convinced Communists have largely disappeared. But the problem for Index associated with the Cold War remains, and in its new form becomes more acute. The hostility between free-thinking liberals and religious fundamentalists has a metaphysical basis and is likely to be more long-lasting. The split may even represent an opposition within human nature which is permanent and which cannot be expected to disappear. In a recently published book, *Innocence and Experience* (Penguin, 1989), I suggested reasons why this opposition may be permanent: at least that there are reasons to doubt that a free-thinking and liberal enlightenment will steadily and constantly spread across the globe, and that this will everywhere gradually displace religious enthusiasm and extreme forms of nationalism. Because of this doubt, it is more than ever important that the evil of censorship should be explained by reference to principles which are likely to be acceptable outside free-thinking and liberal circles.

It seems unwise to expect that the right to free expression of feeling and of opinion in art and literature will be universally accorded some overriding, or at least very high, priority. Therefore one still has to look for principles that are at least widely acceptable across frontiers, and across different moralities, and which entail the paramount necessity of free expression, even when viewed from different and opposing moral standpoints. I think there is a way of doing this, an argument that may sometimes carry conviction outside liberal circles, although it is probably too much to expect that the most fanatical and earnest proselytes of supernatural causes will be convinced by this one argument alone. If they are certain that they have an assurance from a supernatural authority that all causes and beliefs other than their own are sinful, are they likely to be swayed by an argument defending open debate and free expression, an argument that does not even claim to be compelling and irresistible? Well, the argument has a certain force, and one can only try to present it as forcibly as possible.

First, a distinction has to be made within the central concept of morality, which is the notion of what is just and fair and right: the distinction between a substantial conception of what is just and fair and a procedural conception of justice. An example: a government may ban a book or play or broadcast on two separate grounds: firstly, that it is obscene; and secondly, that it is certain to inflame the already acute racial and religious hostilities in the country. There is then the substantial moral issue of whether it is just and fair that the work should be suppressed, and that these grounds are sufficient to show that it is just and fair. Then there is the procedural question: has there been an adequate and fair discussion in an appropriate forum between those who assert and those who deny that these are adequate grounds for banning? Have both sides to the dispute been sufficiently represented?

A ban is unfair and unjust in the absence of any adversary argument about its justice and fairness. Political parties and governments of utterly different and opposed views about the substantial justice of the ban may reasonably be asked to acknowledge the fairness of a procedure which requires all sides of the case to be stated and discussed in an appropriate forum. Procedural justice requires that the final decision about the banning should be justifiable as the regular outcome of the adversary process: a procedural justification of the outcome, whatever it may be, then takes the place of the substantial reasons alleged by the opposing parties for their opposing views. If the established canonical procedures have been followed, and both sides have had their say in the recognized institution, then the anti-banners have been given a good reason to acquiesce in a ban, if that is the outcome, and those in favour of a ban have a good reason to accept free expression in this case, if that is the outcome. What makes the reason a good reason is that the decision, considered as a process, was not unfair, even though the propositions affirmed may seem to many people clearly wrong.

It will be asked: why should the opposing parties, each with their irreconcilable moral convictions, accept the norm of procedural fairness except when they believe that they will emerge victorious from the adversary procedure? The answer appeals to a notion of rationality which all the opposing parties, however extreme and divergent their moral convictions, unavoidably use in most of their day-to-day activities: it is the notion of reviewing pros and cons, of hearing both sides of a case, of weighing evidence for and against, before deciding. Even the most fanatical believers in supernatural revelations unavoidably try to be rational in making their prudential decisions, and in assessing the evidence relating to matters of fact in the ordinary natural world which they inhabit. In this respect, and to this extent, they cannot afford to behave differently from their liberal enemies. They would otherwise disappear and we should hear no more about their creed. They deliberate and have both inner and public debates about the best courses of

action and about probable happenings in the world around them. They
have public debates even if only with their co-religionists, and they
have built up the institutions in which these debates can be conducted.
Adversary argument, public and private, and hence the idea of rationality, cannot be strange to them. Rather, their situation must be that
there are certain topics of morality and religious observance which have
been put to rest, once and for all, by supernatural authority, and by
some form of revelation, and on these topics there ought not to be any
reviewing of arguments for and against. On these topics, this normal
requirement of rationality is to be suspended because of a superior
source of certainty. Probably they will not even admit that the superiority of the source of certainty is open to debate.

The illiberal fundamentalist, like the convinced Communist before
him, can be in one of two situations: either he lives in a society, roughly
to be called totalitarian, in which fundamental moral questions are
settled by authority or by force and are beyond dispute; or he lives in
a society within which a formidable number of its citizens will not
agree that fundamental moral questions are beyond dispute. Then the
fundamentalist must either resort to force, on the assumption that he
is powerful enough to suppress all free expression; or he must enter
into public arguments, so far accepting the canons of argument which
govern adversary procedures. He is led into a public display of rationality by the existence of fellow citizens who reject the route to moral
certainty through a supernatural and superior authority. He must either
live alone with his fellow believers and not venture out into the world
beyond the Pale, or play a part in the institutions which are established
for adversary argument – such institutions as the law courts, the press,
parliaments, assemblies, councils and party meetings. This is the point
at which mutual awareness, with the new means of communication,
becomes relevant. It is becoming always more difficult to segregate the
believers in a faith from full knowledge of, and normal dealings with,
the rest of humanity.

As the enemy of censorship, *Index* can still preserve its impartiality,
and can avoid being too narrowly identified with a liberal ideology
confined to the West, when it stresses the justice of just and fair procedures, as distinct from substantial conceptions of justice in the allocation of goods within society. The right to free expression does not pick

out one good thing which has a priority among good things available in a country well governed. Rather, it is the only alternative to the imposition by force, or by threat of force, of moral uniformity. Justice requires that there should always be the right of appeal against censorship and the denial of free expression, the right to a day in court or in the appropriate tribunal. Publicity, the exposure of censorship and other denials of free expression, is of the essence of procedural justice, because without publicity, the war of words, adversary argument itself, cannot be expected to begin. It is also true that courts, tribunals and parliaments, all scenes of adversary argument, in part depend for their effectiveness on their proceedings being recorded and reported, or at the very least on not being kept secret.

These are such obvious points about fairness and decency in political procedure that they cannot, I think, plausibly be represented as the prescriptions only of a liberal philosophy. Even in a one-party state, and in a country where a fundamentalist religion is dominant, disputes about the justifiable limits on free expression will naturally arise, and it is evident that fairness in the handling of such disputes demands that the facts of the political or religious censorship be made known, whether the censorship is finally held, after argument, to be justifiable or not. There will always be different opinions about the rightness or wrongness, the fairness or unfairness, of censoring or suppressing particular forms and kinds of free expression, because there are different moralities with different ideas of substantial justice. But there can be a more general respect for fair procedures in settling these conflicts and this requires *Index's* vigilance and publicity.

April 1992

FANG LIZHI

China is a world problem

Fang Lizhi, the distinguished Chinese physicist, was born in Beijing in 1936 and spent the Cultural Revolution years as a miner and farm labourer. In 1986 he was dismissed as Vice-President of the University of Science and Technology of China, sought sanctuary in the American embassy following the Tiananmen Square massacre, and since 1990 has been a visiting scholar at Cambridge, Princeton and the University of Arizona.

In 1989, movements for democracy were successful in Eastern Europe but failed in China. For those concerned with democracy, this has given rise to the question: can China ever achieve democracy?

I am no astrologer who can predict China's future, only an astrophysicist. But one thing I can predict with confidence: China cannot avoid moving towards democracy. My reasons are simple: a democratic China fills the needs of both the Chinese people and of the rest of the world.

People say that because China is a big country as well as a poor one, the first need of the Chinese people is for economic development, not democracy. This is hard to deny; modernization has been the goal of the Chinese people for a long time. Time and again, however, Chinese efforts at modernization have ended in failure. The most recent example was the reform movement that began in the late 1970s. The movement achieved some success in the first five years of the 1980s, but by 1987, step by step, it was moving towards failure.

Why do Chinese efforts at modernization fail? Why do reforms fail? Why has the Chinese economy remained largely inaccessible? Obviously, it is not because the Chinese people are not hard-working or fail to understand economics and doing business. The success of overseas Chinese around the world belies such a conclusion. The problem has to do with the authoritarian political system in China. The Chinese people need democracy since without the reform of China's autocratic political system it will be impossible to bring about modernization.

The Chinese people's need for democracy is not only a result of the economic failure of their current Communist system, it also comes from the extreme inhumanity of that system, which has trampled upon the most basic dignities, rights and freedoms of its citizens. This explains why the movements that have opposed such regimes have always been movements specifically for democracy and human rights. The pattern has been the same whether in Eastern Europe, the Soviet Union or China.

The true record of human rights in China has been hidden: the Chinese authorities have blocked any communication about it. Some have been misled into believing that China has been free of human rights violations. No record at all can be the worst record of all. The Tiananmen massacre of 1989 shocked many people; it also marked the first time the outside world could see for itself how cruel and violent the behaviour of the Chinese authorities can be. But the Tiananmen incident is only the tip of an iceberg. I cannot describe the rest of the iceberg in its terrible entirety, but will mention just one item: according to incomplete statistics, there are at least 976 labour reform camps in China. It is hard to say exactly how many people are in them, but we do know that the inmates of certain camps in Xinjiang Province number between 50,000 and 80,000. How many of these are political prisoners? Again we do not know, but one informed researcher has estimated that 10% are political prisoners.

In a word, Chinese history teaches us that modernization needs democracy; human rights need democracy.

The world also needs a democratic China. In today's world, the human race lives within one unified human environment. The exchange of news, knowledge and culture is the current that flows within that single environment. It is no longer possible to keep China's affairs separate from those of the rest of the world.

A democratic China would contribute greatly to stability in East Asia and in the entire Pacific region. The Cold War is over, Eastern Europe has embarked on a new road, even the two Koreas are talking to each other, but China is still a country divided since 1949; it is formally in a state of civil war.

In our small global village, more and more world-wide problems have appeared on the agenda: population, energy, the environment, global warming and deforestation. The human rights problem is another global problem, and an important one. When it is a matter of relationships within our global village, we must ask where the problem lies. As long as there exists anywhere in the world a government that can be proud of the Tiananmen massacre, or a dictatorship that refuses to apply universally recognized principles to control its own behaviour, it will remain difficult to imagine the possibility of world understanding. History teaches us that to indulge a government that is proud of murder at home eventually confronts the rest of mankind with major dilemmas. China's democracy and human rights problems, therefore, are also the world's problems. The Tiananmen massacre not only caused China to suffer; it also polluted the world environment. Without the gradual improvement of the world's human rights environment, solutions to the problems of our global village cannot be guaranteed.

It is clear that the struggle for freedom and democracy in China is far from over. The road to Chinese freedom and democracy has already been long and difficult and is likely to remain so for many years to come. It may take a decade, a generation, even longer. But it will be difficult to reverse the trend towards democracy, freedom and human rights that has been set in motion. The historic demonstrations in Tiananmen Square have revealed the enduring truth that the time for freedom and democracy in China will eventually come.

China's twentieth-century history has closely paralleled world trends. At the beginning of the century, when Communism was on the rise world-wide, it also gained ground rapidly in China. By mid-century, when many countries were becoming 'proletarian' dictatorships, China followed the trend. Today, with the Communist system in decline, Communism in China is also losing its reputation. We can predict with confidence that China, as part of a world-wide historical trend, will eventually move away from authoritarian rule and towards more democratic government.

The world will never forget the men and women of Tiananmen who paid with their lives for freedom and democracy in China. Despite the many frustrations and disappointments in today's China, I still view China's future with hope.

September 1992

RADE RADOVANOVIĆ

Not a special case

Rade Radovanović, playwright and screenwriter, was a founder member of the Serbian Independent Union of Journalists. His screenplay for *The Original Lie* was nominated for an Oscar in 1991. He spoke to *Index*'s Ursula Ruston at a meeting of journalists in Düsseldorf in August 1992, to discuss their misgivings about the journalists' role in the Yugoslav conflict.

'The situation facing journalists is very complicated and dangerous, with journalists facing blackmail on a daily basis. Some are told that they are on deathlists of one or other organization. Nothing is certain, but the psychological pressure is intense.

'There has been a direct attempt by the government to break our union. Our members are singled out for attack and threats against us often mention the fact of our union activities. Meanwhile, the official union is given money by the state to feed its members and is able to give them sugar and meat as an incentive not to join us. They have to submit to strict censorship by the state. Our members are suffering because many have not been paid by the state for several months because of their union activities. Because of the sanctions the prices are rising and food is scarce. The pressure on them from their families to give up their resistance to government control is intense. We feel it is inhuman and disgusting to blackmail people with hunger.

'I am concerned now about the kidnapping of political opponents which has started in Serbia. Jovan Mandic, an engineer who was responsible for switching out the lights in Belgrade in support of a student protest against Milošević in July, was kidnapped the day after, on 8 July 1992, blindfolded so that he could not identify his attackers, and taken to an interrogation centre outside Belgrade where he was

beaten and questioned for 20 hours. After his release he was hospital-
ized for his injuries. He is now in Düsseldorf with his family as a
refugee.'

October 1992

JUDY BLUME

Gentle reader

Judy Blume, who writes novels for children and young adults and is a
member of the board of the American PEN Centre, here describes her own
experience of what happened to American writers when, in 1980, the moral
majority's censors 'crawled out of the woodwork, seemingly overnight,
organized and determined'.

It never occurred to me, when I started to write more than 20 years
ago, that what I was writing was controversial. Much of it grew out
of my own feelings and concerns when I was young.

There were few challenges to my books then, although I remember
the night a woman phoned, asking if I had written *Are You There God?
It's Me, Margaret*. When I replied that I had, she called me a Communist
and slammed down the phone. I never did figure out if she equated
Communism with menstruation or religion, the two major concerns
in 12-year-old Margaret's life.

But in 1980 the censors crawled out of the woodwork, seemingly
overnight, organized and determined. Not only would they decide what
their children could read, but what all children could read. Challenges
to books quadrupled within months, and we shall never know how
many teachers, school librarians and principals quietly removed books
to avoid trouble.

Censorship grows out of fear and, because fear is contagious, some
parents are easily swayed. Book banning satisfies their need to feel in
control of their children's lives. This fear is often disguised as moral
outrage. They want to believe that if their children do not read about
it their children will not know about it. And if they do not know about
it, it will not happen.

Today, it is not only language and sexuality (the usual reasons given
for banning my books) that will land a book on the censors' hit list.

It is Satanism, New Age-ism and a hundred other 'Isms', some of which would be laughable if the implications were not so serious. Books that make kids laugh often come under suspicion; so do books that encourage kids to think, or question authority; books that don't hit the reader over the head with moral lessons are considered dangerous. My book *Blubber* was banned in Montgomery County, Maryland, for 'lack of moral tone' and, more recently, challenged in Canton, Ohio, for allowing evil behaviour to go unpunished. But in New Zealand it is used in teacher-training classes to help explain classroom dynamics. Censors do not want children exposed to ideas different from their own. If every individual with an agenda had his or her way, the shelves in the school library would be close to empty.

But I am encouraged by a new awareness. This year I have received a number of letters from young people who are studying censorship in their classes. And in many communities across the country, students from elementary through high school are becoming active (along with caring adults) in the fight to maintain their right to read and their right to choose books. They are speaking before school boards, and, more often than not, when they do the books in question are returned to the shelves.

Only when readers of all ages become active, only when readers are willing to stand up to the censors, will the censors get the message that they cannot frighten us.

January 1993

DUBRAVKA UGREŠIĆ

Goodnight, Croatian writers

Dubravka Ugrešić is a Croatian novelist and essayist, several of whose books have been published in Britain by Virago Press and Jonathan Cape. This piece, written when she was living in Zagreb during the war with Serbia, takes its title from a phrase which was repeated at the end of the evening news broadcasts on Croatian television.

The life of a Croatian writer in these difficult times is not easy. When the fundamental coordinates of everyday reality have become staying alive and surviving, the Croatian writer's situation is somewhat more complex. He would also like to write – and writing, to put it at its simplest, means thinking. Why is this so hard for some Croatian writers, in particular for the one who concerns us here?

Our Croatian writer is sitting today over a piece of blank white paper as though it were a minefield. Many of his colleagues are on the other side of the field, they are waving to him, calling kindly to him: 'Come over', they say, 'it isn't difficult.' Our writer shakes his head doubtfully; some of his colleagues did not make it, others barely did. Some are standing on the edge, not daring to cross. Others again cross, and have the decency to leave markers after them: BEWARE OF THE MINES! The unwritten pages of white paper lie before our writer and it seems as though everything were teeming with warnings: there are little red 'stop' signs everywhere; narrow green crossings; amber lights urging caution; black death's heads . . .

Our Croatian writer finds himself in a completely new world of communications brought about by the new and terrible reality of war. Sometimes it seems to him that the task of sending artistic messages has been reduced to the mere process of distinguishing noises, removing barriers, to a painful endeavour to explain what he has, in any case, already said. It seems that a small text of a few pages demands twice as many explanatory footnotes. His text is no longer understood as it was before: something gets in the way, the words no longer mean what they used to, each one rebounds in his face.

It seems to our writer that this is because things can no longer be implied, and they cannot be implied because there is no longer a common code, or that such a code has been established and become common to others, but not to him.

Further, it seems to him that this is because the world he knew, for better or worse, has fallen apart leaving everything in pieces. That is why his, the writer's, perspective has been called into question; it too is a victim of the chaos of war. That is why it seems to the writer that he no longer recognizes the orientation of those he is addressing. They have changed, but he has not; or he has and they have not. In any case, in the very nature of things, his message is certainly read differently by those in the trenches, those on one side and those on the other, those without a roof and those with a roof over their heads, those who are hungry and those who have enough to eat, those who have experienced the new-style concentration camps and those who have only seen pictures of war on television.

In this new communications order our writer is called upon to build into his text the clear signals which his readers expect: they too want to find their way through the text, read it from the 'right' angle.

The starting signal – which in the present situation determines the text – is the writer's origin. If he is a Croat he will be condemned but forgiven for a critical stance towards the new-style reality. He is 'one of us' after all, thinks the reading public contentedly. If he is a Serb, a Croatian Serb, of course he will never be forgiven – for a long time he will simply not be forgiven for being a Serb – but at least it will be perfectly clear which way the wind is blowing. If no one knows who he is, he will be publicly labelled: someone will know, or think he knows – no distinction is made between 'thinking' and 'knowing'.

In the map of the world according to blood group, the fundamental marker for every public act, for an ordinary 'Good morning' to a neighbour, is the Holy Blood Group. In a system of generally induced paranoia, one's national origin is the essential fact, the measure of all things. It determines perspective, it is the most fundamental assumption in the relation between sender and recipient. The first demand made of the writer and his text is the clear and public expression of that primary assumption. For fear of not being understood, in the desire to be understood no matter what, the writer makes his first signal. The message now slips differently along the channel of communication. We understand one another, we belong, even when we don't understand one another; or we don't belong, even when we do understand one another.

Another exceptionally important signal in understanding the text – or even that ordinary 'Good morning' to a neighbour – is the social origin of the writer, or at least his implicit or explicit adherence to various political options.

Yugo-nostalgia is one of the most loaded signals of political qualification in a paranoid communications system. It is more loaded than many other labels in use today, such as Chetnik, nationally colour-blind person, Commie, Great Serb and the like. This little term conceals many dangerous things. It conceals a perfidious doubt in the new system; the old one, the Commie one was better. Doubt in the new system is a hostile act against the new state, questioning its values, implying condemnation of the war, accepting the option that our enemies are also people. It also implies subscribing to Communism and the whole ideological package it carried with it. But, most of all, nostalgia is dangerous because it encourages remembering. In the newly-established reality, everything starts again from scratch. And to start from scratch, everything that came before must be forgotten.

That is why the writer more or less joyfully builds additional signals into his text. They are clear or cryptic, depending on his background and style, but essential if the text is to reach its audience. Hence, I am not a 'Yugo-nostalgic', I am not in favour of 'the prison of nations'; I was not a 'Communist', or I was, but only for a short time; or I was, but I always had a low opinion of them. And so on.

Just as ordinary people wear badges which will smooth communication with others and put things in their proper place – crosses round necks, stickers with the Croatian coat-of-arms on the windows of flats, on cars – a similar system of signals, simple and comprehensible to all, is also expected of the writer. He is the sender of messages and his message must reach the recipient without hindrance.

But the recipient today no longer seems to be the reading public but the people. And our writer, like it or not, suddenly finds himself in the completely new situation of sending messages to the people! He becomes, by chance or intention, like it or not, a writer of the people. And what exactly that is our writer doesn't know, just as he doesn't know exactly what 'the people' is. His literary memories search and strain, connecting that whole vague complex with 'popular' novels, with the nineteenth century, with the theory of 'commission', with patriotism, with 'the role of the intellectual' in difficult times. And why is 'the people' suddenly doing the commissioning, grumbles the writer, when there are so few books in any case, and when 'the people' are not too concerned that there are so few, when culture in these unhappy times is in any case reduced to the level of communication of hearsay!

Our writer knows that the war has changed everything: no one is the same any more; even his own reality, his own norms, have vanished. In their place a new reality is coming into being before his eyes: new values are being established, a new world is being built into which life will be breathed once it is named.

The business of building begins with naming. This is a house; this is the homeland; this is black; this is white. Our writer is confused. He humbly recalls that naming is the work of God. He is surprised by this passion for naming; it appears to be intended to convince oneself and others of the actual existence of the new reality. It is only in firm coordinates, in a clear and named world, that we shall not be lost, not threatened by the chaos of madness, ambiguity, multiple truths. Because we are at the beginning, we need ONE truth.

An alarm bell rings in our writer's head: his work, that of a writer, is not, and cannot be, adherence to one truth. But in the new relationship between him and his audience, there is room for only ONE truth – or what has been proclaimed the truth. Everything else is a lie.

Our writer finds himself in a new communicative situation akin to that of the photographic, in which, like a double exposure, things overlap even within himself: he no longer knows where the private person ends and the writer begins, where the boundaries between his heart and his mind lie. In this fragmented state, he is being asked to provide something he does not understand and that is beyond his strength: he is being asked to be the spokesman of his people, the loudspeaker and conveyor of 'correct' political truths, a soothsayer and a leader, a popular singer and healer, examiner of the 'national being' and its spiritual renovator.

Our writer is disconcerted, inner alarm bells ring wildly in him, the memory of his 'genetic' password, the password of his 'people', the writer's people. He remembers decades, centuries, times filled with the sweet appeal of national community and bitter rejection. He recalls the consequences of agreeing to roles; remembers the history of careers, the words, those before and those after, spoken by the same lips, written by the same pens; recalls both the shameful and the glorious moments from the general history of the writer's craft.

Our writer is a Croatian citizen: he has a heart connected to the mega-bloodstream of general suffering. His world is split in two, reality unfolds before his eyes like a grotesque nightmare. One half of him, the writer in our writer, resists the proposed strategies: naming terrorism by forgetting; the new utopia projected on the ruins of the old; unambiguous language; mental florets which come to life in the consciousness like new blades of grass. All this has been done already, not so long ago; he has learned about it from the history of the link between culture and politics. The other half, the citizen in our writer, is torn apart by the numerous miseries of his countrymen, his present and that former country. How can he separate them, and how connect them? How go on?

In his search for answers, our writer turns to his colleagues: writers, journalists, intellectuals. Of those who still make their voices heard these days, his colleagues, the majority of them, have adapted. They have accepted the codes of behaviour of a changed communications order and a newly-established reality: they have preserved the old mechanisms of their guild life. With little artistic or moral difficulty they reproduce the same language, the same mental and linguistic formulae, the same articulation of the unhappy reality which has affected everyone equally. From the outside, they appear to be innocently and contentedly submerged in the warm, smoke-filled, sweet collectivity. It is as though they have no inkling that what is in store for them is the destiny they have already lived through – as though a benevolent amnesia had wiped out all their memory.

Our writer sees his colleagues arguing, with a zeal that sometimes surprises themselves, over what needs to be done: should the greatest classic writer of Croatian literature be published in full, or should his political essays be omitted, particularly the ones dealing with Yugoslavism (is it the right political moment?); should such a writer be published at all? He watches his colleagues zealously discussing whether another colleague (who has in any case been getting up their collective nose for some time) should be destroyed. He sees them forget that they used to be guided by one set of principles and now subscribe to another, that this is what used to be done to them. His colleagues discuss things in corridors, hatch plots in almost non-existent editorial boards, accuse one another, the true believers accusing the heretical.

In the newly-established and paranoid communications order, in their everyday life, his colleagues are suddenly waging invisible wars for the right way, the right idea. They are suddenly surrounded by a self-styled army of little patriot-informers who slip them reports about the antipatriotic behaviour of this or that colleague. What is at stake is what is right, what is at stake are sincere patriotic feelings and all methods are permissible. Forget methods: this is being done in the name of the homeland, which is in danger. Without noticing it, his colleagues are slowly becoming policemen, courtiers who take the collective patriotic pulse. With the serious, grey mask of true believers, unconsciously copied from their predecessors, on their faces, his colleagues are turning themselves into executives. In collective systems which confirm their vitality simply by hunting down individuals, by collective lynching, it is a logical assumption that one day the executioners will become the victims. And *vice versa*. Because they, the vital ones, leap up more swiftly than maize from popcorn machines. And while his colleagues raise their spear-pens with holy, dedicated concentration and aim them at their enemies, while they click their carefully sharpened censor's scissors (temporary only: it is not the right moment), convinced that they are doing it for the first time (it's our lives, our freedom, our future that are at stake), behind their backs rises the supple shadow of a younger and more skilful hunter.

I, too, the author of this text, am a Croatian writer. I have no alternative, it was not my decision. But as I write on these white sheets of paper, I have at least decided not to take note of labels. I am prepared for the explosive consequences; I am not complaining. Everyone chooses his path. Of course, I allow that in these unhappy times everyone, from the ordinary citizen to the State President, from the arms smuggler to the fighter, believes that he has the right to expect the writer to fulfil his duty to the homeland, to be the spokesman of the people, to be a loyal son (where are the daughters?) of his Croatian homeland, that he declare his love for it, out loud, clearly and publicly. But I shall allow myself to refuse such demands.

From the history of my people, this writer's people, I have learned what misfortunes result from confusing roles: for the writers them-selves, for their people, for freedom of speech, for literature itself. Therefore, as a writer I shall not defend the barricades of my homeland. I prefer to stroll along the barricade of literature or sit awhile on the barricade of freedom of speech.

I am still not sure whether I should quite believe Osip Mandelstam, who considered that the writer was 'a parrot in the deepest sense of the word.' 'A parrot does not belong to any time,' says Mandelstam, 'it does not distinguish day from night. If it bores its owner, the latter will cover it up with a black cloth, and that becomes a surrogate of night for literature.' I am equally not sure whether it has become completely dark here yet. But, just in case, goodnight, Croatian writers, wherever we may be.

Translated by Celia Hawkesworth

May/June 1993

RONALD DWORKIN

A new map of censorship

Ronald Dworkin, professor of jurisprudence at Oxford since 1969, is a leading theorist of civil rights requirements and responsibilities. Among his many books are *Taking Rights Seriously* (1977), *A Matter of Principle* (1985), *A Bill of Rights for Britain* (1990) and *Freedom's Law* (1996). This essay marked *Index*'s relaunch in 1994 under the editorship of Ursula Owen.

Is freedom of speech a universal human right? Or is it, after all, just one value among others, a value cherished by middle-class intellectuals in Western democracies, but one which other cultures, drawing on different traditions, might well reject as unsuitable for them, and which radical groups within those Western democracies might well challenge as no longer central even there?

Index was founded in the first conviction: that freedom of speech, along with the allied freedoms of conscience and religion, are fundamental human rights that the world community has a responsibility to guard. But that strong conviction is suddenly challenged not only by freedom's oldest enemies – the despots and ruling thieves who fear it – but also by new enemies who claim to speak for justice not tyranny, and who point to other values we respect, including self-determination, equality, and freedom from racial hatred and prejudice, as reasons why the right of free speech should now be demoted to a much lower grade of urgency and importance.

In part, this new hostility reflects reluctance to impose Western values on alien cultures. Free speech may be important within our own secular traditions, some critics say, but it would make no sense to graft it on to very different styles of life. We cannot reasonably ask peoples whose entire social structure and sense of national identity are based on the supreme authority of a particular religion to permit what they believe to be ridicule of that religion within their own borders.

How can we expect people who are committed to a particular faith, as a value transcending all others, to tolerate its open desecration?

Other critics insist that free speech is overvalued even within Western democracies, and particularly within the USA. When the Supreme Court ruled, in the Skokie case, that the Constitution's First Amendment protected neo-Nazis who wanted to carry swastikas through a town of Holocaust survivors in Illinois, many people of good will wondered how justice could require people to accept such a grotesque insult. In the decades since the Skokie decision, moreover, Americans have become even more aware of the malign, chilling force of hate-speech and hate-gesture. That kind of speech seems particularly odious in universities, where it has been directed against women and minority students and fuelled by a backlash against the affirmative-action and other special recruiting programmes such universities adopted to increase the number of such students.

Officials at some of these universities have adopted 'speech codes' to prohibit remarks that are sexist or derogatory of a particular race or religion or sexual orientation; they defend that apparent violation of freedom of speech by insisting that the regulations are necessary to protect the dignity and equal status of all students. Some speech code supporters have taken the opportunity not just to argue for an exception to free speech, however, but to deny its importance in principle. They say that though the right of free speech has been much prized by liberal writers who profit from it, it has proved of little value to the poor and disadvantaged, and has often acted as an excuse for their oppression. One such critic, Stanley Fish, declared that, 'There's no such thing as free speech, and a good thing too.'

But the strongest new attack on freedom of speech, within democracies, has been organized by those feminists who are anxious to outlaw pornography or to make its publishers liable for punitive damages if a rapist or other criminal convinces a jury that pornography made him act as he did. They say that pornography contributes to a general cultural environment in which women are treated only as sexual devices, and subordinated to men in every way. One such American feminist, Catharine MacKinnon, is contemptuous of the objection that such censorship violates an important right; she says that Americans elevate freedom of speech to an absurd level of importance, and that more sensible people, in other parts of the world, recognize that it is to be tolerated only so long as it does not jeopardize more important goals.

Even Tom Stoppard, a distinguished and long-standing Patron of *Index*, has joined in this recent demotion of free speech. Speaking at an anniversary of Khomeini's hideous *fatwa* against Salman Rushdie, Stoppard said that though it was of course outrageous for Iran's priests to suppose that they had a right to order a murder in Britain, it was nevertheless a mistake to regard freedom of speech as a 'fundamental' human right. 'The proscription of writing which seeks to incite race hatred sits as comfortably in the Western liberal conscience,' he said, 'as the proscription against falsely shouting "Fire!" in a crowded theatre.'

These are all thoughtful opinions that will strike many people as reasonable. They signal, just for that reason, a new and particularly dangerous threat to free speech, for we are more likely to relax our defence of that freedom when its betrayers are foreign, or when the speech in question seems worthless or even vile. But if we do, then the principle is inevitably weakened, not just in such cases, but generally. So we must try to abstract from the particular challenges to free speech that now dominate the argument, and return to the wider question I began by asking. Is free speech a universal human right, a right so important that we must work to secure it even in nations where it is unfamiliar and alien? Is it so important that we must tolerate, in its name, despicable and harmful speech in our own society?

I do not mean, by posing that last question, to agree that bad speech has had the malign consequences that have recently been claimed for it. Many of those claims are inflated and some are absurd. But if free speech really is as fundamental as many of its defenders have supposed in the past, we must protect it even if it does have bad consequences, and we must be prepared to explain why. We must explain this, moreover, bearing in mind everything that, if we are right, must be tolerated. It may seem easy to defend the rights to investigative reporters exposing corruption or serious novelists exploring literary and intellectual boundaries. But free speech, if it is a universal right, also protects pornographers hawking pictures of naked women with their legs spread, and bigots sporting swastikas or white hoods and selling hatred.

We must start by recognizing that the most famous and honoured defence of free speech – John Stuart Mill's argument in *On Liberty* –

cannot support a right with that scope. Mill said that we should tolerate even the speech we hate because truth is most likely to emerge in a free intellectual combat from which no idea has been excluded. People with passionate religious convictions think they already know the truth, however, and they can hardly be expected to have more confidence in Mill's doubtful epistemology than in their own Bibles. Nor could Mill's optimism justify, even to us, tolerating everything that those who believe free speech is a basic human right insist should be tolerated. Pornographic images hardly supply 'ideas' to any market place of thought, and history gives us little reason for expecting racist speech to contribute to its own refutation.

If freedom of speech is a basic right, this must be so not in virtue of instrumental arguments, like Mill's, which suppose that liberty is important because of its consequences. It must be so for reasons of basic principle. We can find that basic principle, moreover. We can find it in a condition of human dignity: it is illegitimate for governments to impose a collective or official decision on dissenting individuals, using the coercive powers of the state, unless that decision has been taken in a manner that respects each individual's status as a free and equal member of the community. People who believe in democracy think that it is fair to use the police power to enforce the law if the law has been adopted through democratic political procedures that express the majority's will. But though majoritarian procedures may be a necessary condition of political legitimacy, they are not a sufficient condition. Fair democracy requires what we might call a democratic background: it requires, for example, that every competent adult have a vote in deciding what the majority's will is. And it requires, further, that each citizen have not just a vote but a voice: a majority decision is not fair unless everyone has had a fair opportunity to express his or her attitudes or opinions or fears or tastes or presuppositions or preju-dices or ideals, not just in the hope of influencing others, though that hope is crucially important, but also just to confirm his or her standing as a responsible agent in, rather than a passive victim of, collective action. The majority has no right to impose its will on someone who is forbidden to raise a voice in protest or argument or objection before the decision is taken.

That is not the only reason for insisting on freedom of speech as a condition of political legitimacy, but it is a central one. It may be objected that in most democracies that right now has little value for many citizens: ordinary people, with no access to great newspapers or television broadcasts, have little chance to be heard. That is a genuine problem; it may be that genuine free speech requires more than just freedom from legal censorship. But that is hardly an excuse for denying at least that freedom and the dignity it confirms: we must try to find other ways of providing those without money or influence a real chance to make their voices heard.

This argument entails a great deal more than just that governments may not censor formal political speeches or writing. A community's legislation and policy are determined more by its moral and cultural environment – the mix of its people's opinions, prejudices, tastes and attitudes – than by editorial columns or party political broadcasts or stump political speeches. It is as unfair to impose a collective decision on someone who has not been allowed to contribute to that moral environment, by expressing his political or social convictions or tastes or prejudices informally, as on someone whose pamphlets against the decision were destroyed by the police. This is true no matter how offensive the majority takes these convictions or tastes or prejudices to be, nor how reasonable its objection is.

The temptation may be near overwhelming to make exceptions to that principle – to declare that people have no right to pour the filth of pornography or race-hatred into the culture in which we all must live. But we cannot do that without forfeiting our moral title to force such people to bow to the collective judgements that do make their way into the statute books. We may and must protect women and homosexuals and members of minority groups from specific and damaging consequences of sexism, intolerance and racism. We must protect them against unfairness and inequality in employment or education or housing or the criminal process, for example, and we may adopt laws to achieve that protection. But we must not try to intervene further upstream, by forbidding any expression of the attitudes or prejudices that we think nourish such unfairness or inequality, because if we intervene too soon in the process through which collective opinion is formed, we spoil the only democratic justification we have for insisting that everyone obey these laws, even those who hate and resent them.

215

Someone might now object that my argument shows, at most, only that free speech is essential to a democracy, and therefore does not show that it is a universal human right that may properly be claimed even in non-democratic societies. We may want to reply, to that objection, that democracy is itself a universal human right, and that non-democratic societies are tyrannies. But we need not rely on that claim, because we can distinguish democracy, as a form of political organization, from the more basic obligation of government to treat all those subject to its dominion with equal concern, as all people whose lives matter. That plainly is a basic human right; and many of the more detailed human rights we all recognize flow from it. And so does a right of free speech. Even in a country ruled by prophets or generals in which ordinary citizens have no real vote, these citizens must nevertheless have the right to speak out, to cry for the attention or to buy the ear of those who will decide their fates, or simply to bear witness, out of self-respect if nothing else, to what they believe to be wicked or unfair. A government that deems them too corrupt or debased or ignoble even to be heard, except on penalty of death or jail, can hardly pretend that it counts their interests as part of its own.

It is tempting, as I said, to think that even if some liberty of speech must be counted a universal right, this right cannot be absolute; that those whose opinions are too threatening or base or contrary to the moral or religious consensus have forfeited any right to the concern on which the right rests. But such a reservation would destroy the principle: it would leave room only for the pointless grant of protection for ideas or tastes or prejudices that those in power approve, or in any case do not fear. We might have the power to silence those we despise, but it would be at the cost of political legitimacy, which is more important than they are.

Any such reservation would also be dangerous. MacKinnon and her allies failed in the USA: the courts held their statute unconstitutional. But they persuaded the Canadian legislature to adopt a severe censorship law, and the law was upheld against constitutional challenge there. As liberals had warned, the first authors to be banned under the new Canadian statute were not those the feminists had in mind. They were, in fact, prominent homosexual and lesbian authors, a radical black feminist accused of stirring up hatred against whites, and, for a time,

Andrea Dworkin, MacKinnon's main ally in the feminist censorship movement, herself. Principle is indivisible, and we try to divide it at our peril. When we compromise on freedom because we think our immediate goals more important, we are likely to find that the power to exploit the compromise is not in our hands after all, but in those of fanatical priests armed with *fatwas* and fanatical moralists with their own brand of hate.

May/June 1994

NOAM CHOMSKY

Sweet home of liberty

Noam Chomsky, one of the leading scholars in the field of linguistics, with a chair for it at MIT since 1976, is also America's foremost political dissident, a trenchant and always controversial critic of his country's foreign and domestic policies. His books include Human Rights and American Foreign Policy (1978), Towards a New Cold War (1982), Language and Problems of Knowledge (1987) and Powers and Thought (1996).

In his preface to Animal Farm, George Orwell turned his attention to societies that are relatively free from state controls. 'The sinister fact about literary censorship in England,' he wrote, 'is that it is largely voluntary. Unpopular ideas can be silenced, and inconvenient facts kept dark, without any need for any official ban.' The outcome is in part ensured by control of the press by 'wealthy men who have every motive to be dishonest on certain important topics,' but more significantly, by the 'general tacit agreement that "it wouldn't do" to mention that particular fact.' As a result, 'Anyone who challenges the prevailing orthodoxy finds himself silenced with surprising effectiveness.' The preface was published 30 years after the book appeared.

In the case under discussion here, the 'prevailing orthodoxy' is well summarized by historian Michael Howard: 'For 200 years the United States has preserved almost unsullied the original ideals of the Enlightenment . . . , and, above all, the universality of these values,' though unfortunately it 'does not enjoy the place in the world that it should have earned through its achievements, its generosity, and its goodwill since World War II' – indeed, 'for 200 years.' The record is unsullied by the treatment of 'that hapless race of native Americans, which we are exterminating with such merciless and perfidious cruelty' (John Quincy Adams) and the slaves who provided cheap cotton to allow the industrial revolution to take off 'through market forces'; by the fact that US aid 'has tended to flow disproportionately to Latin American governments which torture their citizens . . . to the hemi-sphere's relatively egregious violators of fundamental human rights' (Lars Schoultz, the leading academic specialist on human rights in Latin America); by the terrible atrocities the US was once again conducting in its 'backyard' as the praises were delivered; or by the fate of Filipinos, Vietnamese, and a few who might have a different story to tell.

A natural starting point for an inquiry into Washington's defence of 'the universality of [Enlightenment] values' is the Universal Declaration of Human Rights [UD] adopted by the UN General Assembly on 10 December 1948, accepted generally as a human rights standard and, in US courts, as 'customary international law'. The UD became the focus of great attention in June 1993, during the international conference on human rights in Vienna. A lead headline in the *New York Times* read: 'At Vienna Talks, US Insists Rights Must be Universal'. Washington warned 'that it would oppose any attempt to use religious and cultural traditions to weaken the concept of universal human rights', the *Times* reported. Secretary of State Warren Christopher declared that 'the United States will never join those who would undermine the Universal Declaration', and will defend their universality against those who hold 'that human rights should be interpreted differently in regions with non-Western cultures,' notably the 'dirty dozen', with Indonesia their advocate.

Washington's decisiveness prevailed. The 'challenge of relativity' was beaten back, the *New York Times* reported. The conference declared that 'the universal nature of these rights and freedoms is beyond question'; there will be no 'retreat from the basic tenets' of the UD.

The impressive rhetoric was rarely besmirched by inquiry into the observance of the UD by its defenders or even its actual provisions. These matters were raised in Vienna in a Public Hearing, held to break through the wall of silence erected to protect Western power from 'inconvenient facts'. Citizens of the free world are fortunate to have readily available to them the concerns of the vast majority of the world's people, in the report of the Public Hearing, *Justice Denied!*, published in an edition of 2,000 copies in Kathmandu.

Some of the provisions of the UD are familiar in the United States. The most famous by far is Article 13 (2), which states that 'Everyone has the right to leave any country, including his own'. Article 13 was invoked with much passion every year on Human Rights Day, 10 December, with public demonstrations and indignant demands that the Soviet Union let Russian Jews leave. To be exact, the words just quoted were invoked, but not the phrase that follows: 'and to return to his country'. The significance of the omitted words was spelled out on 11 December 1948, the day after the UD was ratified, when the General Assembly passed Resolution 194, which affirms the right of Palestinians to return to their homes or receive compensation, if they chose not to return. But it was always understood that it 'wouldn't do' to mention the omitted words, let alone the glaringly obvious fact that the most passionate opponents of Article 13 were the people exhorting the Soviet tyrants to observe it, to much acclaim.

It is only fair to add that the cynicism has now been overcome. At the December 1993 UN session, the Clinton administration for the first time joined with Israel in opposing UN 194, which was reaffirmed by a vote of 127-2. As is the norm, there was no report or comment. But at least the inconsistency is behind us: the first half of Article 13 (2) has lost its relevance, and Washington now officially rejects its second half.

Let us move on to Article 14, which affirms that 'Everyone has the right to seek and to enjoy in other countries asylum from persecution.' Haitians, for example, including the 87 new victims captured in Clinton's blockade and returned to their charnel house as the Vienna conference opened. The US has upheld Article 14 in this manner since the 1970s, the Duvalier dictatorship being a respected ally helping to convert Haiti to an export platform for US corporations seeking super-cheap labour. The practice was ratified in a Reagan–Duvalier agreement. When a military coup overthrew Haiti's first democratically elected president in September 1991, renewing the terror, the Bush administration imposed a blockade to drive back the flood of refugees to the torture chamber where they were to be imprisoned.

Bush's 'appalling' refugee policy was bitterly condemned by candidate Bill Clinton, whose first act as President was to tighten the illegal blockade while extending Bush's decision to exempt US firms from the OAS embargo. Trade with Haiti in violation of the embargo remained high in 1992 and increased by almost half under Clinton, including purchases by the US government and a large increase in export of food from the starving island. These are among the many devices adopted to ensure that the popular forces that swept President Aristide to power will have no voice in any future 'democracy,' no surprise to people who have failed to immunize themselves from 'inconvenient facts'.

Again, fairness requires that we recognize that Washington did briefly depart from this systematic rejection of Article 14. During the seven months of democracy, Washington gained a sudden and short-lived sensitivity to Article 14 as the flow of refugees declined to a trickle – in fact, reversed, as Haitians returned to their country in its moment of hope. Of the more than 24,000 Haitians intercepted by US forces from 1981 to 1991, 11 were granted asylum as victims of political persecution (in comparison with 75,000 out of 75,000 Cubans). In these years of terror, Washington allowed 28 asylum claims. During Aristide's tenure, with violence and repression radically reduced, 20 were allowed from a refugee pool perhaps 1/50th the scale. Practice returned to normal after the military coup and the renewed terror.

Concerned that popular pressures might make it difficult to sustain the blockade, the administration has been pleading with other countries to relieve the US of the burden of accommodating refugees. Curiously, debate over this issue has missed the obvious candidate: Tanzania, which has been able to accommodate hundreds of thousands of Rwandans, and could surely come to the rescue of the beleaguered USA by accepting a few thousand more black faces.

Article 25 of the UD states that 'Everyone has the right to a standard of living adequate for the health and well-being of himself and his family, including food, clothing, housing and medical care and necessary social services, and the right to security in the event of unemployment, sickness, disability, widowhood, old age or other lack of livelihood in circumstances beyond his control.' It is unnecessary to dwell on the defence of these principles in the world's richest country, with unparalleled advantages – and a poverty level twice that of England, which has the second worst record among the industrial societies. In the USA, 30 million people suffer from hunger, an increase of 50% since 1985; 40% of children in the world's richest city fall below the poverty line, deprived of minimal conditions that offer some hope of escape from misery, destitution, and violence; and on, and on.

Given its extraordinary advantages, the USA is in the leading ranks of opposition to the universality of the UD by virtue of this Article alone, with Britain not far behind.

Article 23 declares that 'Everyone has the right to work, to free choice of employment, to just and favourable conditions of work and to protection against unemployment,' along with 'remuneration ensuring for himself and his family an existence worthy of human dignity, and supplemented, if necessary, by other means of social protection.' Again, we need not tarry on the devotion to this principle. Furthermore, 'Everyone has the right to form and to join trade unions for the protection of his interests.'

The latter right is technically observed in the USA, though it is efficiently undermined by an array of legal and administrative mechanisms. Reviewing some of the methods, Business Week reports that 'Over the past dozen years, in fact, US industry has conducted one of the most successful anti-union wars ever, illegally firing thousands of workers for exercising their rights to organize. Unlawful firings occurred in one-third of all representation elections in the late '80s, versus eight per cent in the late '60s.' Workers have no recourse, as the Reaganites converted the increasingly powerful state they nurtured to an expansive welfare state for the rich, defying US law as well as the customary international law enshrined in the Universal Declaration.

Under popular pressures rooted in the ferment of the 1960s, the US Congress has imposed human rights conditions on military aid and trade privileges. These actions have compelled the White House to find various modes of evasion, which became farcical during the Reagan years. The contortions on China are a recent example, though it is worth noting that many critical issues were not even raised: crucially, the horrifying conditions that 'free labour' is forced to endure, with hundreds of workers, mostly women, burned to death locked into factories, some 15,000 deaths from industrial accidents in 1993, and other gross violations of international conventions.

The role of sanctions is well illustrated by the case of the voice of the 'dirty dozen,' Indonesia. Its horrendous human rights record at home and near-genocidal aggression in East Timor has not led to sanctions, though Congress did cut off aid for military training in reaction to the Dili massacre. The aftermath followed the familiar pattern: delicately selecting the anniversary of the Indonesian invasion, Clinton's State Department announced that 'Congress's action did not ban Indonesia's purchase of training with its own funds', so it can proceed despite the ban. Rather than impose sanctions, or even limit military aid, the USA, UK and other powers have sought to enrich themselves as much as possible by participating in Indonesia's crimes.

World leaders do recognize some limits, however. In November 1993, on behalf of the non-aligned movement and the World Health Organization, Indonesia submitted to the UN a resolution requesting an opinion from the World Court on the legality of the use of nuclear weapons. In the face of this atrocity, the guardians of international morality leaped into action. The USA, UK and France threatened Indonesia with trade sanctions and termination of aid, the Catholic Church press reported, unless it withdrew the resolution, as it did.

Meanwhile, terror and aggression continue unhampered, along with harsh repression of labour in a country with wages half those of China. The administration suspended review of Indonesian labour practices, commending Indonesia for 'bringing its labour law and practice into closer conformity with international standards' (Trade Representative Mickey Kantor), a witticism that is in particularly poor taste.

As the most powerful state, the USA makes its own laws, using force and conducting economic warfare at will. It also threatens sanctions against countries that do not abide by its conveniently flexible notions of 'free trade'. Recently Washington has employed such threats with great effectiveness (and GATT approval) to force open Asian markets for US tobacco exports and advertising, aimed primarily at the growing markets of women and children. The US Agriculture Department also gives grants to tobacco firms to promote smoking overseas. Asian countries have attempted anti-smoking campaigns, but they are overwhelmed by the miracles of the market, reinforced by US power through the sanctions threat. Oxford University epidemiologist Richard Peto estimates that among Chinese children under 20 today, 50 million will die of cigarette-related diseases, an achievement that ranks high even by 20th century standards.

While state power energetically promotes the most lethal known form of substance abuse in the interests of agribusiness, it adopts highly selective devices in other cases. On the pretext of the war against drugs, the US has been able to play an active role in the vast atrocities conducted by the security forces and their paramilitary associates in Colombia, now the leading human rights violator in Latin America, and now the leading recipient of US aid and training, increasing under Clinton – again, no surprise in the real world. The war against drugs is 'a myth', Amnesty International reports, agreeing with other investigators. Security forces work closely with narcotraffickers and landlords while targeting the usual victims, including community leaders, human rights and health workers, union activists, students, the political opposition, but primarily peasants, in a country where protest has been criminalized.

Subsequent International Covenants are respected in much the manner of the UD. The Convention on the Rights of the Child has been ratified by 159 countries, including every country of the Americas apart from the USA. After delaying for decades, it did endorse the International Covenant on Civil and Political Rights, 'the leading treaty for the protection' of the narrow category of rights that the West claims to uphold, observe Human Rights Watch and the American Civil Liberties Union in their report on US non-compliance with its provisions.* The Bush administration ensured that the treaty would be inoperative by eliminating provisions that might expand rights and declaring the US in full compliance with the remaining ones. The treaty is 'non-self-executing' and accompanied by no enabling legislation, so it cannot be invoked in US courts and ratification was 'an empty act for Americans,' the HRW/ACLU report continues.

The exceptions are crucial, because the US violates the treaty 'in important respects,' the report observes, giving numerous examples. To cite one, the US entered a specific reservation to Article 7, which states that 'No one shall be subjected to torture or to cruel, inhuman, or degrading treatment or punishment.' The reason is that conditions in prisons in the USA – which leads the world in imprisoning its population, the numbers almost tripling during the Reagan years – violate these conditions as generally understood, just as they seriously violate the provisions of Article 10 on humane treatment of prisoners

---

* *Human rights violations in the United States: a report on US compliance with the International Covenant on Civil and Political Rights* (Human Rights Watch/American Civil Liberties Union, December 1993).

and on the right to 'reformation and social rehabilitation,' which the US flatly rejects. Another US reservation concerns the death penalty, which is not only employed far more freely than the norm but also 'applied in a manner that is racially discriminatory,' the HRW/ACLU report observes, reiterating the conclusions of many studies.

Other International Covenants submitted to Congress also were restricted as 'non-self-executing.' In the case of the UN Convention Against Torture and Other Forms of Cruel, Inhuman or Degrading Treatment or Punishment, the Senate imposed this restriction, in part to protect a Supreme Court ruling allowing corporal punishment in schools.

The USA is a world leader in defence of freedom of speech, perhaps unique in realising Enlightenment values at least since the 1960s. With regard to civil-political rights and 'anti-torture' rights, the US record at home ranks well by comparative standards, though a serious evaluation would have to take into account the capacity to uphold such rights, including the extraordinary advantages the country has enjoyed from its origins. The social and economic provisions of the UD and other conventions are operative only insofar as popular struggle over many years has given them substance. The point generalizes; as James Madison observed, a 'parchment barrier' will not protect freedom and rights. The earlier record within the national territory is hideous, and the human rights record abroad is a scandal, though it has somewhat improved as popular forces have placed limits on state terror.

But the realities are for the most part 'kept dark, without any need for any official ban,' much as Orwell understood.

July/August 1994

NADINE GORDIMER

Standing in the queue

Nadine Gordimer wrote this moving account of South Africa's first free elections under universal suffrage for *Index* in 1994.

Is there any South African for whom this day will be remembered by any event, even the most personal, above its glowing significance as the day on which we voted? Even for whites, all of whom have had the vote since they were eighteen, this was the first time. This was my overwhelming sense of the day: the other elections, with their farcical show of a democratic procedure restricted to whites (and, later, to everyone but the black majority), had no meaning for any of us as *South Africans*: only as a hegemony of the skin.

Standing in the queue this morning, I was aware of a sense of silent bonding. Businessmen in their jogging outfits, nurses in uniform (two, near me, still wearing the plastic mob-caps that cover their hair in the cloistered asepsis of the operating theatre), women in their Zionist Church outfits, white women and black women who shared the mothering of white and black children winding about their legs, people who had brought folding stools to support their patient old bones, night watchmen just off duty, girl students tossing long hair the way horses switch their tails – here we all were as we have never been. We have stood in line in banks and post offices together, yes, since the desegregation of public places; but until this day there was always the unseen difference between us, far more decisive than the different colours of our skins: some of us had the right that is the basis of all rights, the symbolic X, the sign of a touch on the controls of polity, the mark of citizenship, and others did not. But today we stood on new ground.

The abstract term 'equality' took on materiality as we moved towards the church hall polling station and the simple act, the drawing of an

X, that ended over three centuries of privilege for some, deprivation of human dignity for others.

The first signature of the illiterate is the X. Before that there was only the thumb-print, the skin-impression of the powerless. I realized this with something like awe when, assigned by my local branch of the African National Congress to monitor procedures at a polling booth, I encountered black people who could not read or write. A member of the Independent Electoral Commission would guide them through what took on the solemnity of a ritual: tattered identity document presented, hands outstretched under the ultra-violet light, hands sprayed with invisible ink, and meticulously folded ballot paper – a missive ready to be despatched for the future – placed in those hands. Then an uncertain few steps towards a booth, accompanied by the IEC person and one of the party agents to make sure that when the voter said which party he or she wished to vote for the X would be placed in the appropriate square. Several times I was that party agent and witnessed a man or woman giving his signature to citizenship. A strange moment: the first time man scratched the mark of his identity, the conscious proof of his existence, on a stone must have been rather like this.

Of course nearby in city streets there were still destitute black children sniffing glue as the only substitute for nourishment and care; there were homeless families existing in rigged-up shelters in the crannies of the city. The law places the gown of equality underfoot; it did not feed the hungry or put up a roof over the head of the homeless today, but it changed the base on which South African society was for so long built. The poor are still there, round the corner. But they are not The Outcast. They can no longer be decreed to be forcibly removed, deprived of land, and of the opportunity to change their lives. They count. The meaning of the counting of the vote, whoever wins the majority, is this, and not just the calculation of the contents of ballot boxes.

Even if to be alive on this day was not Wordsworth's 'very heaven' for those who have been crushed to the level of wretchedness by the decades of apartheid and the other structures of racism that preceded it; if they could not share the euphoria I experienced, standing in line, to be living at this hour has been extraordinary. The day has been captured for me by the men and women who couldn't read or write, but underwrote it at last, with their kind of signature. May it be the seal on the end of illiteracy, of the pain of imposed ignorance, of the deprivation of the fullness of life.

July/August 1994

IRFAN HOROZOVIC

The Bosnian bull

Irfan Horozovic's 'The Bosnian bull' was written in response to the proposal by Haris Pasovic, the Sarajevo theatre director, for a series of stories to be read simultaneously in Sarajevo and other European cities, a symbol of solidarity in time of conflict that came to be known as 'Scheherazade 2001'.

He didn't notice the Butcher approach. Images of the world took on hazy shapes in his drowsy eyes. That made the blow all the more terrible. His head suddenly felt severed from his body, fertility from foreboding, his tail powerless against all former and future leeches.

Never had that little bull felt as big as now, with this growing pain.

He was not dead. Murky, dark senses were aroused when the steel jaws began to bite, tear and chew, when his flesh, his life became food, food for the insatiable tooth, food which watches itself being eaten! He saw the towns through which his flesh was being hauled. He saw the villages in the eyes of his raped shepherdesses. He saw the destroyed houses and the old men who resembled scorched tree stumps which glow in the night. He saw the throngs of people streaming into exile like blood from his body.

He saw. And he tried to stand up.

The game had only just begun.

Just like the Spanish theatre of sacrifice, his little meadow became peopled with observers, supporters and advisers. The loud scream produced a sudden hush. The medicinal herb he had unconsciously bitten into, its juice mixing with his own blood, took his attention away from the spear-throwers who were approaching with their quivering muscles, taking aim at his pulse, his arteries, his heart. The iron rhinos made for his stomach and shoulder blades. Their riders held charts of the bull's flesh, reproduced at the Great Butcher Shop. They knew who would get the ribs, who the shanks, who the legs and the tail, who the heart, who the eyes, the brain and the tongue. They knew and they quarrelled.

Drawing his strength from unplumbed memory, the bull rose to his feet. In that same instant, the iron, toothed horn knocked him down, and pinned him to the ground, to the trampled secret grass. Now he resembled a living monument who served as a target for the steel birds which fired their vapours at him from the very firmament above. He no longer heard a thing. No shouts of delight or of displeasure. He did not notice how the iron rhinos had been removed so as not to block the view while the performance of the steel birds was on. Only the one pinning him down remained, while the others circled around, waiting for their moment to come.

Finally, his head slumped, his chest, his legs.

The butchers quarrelled over the various pieces, they threatened each other with their teeth and toothed horns, they cited the promises and secret agreements made in the Great Butcher Shop. The observers joined in the fight. The supporters created an unbearable racket, completely covering a dark sound which emanated from the bull's severed head, from his slit throat. It was a death rattle in which one sensed something like memory, something like the trumpet of a parallel world, something like birth.

The decimated bull rose to its feet.

He stood there like that, awkward and desperate, trying to understand.

After their initial surprise, the butchers, the iron rhino masters, the steel bird drivers, and the observers all rushed in. The butchers killed the severed pieces which still clung to the body, if only in foreboding; they cut up the bones, the nerves, directing their knives at the fore-boding itself.

The bull stood there and screamed.

The observers, the supporters and the advisers returned to their places behind the fence and continued watching the show which defied every known rule. They watched the killing which emerged from the killing, the killing which turned into the next killing, the killing and decimation, the decimation and killing. They watched and they waited. Time stopped. Time stopped behind the fence. The pulse of pain.

Everybody waited to see the little decimated bull knuckle under, its magnificent horns of a herbivore raised to the sky.

Translated by Christina Pribichevich-Zoric

September/October 1994

WOLE SOYINKA

The last despot and the end of Nigerian history?

Wole Soyinka's pungent account of the devastation of the land of the Ogoni people of south-eastern Nigeria, and of the crudely manipulative policies of Nigeria's despotic ruler, General Sani Abacha, was written one year before the execution of the Ogoni writer and spokesman Ken Saro-Wiwa, long held 'incommunicado in a hidden prison ... totally at the mercy of a gloating sadist, a self-avowed killer and torturer of the military kind, specially selected for the task of total "pacification" of Ogoniland.' Soyinka was then himself sentenced to death in absentia.

There was once a thriving habitation of some half a million people in south-eastern Nigeria, the land of the Ogoni. It is an oil-producing area that had suffered much ecological damage. That damage has received world publicity largely due to the efforts of a feisty and passionate writer called Ken Saro-Wiwa, himself an Ogoni. A leader of the Movement for the Salvation of the Ogoni People, MOSOP, he exposed the plight of the Ogoni to the United Nations Minorities Council, calling for the recognition of the Ogoni people as one of the world's endangered minorities. He agitated for compensation for damaged crops, polluted fishing ponds and the general destruction of what was once an organic economic existence of his people.

That at least was in the beginning, some two or three years ago. Now, Ken Saro-Wiwa is held in chains in a hidden prison, incommunicado. He is seriously ill – he suffers from a heart condition – and is totally at the mercy of a gloating sadist, a self-avowed killer and torturer of the military species, specially selected for the task of total 'pacification' of Ogoniland. Saro-Wiwa's people have taken to the surrounding forests and mangrove swamps to survive. Those who remain in townships and villages are subjected to arbitrary displacement, expropriation of their property, violence on their persons and the rape of their

232

womanhood. Ogoniland has been declared a 'military zone' under the direct rule of a 'Task Force on Internal Security'. Within this enclave, reporters, foreign or local, are made unwelcome and, in some cases, brutalized. In any case, the stable of an effective Nigerian press is being constantly reduced through illegal closures by the police on orders from the military. Before long, even those who penetrate the iron curtain of Sani Abacha's militarized enclave will have no media through which to remind the Nigerian populace of the atrocities daily inflicted on their Ogoni compatriots.

One ongoing actuality of repression very easily obscures another; it is a familiar and understandable pattern, one that dictatorships, especially of the most cynical kind, exploit most effectively. For the majority of Nigerians, Ogoni is only some localized problem remote from the immediate, overall mission of rooting out the military from Nigerian politics, rescuing the nation's wealth from its incontinent hands and terminating, once for all, its routine murders of innocent citizens on the streets of Lagos and other more visible centres of opposition. The massacres in Ogoni are hidden, ill-reported. Those that obtain the just publicity of horror, mostly in government-controlled media, are those that are attributed to the Ogoni leadership movements, such as MOSOP.

Yet the accounts of such incidents, and careful investigations, lead to more than mere suspicions of dirty tricks, of covert military operations designed to discredit the leadership, throw the movement in disarray and incite ethnic animosity between the Ogoni and their neighbours, thus instigating an unceasing round of blood-letting . . .

Ogoniland is the first Nigerian experimentation with 'ethnic cleansing', authorized and sustained by the Nigerian despot, General Sani Abacha. His on-the-spot operatives, Lt Colonel Dauda Komo and Major Paul Okutimo, are Nigeria's contribution to the world's shameful directory of obedience to orders over and above the call of duty. The so-called 'Task Force on Internal Security' is doomed to be Abacha's sole legacy to the nation, Nigeria's yet unheralded membership card of the club of the practitioners of 'ethnic cleansing' . . .

Ogoniland is, alas, only the model space for the actualization of a long-dreamt totalitarian onslaught on the more liberated, more politically sophisticated sections of the Nigerian polity, which have dared expose and confront the power obsession of a minuscule but obdurate military-civilian hegemony. Ogoni people are, alas, only the guinea-pigs for a morbid resolution of this smouldering inequity that was instituted by the British as they planned for their departure. The beneficiaries remain, till today, a minority made up of a carefully nurtured feudal oligarchy, and their pampered, indolent and unproductive scions.

The carefully propagated myth of an uncritical, political solidarity within this section of the populace, the 'North', was only recently exploded however . . . In a sense, it was not until the national elections of 12 June 1993 that the collapse of that fiction became irrefutable, thanks to the conduct of those elections which was universally acclaimed a model of fairness, order and restraint.

The pattern of voting also made it abundantly clear to the entire world that the so-called gulf between the North and the South was a deliberate invention of a minor power-besotted leadership and its divisive gamesmanship. There is indeed a line of division in the North, but it was drawn between the workers, peasants, civil servants, petty traders, students and the unemployed on the one hand, and the parasitic elite and feudal scions on the other. These last, the beneficiaries of that ancient deception, are now traumatized. They cannot cope with this stark revelation of a nationalist political consciousness, so triumphantly manifested in the 12 June elections . . .

After the initial noises of realism and surrender to a popular, democratic will, the reprobates of the old order recovered their breath and recollected their endangered interests, regrouped, and ranged themselves behind a mouldy concept of an eternal right to governance and control. The latest instrument of their feudal, despotic will is General Sani Abacha, the last in the line of the reign of deception, of obfuscating rhetoric and cant in the service of a straightforward will to domination by an anachronistic bunch of social predators. Their notion of a historic mandate of power is not only warped and mindless; it may prove terminal to the existence of the nation if its most faithful facilitator to date, General Sani Abacha, succeeds in clinging to office for another six months, maybe less. That is our reading of this crisis of nation-being, and then Nigeria goes down as yet another forgotten smear on the geographical atlas of the world.

*   *   *

Of late, the Nigerian media have virtually waxed hysterical over the increasing arrogance and obduracy of this minority, thanks largely to the boastful performances of their most disreputable members. One notorious example is the lately returned fugitive Umaru Dikko, the Task Force specialist on rice importation, who barely escaped being crated back to Nigeria to face military justice under General Buhari. In denouncing the activities of this minority, described variously and often imprecisely as the Sokoto Caliphate, the Northern Elite, the Kaduna Mafia, the Hausa-Fulani oligarchy, the Sardauna Legacy, the Dan Fodio Jihadists etc etc, what is largely lost in the passion and outrage is that they do constitute a minority, a dangerous, conspiratorial and reactionary clique, but a minority just the same. But their tentacles reach deep, and their fanaticism is the material face of religious fundamentalism.

But it is not just the Nigerian free media – and perhaps, before it is too late, our nettled general of the occupation forces of media houses will be made to realize this. Public debate – in bars, bus stops, the markets, the motor garages, staff and student clubs, government offices etc etc, largely in the South, naturally – has catapulted the activities of this minority to the heart of the national crisis, resulting in questioning the hitherto assumption (and 12 June affirmation) of the nation as a single entity. And the military, by its sectarian alliance with these claimants of divine attribution of power, has lost the last vestiges of any claims to neutrality in all areas of the contest for civic power. On 23 June 1993, the day of the arbitrary annulment of the national presidential election, the military committed the most treasonable act of larceny of all time – it violently robbed the Nigerian people of their nationhood.

Those who still advocate, therefore, that Sani Abacha has inaugurated his own programme of transition to civil rule from a 'sincere interest of the [Nigerian] nation at heart', are bewildering victims of a carefully nurtured propaganda that began with the erstwhile dictator of Nigeria, General Ibrahim Badamosi Babangida (IBB). It was this propaganda, waged on an international scale, and funded to the tune of millions of dollars, that enabled quite a few, normally intelligent analysts at the Africa desk of foreign powers to propose that the expensive, impossibly tortuous transition-to-democracy programme of Abacha's predecessor was a well-considered, disinterested programme that objectively

recognized the peculiar nature of Nigerian politicians, to which abnor-
mality the good General was merely responding . . .

But IBB was at least an original. What Nigeria is confronting today
is a species of mimic succession that considers itself innovative. The
imposition of a Constitutional Conference by General Sani Abacha, as
a 'solution' to the artificial crisis developed from a free and fair election,
is really a pitiable compliment to I. B. Babangida, who at least played
that con game with panache, milking it eventually to death. In Abacha's
hands, it is a squeezed-dry, humourless patent for any would-be dictator. It is a fair assessment of the IQ of Sani Abacha that he actually
imagines that this transparent ploy for self-perpetuation would fool the
market woman, the roadside mechanic, the student, factory worker or
religious leader of whatever persuasion. Even the village idiot must
marvel at such banal rivalry of a disgraced predecessor.

Nigerians simply do not believe for one single moment in this conference, not even the propagandist who must churn out the government
line; even less the volunteers and conscripts he has gathered together
in Abuja for this non-event. The participants are mostly economically
exhausted politicians, who cannot resist a six-month sabbatical without
obligations, all expenses paid and some; they are chronic wheelers and
dealers looking for a quick financial chance – from the inexhaustible
(but drastically devalued) government purse; politicians seeking a free
and painless venue for some horse-trading against the resumption of
civilian party politics etc etc. There are, of course, also the anti-
democratic die-hards, the aforesaid guardians of the very private pre-
cinct of power, for whom the very notion of an actualized 12 June
election, that declaration of national unity, must be expunged from
memory for all eternity . . .

Not to be forgotten – however academic it may sound, given the
nature of military rule – is the fact that Abacha's administration is
patently illegal, and has been thus proclaimed by the Nigerian law
courts . . .

We have gone to court once again to obtain a separate declaration
on Abacha himself. This move involves more than an academic exercise
however. The Nigerian populace is being primed for a campaign of
comprehensive civil disobedience. They are being reinforced in their

conviction that their cause, and their acts, are backed by law; that it is an outlaw who presently inhabits Aso Rock; that his closures of media houses and confiscation of passports are illegal – nothing but plain thuggery; that his seizure and operation of the nation's treasury and revenues are nothing but acts of banditry; that his imagined authority to try anyone for treason is the ultimate ridicule of a judiciary that his very presence in Abuja (and contemptuous flouting of court orders) subvert; that his detention of any Nigerian citizen is nothing but the hostage-taking tactics of two-a-penny terrorists . . . ; that, in short, he may exercise power through the gun, but he lacks authority even in the most elastic sense of the word, and that this emptiness must be made increasingly manifest in public acts of rejection . . .

Abacha's recent address to the nation, one which re-emphasized his determination to decide our destiny through this still-born conference, was, of course, not unexpected. This particular despot differs from his predecessor in his inability to cope with more than one line of thought, or anticipate more than one course of action or response in any given month. His address, however, fell short, for now, of the scorched-earth policy that we had expected him to declare – the proscription of the striking trade unions, imposition of a state of emergency, the closure of more media houses and yes, even detention camps for dissidents.

The blueprint for these measures has been worked out, and military units – veterans of random slaughter of civilians – even deployed to opposition strongholds for a ruthless clamp down on the populace. The necessary decree was drafted – no, not from the Attorney-General's office, that misguided lawman had long been sidelined – but from the Presidency itself, where the Secretary to the Government, one Alhaji Aminu Saleh, an unabashed 'capo' of the notorious minority, has taken over the functions of law-drafting, recruiting private lawyers to do the dirty work that the AG had shown increasing reluctance to undertake. The government prosecutors of the President-elect, Basorun M. K. O. Abiola, were, for instance, recruited lawyers from private practice, contracted not by the Attorney-General's office, but by Aminu Saleh. His bold, unchallengeable incursions into the zone of authority even of generals within the cabinet are already public knowledge.

It is necessary to alert the world now that this plan has merely been shelved, not abandoned. Abacha, let no one be in any doubt, has resolved to subjugate the strongholds of opposition in an even more ruthless manner than he did last year when, as Babangida's hatchet-man, he succeeded in murdering over 200 pro-democracy demonstrators. . . . This time round, a far more systematic response has been outlined: Nigeria, especially the south-west and the oil-producing south-east, are to be 'Ogonized' in a thoroughgoing blitz. The trade union leaders, the intellectual and professional opposition are to be sequestered and subjected to absolute military control under the clones of the Dauda Komos and Paul Okutimos.

Abacha is resolved to spread the 'Ogoni' solution throughout southern Nigeria. A minuscule being and matching mind, but with a gargantuan ego, he feels personally insulted by the resistance to his delusions and has sworn, if it came to the crunch, to 'wipe out the very oil wells those labour unions are using to blackmail us.' That statement is a very reliable quote. Abacha is out to out-Saddam Saddam's parting gift to Kuwait. Anyone who believes that Abacha will not kill the goose that lays the golden egg forgets that, in any case, the General's private barn is already bursting with a vast deposit from Nigeria's obliging goose.

Those who wish to understand the catastrophe towards which the Nigerian nation is being propelled will do well to study the personalities of the present and the immediate past Nigerian military despots . . . Babangida's love of power was visualized in actual terms – power over Nigeria, over the nation's impressive size, its potential, over the nation's own powerful status (despite serious image blemishes) within the community of nations. The potency of Nigeria, in short, was an augmentation of his own sense of personal power. It corrupted him thoroughly, and all the more disastrously because he had come to identify that Nigeria, and her resources, with his own person and personal wealth.

Not so Abacha. Abacha is prepared to reduce Nigeria to rubble as long as he survives to preside over a name – and Abacha is a survivor. He has proved that repeatedly, even in his internal contests with Babangida. Totally lacking in vision, in perspectives, he is a mole trapped in a warren of tunnels. At every potential exit he is blinded by the headlamps of an oncoming vehicle and freezes. When the light has veered off, he charges to destroy every animate or inanimate object within the path of the vanished beam. Abacha is incapable of the faculty of defining that intrusive light, not even to consider if the light path could actually lead him out of the mindless maze.

Abacha has no IDEA of Nigeria; beyond the reality of a fiefdom that has dutifully nursed his insatiable greed and transformed him into a creature of enormous wealth, and now of power, Abacha has no NOTION of Nigeria. He is thus incapable of grasping what is being said to him by some entity that speaks with the resolute voice of the Civil Liberties Organization, the Campaign for Democracy, the National Democratic Coalition, the market women, civil servants, student unions, labour unions, the press etc, etc. None of these could possibly be part of his Nigerian nation, and it is only by eliminating them in toto, by silencing such alien voices, that Nigeria can bemoan the entity that he recognizes . . .

Abacha will be satisfied only with the devastation of every aspect of Nigeria that he cannot mentally grasp, and that is virtually all of Nigeria. He will find peace and fulfilment only when the voices whose nation-language he cannot interpret are finally silenced, only when, like the Hutus, he cuts off the legs of the Tutsis so that Nigeria is reduced to a height onto which he can clamber.

These voices however, and the history that brought them into being, and with such resolve, have already ensured that Abacha is the last despot that will impose himself on the Nigerian nation. Of course, there will be others who will yield to temptation and attempt to tread the same path of illusion, but their careers will be so short-lived that they will hardly be noticed in passing. The strategy of the present struggle is such that the people are attaining an unprecedented level of self-worth within a national being that defines anti-democrats as treasonable conspirators, and precludes any future automatic sub-mission to the sheerest suspicion of military despotism, even of a messianic hue.

The danger, the very real danger however, is in the character of this last torch-bearer for military demonology, the puny Samson whose arms are wrapped around the pillars, ready to pull down the edifice in his descent into hell. That hell that is Ogoniland today is the perception of nation compatibility of which Abacha's mind is capable. What does not readily yield to his obsessive self-aggrandizement both in power and possessions is alien and must be subjugated and 'sanitized'. In Sani

Abacha's self-manifesting destiny as the last Nigerian despot, we may be witnessing, alas, the end of Nigerian history.

November/December 1994

ALBERTO MANGUEL

Daring to speak one's name

A reflection on gay censorship

Alberto Manguel is the author of *A History of Reading* and the novel *News From a Foreign Country Came*. This essay introduced *Index*'s special feature on gay rights and censorship.

In most of my reading, they were invisible. Mr Pickwick, who saw everyone, never saw them; Monsieur Bovary, who met everyone, never met them; Anna Karenina, who thought she knew everything about her ungracious lover, never noticed them among his acquaintances; they were absent in Captain Nemo's intimate submarine and on Professor Challenger's expedition to the Lost World. They were never small children like Masie Farange, or adolescents like Holden Caulfield. They never fought in wars like Malraux's heroes or scoured the seas like Captain Ahab. They never became their own nightmares, like Gregor Samsa, or their own happiness, like Beckett's Winnie. Their days were never chronicled, let alone with the minuteness of Leopold Bloom's or Mrs Dalloway's. They lived anonymously and died in unmarked graves. They were those through whose denial our society defined its sexual tenements. They stood behind the door that held this warning: 'Beyond you shall not go.'

Readers are a persistent lot. Eventually, as I became aware of my own sexuality, and since I had found in literature echoes of everything I was or was to become, I sought them out in the pages of my books. A gesture there, a hint here, like summoned spirits, they occasionally began to give signs of life. But those who materialized seemed to be in agony: wandering through the third ring of the seventh circle of Hell, like Dante's old teacher, Brunetto Latini; embodying the decay of fin-de-siècle society, like the Baron Charlus; predating wickedly on the

241

young, like Inspector Vidocq; horribly punished with death like Marlowe's Edward II; destined to suicide like the boy lover in Peyrefitte's *Les amitiés particuliers*. It seemed as if they were allowed to appear only as condemned penitents, made to carry the name coined for inhospitable people, portrayed as caricatures, as hideous examples.

The story of my reading, in a succession of book-lined rooms in so many different countries, is also the story of the censorship of my reading. Every reader is engaged, at the time of reading, in two activities: one private, in which the text is transformed through personal experience, and modifies or supplants that experience through the illusion of a fictional memory; and one in which the reading is shared with that vast and loud community of readers which we call our society, readers who incessantly label, qualify, restrict, attribute, condemn or glorify a certain text. Over the shoulder of every reader is a censor, praising this, concealing that, distorting something else. At times, the reader submits to this authoritarian judgement; at others, the reader becomes a kabbalist, secretly looking for that which the censor has hidden. Sometimes the censor is grossly obvious, marking off the limits with laws and signs of 'No Trespassing'. Sometimes the censor becomes devious, allowing representations of forbidden things while at the same time undermining their significance. Tolerant regulations (which always presuppose a hierarchy, since tolerance implies someone entitled to give permission to someone else) coexist with exclusionary statutes; I learned to read being told that nothing was forbidden, in libraries where certain books had never been allowed to enter, or had been classified under innocuous headings, or had been cleansed before being offered for consumption. Léopold Sédar Senghor says that, as a boy, he read *Les Misérables* as if Jean Valjean were black, because French literature lacked, for him, mirrors. I too tried to teach myself the art of creative reading.

Today, and in the Anglo-Saxon world at least, the effort would seem hardly necessary. The bookshelves themselves appear to have changed. Gay writing is curiously visible. Gay literary magazines, gay short-story anthologies, gay fiction series, gay biographies, fill whole sections of general bookstores. So recent is the appearance of these books that the label still requires definition: vaguely, 'gay' signals a homosexual subject – usually male since female homosexualities apparently prefer to be known as lesbian. Those who employ 'gay' for both male and female have been accused of displaying linguistic arrogance by including women in their definition (since 'gay' is primarily a term to designate a male homosexual) and of ignoring their different histories. On the other hand, those who divide homosexualities into 'gay' for male and 'lesbian' for female have been seen as ignoring their common source of persecution, and weakening the strength of shared resistance. The definition is further complicated by the fact that a 'gay' book may designate not the subject but the author: is *Lady Windermere's Fan* a 'gay' play because it was written by Oscar Wilde? Or should 'Divorce in Naples' — a short story on a gay theme — be removed from the 'gay' shelf because it was written by William Faulkner?

This is where the censor's eye is useful. In an effort to condemn, the censor needs to define, however fallaciously, its victim. 'Gay' therefore is everything that in any way presents homosexuality in a favourable light, whether in the telling of a supposedly heterosexual author, or in that of a supposedly homosexual one, who might be considered exemplary simply by writing well. Sometimes it is the recipient who defines — in the censor's eye — the forbidden subject, as when books destined for a gay bookstore are stopped at customs because of their destination. The censor's eye is extraordinarily eclectic.

Whatever the chosen definition, the recent explosion of so-called gay literature calls attention to at least two facts: first, that here is an entire literary realm seemingly non-existent in centuries of previous writing; second, that most of the rest of the world still continues to ignore it. Yes, and both facts are fallacies.

Since societies define themselves as much by what they include as by what they leave out, acts of censorship belong to the same history as their subjects; they don't supplant them. Gay history extends along a road largely lit by the bonfires of the censors.

For centuries, gay subjects were not excluded from literature. For the Greeks and Romans, a fluid sexuality was the norm, while allowing for a distinction between free love and prostitution. Homosexuality (for which the ancients had no word; the pseudo-scientific term was coined in the nineteenth century) was not a particularity of human sex, but one of the unnamed modes, loosely established, of our sexuality. What mattered to the contemporaries of Homer and of Caesar was not with whom one made love, but how and under what circumstances. Achilles and Patroclus were exemplary lovers; Zeus is unfaithful to Hera with both Leda and Ganymede; different and same-sex tangles are equally derided by Martial and Catullus; the characters of Petronius roam about in a world where the sex of each partner must be specified because heterosexuality is not compulsory.

The historian John Boswell, in his masterly study *Christianity, Social Tolerance and Homosexuality*, has pointed out how censorship of gay themes was almost unknown in the ancient world. Only with the shift in public morality that followed the decline of the Roman Empire in the West did the repression of all 'other' sexualities become widespread. The classical texts that survived the *auto-da-fés* of Pope Gregory VII and his successors were pruned and altered to suit the new Christian morals. According to Boswell, ignorance was the major cause for most deletions and criminal changes: for instance, Plato's *Symposium* was transformed into a debate on heterosexual love because Socrates' dining companions were assumed to be female.

But there was also a deliberate attempt to modify uncomfortable meanings, as when, in a mediaeval transcription of Ovid's *Art of Love*, the line 'a boy's love appealed to me less' appeared transcribed as 'a boy's love appealed to me not at all' – to which the anonymous scribe explicitly added: 'Thus you may be sure that Ovid was not a sodomite.' For the censor, a work cannot be both worthy and contain material that offends the official norm. (Earlier this century, the critic Van Wyck Brooks explained in his paean to Walt Whitman: 'Homosexuality in the sense of perversion could scarcely have thriven in the climate of his time and place or in one who so liked "manliness" and all that was bracing, hardy and sane and was drawn to the strongly marked of both the sexes.')

Boswell lists several cases in which gay censorship was effected by merely changing the pronouns: Michelangelo's grand-nephew 'corrected' his uncle's sonnets so that they appeared to be addressed to a woman; the Persian fables of Sa'di were 'purified' in an English nineteenth-century translation by Francis Gladwin, transforming the homosexual love stories into heterosexual ones; Fitzgerald's *Rubáiyát* of Omar Kayyám shyly ignored that the loved one is male.

The most famous English series of Greek and Latin classics, the Loeb

Library, refrained for years from translating passages dealing with homosexuality – even in those works which condemned it, such as the writings of the Church Fathers. In the case of Greek texts, Loeb soberly gave a Latin version of the passages and imbedded them in the English, naively composing a homosexual anthology which a skilled reader could peruse by simply jumping from one Latin passage to the other.

Invisibility doesn't mean inexistence.

When Spain invaded the New World it brought with it its imaginary landscapes, peopled with fictional wonders culled from novels of chivalry and fantastical travel books. They saw what they knew they would see. Columbus saw mermaids in the Caribbean waters ('though they are not as beautiful as we have heard tell'); Ferdinand Magellan recognized the giants of old along the coast of Patagonia; Gaspar de Carvajal met the famous Amazons in the forests of Brazil; seeing for the first time the huge anaconda serpents, Lopez de Gomara declared that here were 'the immortal dragons of Andromeda and St Margaret'; the view of the wonderful city of Tenochtitlan reminded Bernal Diaz del Castillo of the magical towers described in that most famous of novels of chivalry, the *Amadis de Gaula*.

Unavoidably, Spain also brought with it the censored, shadow landscapes. Together with the Arcadian New World of wonders, the *conquistadores* saw Paradise riddled with the foulest sins including, of course, the sin of sodomy.

Since the Spaniards burnt the Aztec and Mayan libraries, no written sources of their laws have reached us, but through the condemnatory comments of the *conquistadores*, we can surmise that homosexuality was fairly widespread throughout pre-Colombian America. Mochica and Chimu pottery depicts homosexual acts; Fray Bartolomé de Las Casas (usually an objective witness) reports that Mayan parents supplied their adolescent sons with younger boys to be used as sexual outlets before marriage; Bernal Diaz del Castillo (a faithful chronicler) described the homosexual customs of Aztec priests who counted among their deities the god Xochipili, the patron of male homosexuality. The *conquistadores* responded to what they saw with punishments imagined for their Christian hell: they set dogs on the 'sodomites' (as did Babloa in Panama), or burned them at the stake (in Puerto Viejo and Mexico).

And yet the notion of a pristine Eden continued. Wary of contaminating the New World, the Spanish Inquisition established the first censorship laws of America, both to prevent immoral books from entering the colonies and to forbid any writing in the colonies themselves that might glorify the native past. On the surface, the inquisitorial injunctions had little effect. Fiction, which the Consejo de Indias sought to ban, was smuggled in regularly from Europe. When legislation was set up to prevent a specific literary activity (such as the law decreed in 1557 to stop Fray Bernardino de Sahagún from pursuing his research on Nahua culture and language) it was largely ignored, and books such as Las Casas's *Apologética historia sumaria*, a formidable compendium of native American cultures, were produced and published (even though Las Casas's work had to appear, digested, in Jerónimo Román y Zamora's *Repúblicas del mundo*, itself censored by the Inquisition).

But more deeply, the Spanish invasion created a world of notable absences, in which the censor's task quickly became not one of banning and cutting but of misinforming and misdirecting. The societies established, variously and haphazardly, throughout Latin America shared from the start the patriarchal values of the Spanish gold-seekers. In this world (which, four centuries later, was to become mine throughout my adolescence), male intimacy was regarded as a necessary consolidation of male power, and any sexual connotation was, in this context, simply inconceivable.

The first notable short story written by an Argentinian was Esteban Echeverría's *El matadero* (The Slaughterhouse), published posthumously in 1871. The story, set in the mid-nineteenth century during the dictatorship of Juan Manuel de Rosas, is a fiercely romantic description of the vast cattle-slaughtering grounds that used to occupy the central plaza of Buenos Aires. The hero of Echeverría's story is, like himself, a young intellectual who loathes the tyrant. One morning, walking by the slaughterhouse, he is taunted by the Rosas-loving mob of butchers. They grab hold of him, cut his hair off, pull down his trousers and are about to thrash him, when the young man literally 'bursts with rage' and dies in the hands of his torturers, blood flowing from his mouth and nose. There are no obvious homosexual references in the story, but the contrast between the effete intellectual and the brutal crowd who punish him by undressing him is built on conventional sexual

stereotypes, and foreshadows a long sequence of stories, from Melville's
Billy Budd to Musil's *Young Torless*, in which the rough, ignorant aggressor
is opposed to the young 'cultured' gay. In a curious but fairly common
literary twist whereby the censor's devices to condemn one area are
used to enhance another, Echeverría accepts the clichés with which his
society mocks the 'deviant' – well-dressed, stylish, intellectual – and
uses them to portray the Byronic young rebel – that is to say, himself.

Echeverría is the first example I can think of, in Latin American
literature, in which the traits stereotypically associated with a gay
character serve to describe a 'positive' hero. Since 'homosexual' or
'effeminate' are denigrating terms, the hero's manners account for
neither trait: the hero's manners 'coincide' with those of a homosexual
outcast and only have the appearance of portraying 'it', the forbidden
thing.

Likewise, stemming from a tradition of soldierly camaraderie, the
voluminous theme of male friendship which is essential in so much
Latin American writing was never read as homosexual; even today,
such a reading is, by and large, studiously avoided both by canonizing
critics and the general public.

It is interesting to observe that Argentinian literature can almost be
defined through the subject of male intimacy: from the Argentinian
national epic poem, *Martin Fierro*, to the stories of Jorge Luis Borges.
Martin Fierro, written by José Hernández in the 1870s, concerns a gaucho
who escapes from compulsory military service; the sergeant sent to
capture him, seeing him surrounded by soldiers, says that 'he won't
allow a brave man to be killed in this fashion' and goes over to fight
on the deserter's side. Their friendship became proverbial, and echoed
through other nineteenth-century 'gaucho' literature, as well as through
much twentieth-century fiction: in novels by Ricardo Guiraldes, Bioy
Casares, Osvaldo Soriano. In one of Borges's later stories, 'La intrusa'
(The Intruder), the two friends are also brothers: one of them brings
home a woman who becomes the cause of their first quarrels. In the
end they kill her, so that nothing and no one will intrude any more
on their relationship.

In none of these books is homosexuality in evidence. And yet . . .
The American critic Leslie Fiedler half-playfully suggested that there
might be more than meets the eye in Huckleberry Finn's relationship

to Jim (in Fiedler's essay 'Come back into the raft, Huck, honey'); a curious reader might be able to recognize in the extensive Argentinian male literature something more than asexual companionships. The problem with suppressing a whole area of human experience is that its absence distorts many others. The treatment of male friendship in Argentinian culture suffers from this 'unspeakable' ambiguity – the same as in the field of sports, one of the few areas where males are publicly allowed to come into contact with other male bodies. The homosexual taboo renders the possibility of writing or reading gradations in male intimacy an almost impossible task.

For a reader such as myself, a further difficulty lies in the fact that, after centuries in which the social censor deleted from the permissible artistic realms the figure of the homosexual, it is difficult to know which reading is today valid. Am I, as a contemporary of Manuel Puig and Jean Genet, wishfully and anachronistically introducing an imaginary character into a fictional landscape where he was simply never imagined? Or am I actually recognizing, secreted under conventional heterosexual garbs, a character who has been denied an identity, a vocabulary, a name?

Borges once defined 'the peculiar logic of hatred' which allows one to affirm that a certain character 'never visited China and that in the temples of that country he insulted the gods'. This is the censor's logic: homosexuality never appears in Argentinian tales of male relationships, and yet the homosexual can be stereotyped and caricatured in that same literature. The role he plays then is of an *ersatz* female, a male betraying and betrayed. This allows the reader to make a double assumption: that a male who does not uphold patriarchy is not a male, and that the female role, which the traitor must necessarily embrace, is despicable since it cannot be redeemed by motherhood. (According to the tango, woman is the cause of man's downfall, and the only good woman is the man's mother who is always long-suffering and blameless.)

Roberto Arlt, a popular novelist and playwright of the first half of the century, described such a character in his 1926 novel, El juguete rabioso (The Furious Toy). The protagonist arrives at a cheap hotel and asks for a room. The manager tells him that the only room left is one he must share with a certain young man. As it turns out, this young man has paid the manager to let him know when interesting single gentlemen arrive at the hotel, and then attempts to seduce them in the hope of becoming 'someone's little woman'. The young man is depicted as ridiculously effeminate – a miserable creature who wears soiled women's underwear in the belief that this will arouse 'real' men. Naturally, the protagonist wards him off in disgust. In Marco Denevi's 1955 detective novel, *Rosaura a las diez* (Rose at Ten), the homosexual character – admittedly minor – turns out to be the murderer's accomplice, 'a filthy deviant', a sort of effeminate Uriah Heep. (In Mario Soffici's film based on Denevi's novel, the actor playing him signalled his sexual inclinations by the most stereotypical of all gestures, allowing his hand to go limp at the wrists.) And in Manuel Mujica Lainez's huge historical novel *Bomarzo* of 1962, the hero, the Duke Pier Francesco Orsini, displays a homosexuality so subtle as to be admissible in a society that can therefore afford to overlook it. (When in 1968 Alberto Ginastera's opera *Bomarzo*, based on the novel, was banned by the military government, it was not because of any homosexual connotation but because of a scene in which one of the sopranos was directed to display her naked breasts.)

None of these books was ever banned. In all three cases, the social censor allowed the books to stand because the homosexual portrayed is a monster, a criminal or someone displaying an aristocratic affectation; under such circumstances, a text that might otherwise be forbidden becomes cautionary. Sometimes the censor can work by allowing a text to stand.

It was no coincidence that when Manuel Puig's *La traición de Rita Hayworth* (Betrayed by Rita Hayworth) appeared in 1968, at the beginning of the military dictatorship in Argentina, it was quickly banned. The mild, somewhat autobiographical tale offended not only the official sensibility, but also the sensibility of the common reader: in General Villegas, Puig's home town, the book was burned by the townspeople in the public square. What was offensive to the public (at a time when Arlt's novel was accepted as a 'classic') was that a homosexual lifestyle could be described as happy, or at least not unhappier than that of other small-town lives. In the eyes of the military advisors, Puig's playful tone, not necessarily the narrative itself, justified the censorship. As the mayor of General Villegas remarked at the time: 'At least in *Peyton Place* the sinful life was normal; in Puig's novel, it's an abomination.'

The experience of other Latin American countries is to all appearances similar. There are no gay characters in Gabriel García Márquez's Macondo, nor in the all-boys military school of Mario Vargas Llosa's *La ciudad y los perros* (The Time of the Hero). The important indigenist literature of Rómulo Gallegos, Ciro Alegría, Jorge Icaza, Juan Rulfo, José María Arguedas ignores them. When the gay subject appears in, for instance, Cuban literature (most importantly in José Lezama Lima's magnificent *Paradiso* or in the artful novels of Severo Sarduy), it is under cover of an intricate, self-concealing baroque style – the same which the Counter-Reformation sanctioned to avoid particular discussion of the theological arguments raised by the dissenters of the Reformation.

To my knowledge, there hasn't appeared yet, in Latin America, a gay novel such as the British Alan Hollinghurst's *The Folding Star*, in which 'being gay' – approvingly or disapprovingly – is not the novel's subject. That novel is still to be written, a novel in which the fact of homosexuality is simply taken for granted, as part of the multitudinous universe, neither as literature of the damned nor as literature of the martyred, but merely as literature, our poor immortality.

Sometime in 1941, Jorge Luis Borges noted that in a riddle whose subject is chess, the only word that cannot be mentioned is precisely the word 'chess'. 'To *always* omit a word, to make use of inept metaphors and self-evident paraphrases,' writes Borges, 'is perhaps the most emphatic way of pointing it out.' The paradoxical ability of censorship is that, in its efforts to suppress, it highlights that which it wishes to condemn: it draws attention to clearings of silence in the tangles of our languages and our literatures. Spanish has an idiom, 'it shines through its absence', that precisely describes censorship's innermost failure.

January/February 1995

YAŞAR KEMAL

The dark cloud over Turkey

Yaşar Kemal, whose novels *Mehmet, My Hawk* and *The Wind from the Plain* depict the harshness of Anatolian village life, is Turkey's foremost author and an outspoken defender of human rights. Given a suspended prison sentence in March 1996 on a charge of 'incitement to racial hatred' following publication of this article in which he condemned Turkish oppression of the Kurdish minority, Kemal shouted to the judges as he left the court: 'It is not you who sentence me. I condemn you!'

One of the greatest tragedies in Turkey's history is happening now. Apart from a couple of hesitant voices, no one is standing up and demanding to know what the Turkish government is doing, what this destruction means. No one is saying: 'After all your signatures and promises you are riding towards doomsday, leaving the earth scorched in your wake. What will come of all this?

Turkish governments have resolved to drain the pool to catch the fish; to declare all-out war.

We have already seen how it can be done. The world is also aware of it. Only the people of Turkey have been kept in ignorance; newspapers have been forbidden to write about the drainage. Or maybe there was no need for censorship: maybe our press, with its sense of patriotism and strong nationalist sentiment, chose not to write about it assuming the world would neither hear nor see what was happening. The water was being drained in so horrendous a fashion that the smoke ascended to high heaven. But for our press, deceiving the world and our people – or, rather, believing they had succeeded in doing so – was the greatest act of patriotism, of nationalism. They were not aware that they had perpetrated a crime against humanity. Their eyes bloodshot, their mouths foaming, they were shouting with one voice: 'We will not give one stone, one handful of soil.' Cries of 'Oh God' rose upon the air. Dear loyal patriotic friends, no one wants a single stone, nor a handful of soil from us. Our Kurdish citizens want their language, their language and culture that are being slaughtered.

Our Kurdish brothers are now at war to win their rights. Those Turkish brothers with whom we have always been together in sorrow and in joy. During the War of Independence we fought shoulder to shoulder. We established this state together. Should a man cut out the tongue of his brother?

Oh friend, is there anything in those declarations you signed – the UN human rights treaties, the European Convention, the Conference on Security and Co-operation in Europe and the Helsinki Final Act – to say that if I give my people human rights they will demand their 'independence'? Did you lay down such a condition? In those declarations you signed did it not say that every nation, every ethnic community should determine its own destiny?

The water has begun to dry up. The houses of nearly 2,000 villages have been burnt. Many animals as well as people have been burnt inside them. The world press has written about this, as well as our so nationalistic newspapers. Our ostriches still bury their heads in the sand. The country is awash with blood and how can our illustrious media remove its head from the sand? They burnt people too in many houses . . .

The draining of the waters has cost Turkey and humanity much. And looks like continuing to do so. Already over 1,700 people have been the victims of murder by persons unknown. Intellectuals in the West have begun to debate whether a new genocide is taking place; the possibility of a Human Rights Court for Turkey's politicians and an economic boycott against Turkey is being discussed. Choose between these delightful alternatives!

The most horrific aspect is the inhumanity of outright war for the sake of a few fish. They have burnt almost all the forests of eastern Anatolia because guerrillas hide out in them. Turkey's forests have been burning for years. Not much that could be called forest is left and we are burning the remainder to catch fish. Turkey is disappearing in flames along with its forests, anonymous acts of genocide, and 2.5 million people exiled from their homes, their villages burnt, in desperate poverty, hungry and naked, forced to take to the road, and no one raises a finger.

Turkey's administrators have got so carried away that intellectual crimes have been regarded as among the most serious; people have rotted away in prisons, been killed and exiled for such crimes. Today over 200 people are serving sentences for crimes of thought in our prisons. Hundreds more are on trial. Among these intellectual criminals are university lecturers, journalists, writers and union leaders. Conditions in the prisons are so fearsome that a country, a world, could sink into the earth in shame.

As if a racist, oppressive regime were not enough, there have been three military coups in 70 years. Each coup has made the Turkish people a little more debased, brought them a little lower. They have rotted from the root, with their culture, their humanity, their language. There is no reason at all for this inhuman, purposeless war in Anatolia. I repeat, the Kurds want nothing but human rights. They want to use their language, to have their identity restored, and develop their culture to the same extent as the Turkish people. You will ask if the Turkish people have these rights themselves. If things continue as they are, it will not be long before we encounter waves of resistance from the Turkish people. These 70 years have crushed all the people of Anatolia like a steamroller; not a blade of grass has grown in its path. For the moment, all we can ask is that all the Anatolian people be granted full human rights.

These things I speak of have a single cause: to appropriate the liberty of the Anatolian people. This government has done everything it can to exploit the Anatolians, humiliate them and leave them hungry. There is nothing they have not suffered for the last 70 years. If they have managed to survive such a wind for so long, that is because the soil of Anatolia is so rich in culture.

This world is a graveyard of wrecked languages and cultures. What cultures whose names and reputations we have never even heard have come and gone in this world? As a cultural mosaic, the cultures of Anatolia have been a source of modern cultures. If they had not tried to prohibit and destroy other languages and other cultures than those of the Turkish people, Anatolia would still make major contributions to world culture. And we would not remain as we are; a country half famished, its creative power draining away.

The sole reason for this war is that cancer of humanity, racism. If this were not so, would it be possible for right-wing, racist magazines and newspapers to declare that 'The Turkish race is superior to every other'? The brother of this statement is, 'Happy is he who calls himself a Turk.' I first went to eastern Anatolia in 1951, and saw that on the mountain sides everywhere they had written in enormous letters visible from a distance of three, five and 10 kilometres, 'Happy is he who calls himself a Turk.' They had embellished the slopes of Mount Ararat, too. The entire mountain had become happy to be Turkish. And, worse even, they made the children declare: 'I am a Turk, I am honest, I am hard-working,' every morning.

And much more is happening in Turkey! Having exiled 2.5 million people, now they have put an embargo on food in eastern Anatolia. No one who does not get a certificate from the police station can buy food, because the villagers give food to the guerrillas. The crops, nut and fruit trees of villagers who prefer exile to taking up arms to protect their village from guerrilla attack are burnt along with the forests. Their animals are slaughtered. Why are the villages being burnt and razed? So that they may not harbour guerrillas and be a source of food for them. From what we hear in Istanbul, the guerrillas receive their needs from the village watchmen. A few days ago the newspapers reported that guerrillas had stolen 700 sheep belonging to the village watchmen, the bastion of the state. There are 50,000 paid watchmen in eastern Anatolia; it is the slave of these people. They are the state in eastern Anatolia, they are everything. They can kill, destroy and burn. They recognize no rule of humanity and no law.

What else is happening in Turkey? The village elders of Ovacik who said that soldiers had burnt their village were found dead in the burnt forests nearby a few days later. The government minister [for human rights], Azimet Köylüoğlu, who had claimed that soldiers were burning villages, went back on his words a few days later: 'How can anyone say that the army is burning villages? It is the PKK.' And our 'free newspapers' reported this.

What else is happening in Turkey? I swear that the newspapers wrote this too. I was dumbfounded. Listen, in a district of Van they woke up one morning and found the town covered with red crosses. How could the newspapers resist such a piece of news? The SS had done the same.

And there are no shepherds left in the mountains. They have killed the adult shepherds, and now they send children on the assumption that they won't touch them. But a few days later they gather up the dead bodies of these tiny shepherds from the mountains.

What else is happening in Turkey? God damn them, one is ashamed of being human. I will write this too. One morning a journalist friend of mine rang. We had worked together as journalists for years. 'Do you know what is going on?' he asked. 'What?' I replied. 'The police have taken away everyone who works for *Özgür Gündem* newspaper.' I immediately went to the newspaper offices and saw that police had cordoned off the building. I asked to go in but the police wouldn't let me. There was no one left to produce the newspaper. They had taken all 120 employees into custody. They had even taken the poor tea boy. If it had been summer they would probably have been ordered to arrest the flies at the newspaper.

That is enough. I cannot bring myself to talk longer about the historic achievement of the Turkish Republic. To battle against oppression in Turkey today is a challenge not everyone can take up. There is the risk of going hungry. It is a strong tradition in the Turkish Republic to make a mockery of its opponents. And, and, and, it is only at the risk of your life that you oppose the state today. The cost of opposing the Turkish–Kurdish War is heavy. What can we do but keep silent?

The coup of 12 September 1980 not only forced intellectuals to keep their heads down, not only threw hundreds of thousands of people into prison and tortured them. The entire country cowered in fear, was made degenerate and driven further from humanity. It made informers of ordinary citizens, created bloody wolf-mouthed confessors, and totally destroyed human morality. A country where universal morality has become atrophied is a patient in a coma.

The Constitution which the leader of the coup, Evren Pasha, passed in the shadow of his weapons and bayonets was ratified by 90 per cent of the population in a referendum. For exactly 12 years Turkey has been governed according to this Constitution. Yes, Turkey has a parliament. Its parliamentarians are like kittens, even when they catch them by the neck

255

at the door of parliament and take them to prison. There is even a Constitutional Court. A Constitutional Court that, according to the Military Constitution, decides whether a law shall be enforced or not.

Some people here are scared stiff of the military launching a new coup. What difference does it make? A new coup would not lead to the abolition and repeal of the Evren Constitution.

There will be no coup. There is no need for a coup.

Some of my friends, my old journalist colleagues, friends whom I love and who don't want anything to happen to me, are anxious. Some say I am taking sides

What is more natural than for me to take sides? As long as I can remember I have been on the side of the peoples of Turkey. As long as I can remember I have been on the side of the oppressed, those treated unjustly, the exploited, the suffering and the poor.

I am on the side of Turkish, the language in which I write. I feel the obligation to do what I can, and what I can't, to enrich and beautify Turkish. My greatest cause of anger against Kenan Paşa is his closure of the Turkish Language Institute.

Of course I take sides. For me the world is a garden of culture where a thousand flowers grow. Throughout history all cultures have fed one another, been grafted onto one another, and in the process our world has been enriched. The disappearance of a culture is the loss of a colour, a different light, a different source. I am as much on the side of every flower in this thousand-flowered garden as I am on the side of my own culture. Anatolia has always been a mosaic of flowers, filling the world with flowers and light. I want it to be the same today.

If the people of a country choose to live like human beings, choose happiness and beauty, their way lies first through universal human rights and then through universal, unlimited freedom of thought. The people of countries that have opposed this will enter the twenty-first century without honour.

Saving the honour and bread of our country, and the cultural wealth of its soil, is in our hands. Either true democracy or . . . nothing!

Translated by Judith Vidal-Hall

January/February 1995

MUMIA ABU-JAMAL

A bright, shining hell

Mumia Abu-Jamal is an award-winning American journalist. Despite serious questions about the conduct of his trial for murder, he has spent the last fifteen years on Pennsylvania's death row, where he is now banned from practising journalism under the specially created 'Mumia' ruling. He contributed this piece to Index's examination of the growing use of the death penalty in the USA.

Imagine.

Imagine living, eating, sleeping, relieving oneself, daydreaming, weeping – but mostly waiting – in a room about the size of your bathroom.

Now imagine doing all those things – but mostly waiting – for the rest of your life.

Imagine waiting – waiting – waiting – to die.

I don't have to imagine.

I 'live' in one of those rooms, like about 3,000 other men and women in 37 states across the United States.

It's called 'Death Row'.

I call it 'Hell'.

Welcome to Hell.

Each of the states that have death rows has a different system for its 'execution cases' varying from the relatively open to the severely restrictive.

Some states, like California and Texas, allow their 'execution cases' work, education and/or religious service opportunities, for out-of-cell time up to eight hours daily.

Pennsylvania locks its 'execution cases' down 23 hours a day, five days a week; 24 hours the other two days.

At the risk of quoting Mephistopheles, I repeat:

Welcome to Hell.

A hell erected and maintained by human governments and blessed by black-robed judges.

A hell that allows you to see your loved ones, but not to touch them.

A hell situated in America's rural boondocks, hundreds of miles away from most families.

A white, rural hell, where most of the caged captives are black and urban.

It is an American way of death.

Contrary to what one might suppose, this hell is the easiest one to enter in a generally hellish criminal justice system. Why? Because, unlike any other case, those deemed potential capital cases are severely restricted during the jury selection phase, as any juror who admits opposition to the death penalty is immediately removed, leaving only those who are fervent death penalty supporters in the pool of eligible jurors.

When it was argued that to exclude those who opposed death, and to include only those who supported death, was fundamentally unfair, as the latter were more 'conviction-prone', the US Supreme Court, in the case *Lockhart v McCree*, said such a claim was of no constitutional significance.

Once upon a time, politicians promised jobs and benefits to constituents, like 'a chicken in every pot', to get elected.

It was a sure-fire vote-getter.

No longer.

Today the lowest-level politico up to the president use another sure-fire gimmick to guarantee victory.

Death.

Promise death and the election is yours.

Guaranteed.

Vraiment.

A 'Vote for Hell' in the 'Land of Liberty', with its over one million prisoners, is the ticket to victory.

March/April 1995

FELIPE FERNÁNDEZ-ARMESTO

Rewriting history

Felipe Fernández-Armesto, the Oxford historian and author of *Millennium: A History of our Last Thousand Years*, wrote this introduction to *Index*'s special feature on the rewriting and censoring of history.

In the film *Big*, Tom Hanks played a little boy who, trapped inside a grown man's body, had a brilliant career as a toy designer. One of his inventions was a computer that gave children the power to write and rewrite their own versions of a story under a stock strip of vivid images. History has always been like the *Big* machine, clicking out colliding perceptions of the same events. It mutates according to a law of relativity: just as space and time shrink or expand relative to the speed of the observer, so our impression of the past seems to warp into different shapes according to the angle of approach. When I was a boy, my favourite book was *Pages Glorieuses de l'Armée Française* because it filled familiar wars with exciting battles of which the writers of my English and Spanish books seemed never to have heard. Within a single country or culture, the circumstances and needs of the time of writing become as much a part of the story as the episodes narrated and the people described.

Thanks to a healthy Pyrronist revival, this millennium is twitching to a close amid doubts about whether an objectively true version of the past even exists to be recovered: history, after all, happened to people who experienced it variously at the time, registered it mentally in contrasting patterns and recorded it in mutually contradictory ways. The onlooker is part of the event. Before historical writing disappears as a genre – to be reclassified by librarians alongside other forms of fiction – the approach of the year 2000 creates a useful pretext for trying to track some of its trends. Although our way of counting time is conventional, dates divisible by 10 do, in practice, arrest attention and stimulate the imagination. The habit of thinking in terms of decades and centuries induces a self-fulfilling delusion and the way people behave – or, at least, perceive their behaviour – really does tend to change accordingly. Decades and centuries are like the clock-cases inside which the pendulum of history swings. Strictly speaking, a new millennium begins every day and every moment of every day. Yet both the Royal Albert Hall in London and the Rainbow Room on top of New York's Radio City were engaged for New Year's Eve, 1999, 25 years in advance. Most of the world's top hotels are already fully booked for the same evening and 'the Millenium [sic] Society of London and New York,' the *Daily Mail* reports, 'is planning a party at the Pyramids.'

A scramble to rewrite history in time for the party is already under way. Some kinds of historical revisionism are always with us. From time to time, a paradise gets mislaid or regained, as each period debunks the golden age myths of others and substitutes its own. Saddam Hussein presents his regime as a Babylonian revival; British fantasies, current or recent, are about a crime-free era when the unemployed got on their bikes. Particular groups tend to see their own past as a 'march of history' towards some goal – usually a complacent present – before discarding it when their complacency snaps. I call these stories 'sacred histories' because the obvious model is the Jews' struggle in a role assigned to them by Providence: uniquely among such myths, this Jewish reading of the past has never been discarded, unless the current secularization of Judaism and the 'peace process' in the Middle East amount to its repudiation. Other, less durable examples are rapidly disappearing today: the Whig interpretation of English history (flowing unstoppably towards constitutionalism and democracy) still has a place in politicians' rhetoric but is getting weeded out of textbooks. The open skies over the 'Frontier Theory' – of an America fulfilling a 'manifest destiny' – have got clouded by a new multiculturalism which includes Blacks, Hispanics and Native Americans. Progress through class war to a classless society was seen finally to have lost its thrill when its objective was appropriated for one of John Major's slogans. And the historiography of the 'European Miracle', which spent a long time 'explaining' European superiority over the rest of the world, no longer seems to have anything credible to explain.

While sacred histories falter, classic 'turning-points' get twisted:

events which at one moment seem to be of transcendent importance decline in significance from a perspective of lengthening time. Until recently, for instance, the Russian Revolution inspired cosmic language which now contrasts with the tendency to assume that its effects are already over. Other examples are the Industrial Revolution (the favoured term is now 'industrialization'), the Reformation (now reclassified as a 'transition'), the Fall of the Roman Empire ('the transformation of antiquity') and the Discovery of America (which, of course, never happened at all). We should expect nominations for important events of our own time to get downgraded accordingly: the rise of Japan, perhaps, the invention of the microchip, the Vietnam War, the demolition of the Berlin Wall, the forging of an 'ever closer' European Union, the Middle East peace accord, South African democracy . . .

Meanwhile, idols of previous generations are getting dethroned. We seem to live in an age of iconoclasm which has felled Churchill, Kennedy, Lenin, Mao; but heroes have always come and gone – selected and rejected according to criteria which change with the needs of the times and the exigencies of political propaganda. The few durable examples – Jesus, Mohammed, Alexander – survive because their attributes, like the outfits of an Action Man doll, can be swapped at will to match the peculiar values of any time and place. Alongside the fallen idols stand masked villains – bogeys of one period who get 're-appraised' at another. Villains get transformed by the alchemy of what C. S. Lewis called 'the historical point of view', which sees characters in the context (and according to the criteria) of their own time. Examiners now call this 'empathy' and it is an impassioning issue in the current educational debate in Britain. Reassessment can transmute the images not only of individuals – King John and Genghis Khan, Stalin and Hitler – but also of institutions and social practices. The Inquisition, human sacrifice, capital punishment, genocide – nothing is too bad to be justified by respectable appeals to moral and cultural relativism. One of the great dilemmas of liberal intellectuals in the new millennium will be to defend relativism while resisting its effects.

The biggest opportunities for rewriting history now are in the former Communist world, where topics have emerged from taboo and formerly proscribed versions are being rebuilt from the rubble. In a recent edition of the standard Hungarian historical atlas for schools, the 'Liberation of our Homeland' has been re-labelled 'Military Operations in Hungary, 1944-5'. In an accompanying volume for grown-up readers, postwar interventions in foreign countries by Russia, Cuba, Libya, Indonesia and India are illustrated alongside those of powers formerly classed as 'imperialist'. The Moravian Empire, the greatness of Lithuania in the late Middle Ages, the role of Free Polish forces in World War II are among subjects newly risen or restored to prominence in the historiography of their own countries. 'National' heroes are being re-elevated or invented: Genghis Khan in Mongolia, Alexander the Great in Macedonia, Gjerje Fishta in Albania, János Hunyadi in Hungary.

Meanwhile, the failure of political Marxism and economic Marxism has undermined historians' faith in historical Marxism. Despite agile writhings to deny it, Marx's predictions have proved false. The embitterment of bourgeoisie and proletariat has not happened as he supposed it would: instead the two classes have collaborated in mutual enrichment and, in the process, have become more like each other in manners, values, dress and taste. Some adepts of the old faith remain – indeed, their numbers are sure to recover after a while, as the disappointments of capitalism accumulate. At present, however, most students of the past are filtering Marxism out of their analyses. The eye-catching European political revolutions of the early modern period were once widely seen as the birth-pangs of a new society, struggling bloodstained from the womb of feudalism. Now they are being reallocated as little local difficulties. 'Class struggles' have disappeared from historians' discourse and even 'class' occurs ever less frequently.

The political changes which dethroned Communist regimes have also broken up big states, especially in Europe, where some peoples have recovered or are reasserting ancient identities. Some have attained devolution, autonomy or independence; others are calling or fighting for it. The agglutinative high-politics of Brussels, say, or Moscow, struggle with the amoeba-like micro-politics of the Caucasus or the Pyrenees. Disintegration is happening at the same time as integration. In consequence, instead of history written to legitimate empires and nation-states, we are now getting 'devolutionist' histories, addressed to a world of subsidiarity. When the policy of 'coffee all round' suddenly multiplied regional governments in Spain, cultural departments with budgets of their own invested heavily in identity-building projects for communities which sometimes had shallow historical roots. They became the patrons of scholarly monographs on regional subjects and of superb multi-volume histories of their areas of responsibility. Recent books on the history of European nation-states have reflected fissile experience, typified by Braudel's efforts in L'Identité de la France to do justice to the cultural environments of all those different kinds of cheese.

While we wait for the rest of the world to catch Europe's devolutionary virus, marginalized and minoritarian groups and regions are getting the benefit of some of the historical attention formerly grabbed by metropolis, empire and state. The fashion for world history helps. World history, to me, is what happens at the edges, where cultures and civilizations, like tectonic plates, scrape against each other and set up seismic effects. Admittedly, the project of rehabilitating the overlooked seems sometimes to become just another way of piling up metropolitan history, because what gets recorded and transmitted is usually selected according to the centre's criteria of importance. The Hsiung-nu are known only from Chinese annals. We would know little about the Ranquele Indians were it not for Colonel Mansilla's interest in them. Children, women, the socially underprivileged, the sick, the 'mad' and the ethnic minorities have had to wait for elite perceptions to change before getting historians of their own. Yet work on recovering these 'lost' histories – with skill like a computer buff's retrieving long-deleted files – shows that history does have bigger potential even than the Big machine.

As well as by political change, historical revisionism is being stimulated by science. Historians, who formerly tried to crush the facts to fit Procrustean models and schemes, are beginning to enjoy the respectability of uncertainty. History is coming to be avowed as chaotic: a turbulence which happens at random or in which causes are often, in practice, impossible to trace; or a state of near-equilibrium, punctuated – like evolution, according to a current theory – by spasmodic change. It happens fast, like a snake darting between stones, tracked in glimpses and coiling unpredictably. After the long supremacy of gradualism, 'short-termism' – that vice of economic planners – has become a virtue of historians. Most of the long-term trends and long-term causes conventionally identified by our traditional histories turn out, on close examination, to be composed of brittle links or strung together by conjecture between the gaps.

The experience of changes – bewilderingly fast, barely predicted – in our own time has helped curtail the hunt for long-term trends: empires have vanished like snow in the river; industrialization has leaped to unlikely places with the speed of a computer virus; and ideological fashions have emulated the readiness with which hem-lines rise and fall. Perhaps the most conspicuous trend of historiography in the last generation has been the squashing by revisionists of what were previously thought to be long drawn-out processes into ever shorter spells. The English Civil War, for instance – long held, by a faith compounded of partisanship and hindsight, to be the culmination of centuries of 'progress' – is now thought by most specialists to be best understood in the context of the two or three years immediately preceding its outbreak. The origins of the French Revolution and World War I have been chopped short by similar blades. Even what used to be called the Industrial Revolution is now seen as shuddering to a start, or series of starts, rather than accumulating smoothly.

Meanwhile, the relatively new discipline of historical ecology is breaking one of the oldest of historians' shibboleths. The first adjective has to be dropped from the motto, 'Homo sum et nihil humanum alienum puto.' The inclusion of Nature in the historian's world is an even more radical innovation than the incorporation of marginalized people. That human beings are only imperfectly studied apart from the ecosystems in which our lives are imbedded is a lesson taught to historians by political ecologists and by holistic trends in geography and anthropology. This is potentially revolutionary: though he occupies less of the picture, man is still the focus of historical ecologists' work, but to the historian from Mars, perhaps, it will look as though wheat was the dominant species on our planet during our recorded history – cleverly exploiting human vectors for its propagation and global distribution.

Even as history succumbs to the influence of science, it is becoming less 'scientific' in the conventional sense. Out of structuralism and post-structuralism, a new humanism has evolved that relishes texts as evidence of themselves rather than as means to reconstruct events. A new antiquarianism has arisen, which ransacks middens and treasuries for instructive objects. Historians are getting out of the archives into the open air – walking in the woods, strolling in the streets, making

inferences from landscapes and cityscapes. The avant-garde are incorpo-
rating oral research and personal experience into their work, to the
dismay of those still trapped in the lanes of a race for objective truth.
The best effect of these changes is that there are now again history
books that are works of art as well as of scholarship. Great history, like
great literature in other genres, is written along the fault-line where
experience meets imagination. When well written, it has all the virtues
of egghead fiction, plus better plots. Right now, the past has a great
future.

May/June 1995

ARTHUR C. CLARKE

Beyond 2001

Arthur C. Clarke, doyen of science fiction writers and science popularizers, described for the film centenary issue how advances in electronics and telecommunications were making censorship increasingly impracticable. He also repeated this cautioning qualification: 'I don't believe that a civilization can advance technologically without corresponding moral progress; if they get out of step, it will self-destruct, as ours is in danger of doing.'

It has always seemed to me that limits of censorship are defined by two famous quotations: Voltaire's 'I disagree with everything you say – but will fight to the death for your right to say it' and Chief Justice Holmes's: 'Freedom of speech does not include the liberty to shout FIRE! in a crowded theatre.' In real life, one must attempt to steer a course between these two extremes. Thus I can tolerate astrologers purveying their (usually) harmless nonsense, but not anti-Semites and neo-Nazis hawking their poison. Even here, though, there is a fringe area: should Leni Riefenstahl's brilliant documentaries be banned because of their sponsor? And aren't there some rather embarrassing bits in Birth of a Nation?

As it happens, I have helped to destroy one form of censorship. Quoting from the speech I made at the UN on World Telecommunications Day, 17 May 1983, I pointed out that the development of communications satellites accessible by cheap and portable equipment would mean that 'news gatherers would no longer be at the mercy of censors or inefficient (sometimes non-existent) postal and telegraph services. It means the end of the closed societies and will lead ultimately – to repeat a phrase I heard Arnold Toynbee use 40 years ago – to the unification of the world.'

What I am saying is that the debate about the free flow of information which has been going on for so many years will soon be settled – by engineers, not politicians. (Just as physicists, not generals, have now determined the nature of war.)

Consider what this means. No government will be able to conceal, at least for very long, evidence of crimes or atrocities – even from its own people. The very existence of the myriads of new information channels, operating in real time and across all frontiers, will be a powerful influence for civilized behaviour. If you are arranging a massacre, it will be useless to shoot the cameramen who has so inconveniently appeared on the scene. His pictures will already be safe in the studio 5,000 kilometres away; and his final image may hang you.

Many governments will not be at all happy about this, but in the long run everyone will benefit. Exposures of scandals or political abuses – especially by visiting TV teams who go home and make rude documentaries – can be painful but also very valuable. Many a ruler might still be in power today, or even alive, had he known what was really happening in his own country. A wise statesman once said, 'A free press can give you hell; but it can save your skin.' That is even more true of TV reporting – which, thanks to satellites, will soon be instantaneous and ubiquitous.

That was written more than 12 years ago: the satellite TV news gives hourly proof that this state of affairs has now arrived. Living as I do in Asia, I can also observe the impact of western movies and TV serials upon societies with totally different cultural backgrounds.

Sometimes it is hard not to sympathize with latter-day Canutes attempting to hold back the waves pouring down from the sky; what has been aptly called 'electronic imperialism' will sweep away much that is good, as well as much that is bad. Yet it will only accelerate changes that were in any case inevitable and, on the credit side, the new media will preserve for future generations the customs, performing arts and ceremonies of our time in a way that was never possible in any earlier age.

Recently I had the enjoyable task of using satellite links to address both Rupert Murdoch and Ted Turner (though not simultaneously!). I gave them this advice on the use and misuse of satellite TV. After quoting a British prime minister's famous accusation that the press enjoyed 'the privilege of the harlot – power without responsibility', I added:

> Today, the TV screen is more powerful than newsprint, and whatever the bean-counters may say, responsibility should always be the bottom line.
>
> Though I'm opposed in principle to any form of censorship, my stomach is often turned by the hideous violence shown on so many TV programmes. It's no excuse to say that Hollywood* is an even worse offender, and I know all the arguments about screen violence providing catharsis, and not role models. But you can't have it both ways: if the advertisers really believed that, they'd never buy any air time.
>
> I don't believe that a civilization can advance technologically without corresponding moral progress: if they get out of step, it will self-destruct, as ours is in danger of doing.
>
> Which leads me to an awesome conclusion. We've had TV for 50 years. Therefore a volume of space containing several hundred suns has now been filled with news of our wars, atrocities and crimes – real ones and fictional ones, which an alien intelligence might have great difficulty in distinguishing.
>
> I conclude from this that there's no, repeat no, superior civiliz-ation in our immediate vicinity. For if there was – the cops would already be here, sirens screaming right across the radio spectrum.

To sum up: as this century draws to a close, it looks as if all the old arguments about censorship will be made obsolete by wide-band, person-to-person communications. When you can download anything and everything 'in the privacy of your own home', as certain notorious

---

* And though Hollywood may be the worst offender, it is by no means the only one. I am reminded that A Clockwork Orange was made in England; the only time I ever saw it was when Stanley Kubrick arranged a screening for me at the studio. Although I understand that he has now withdrawn it from exhibition, later highly praised movies have been far more violent, with far less justification.

advertisements used to say, not even entire armies of Thought Police will be able to do anything about it.

The real challenge now facing us through the Internet and the World Wide Web is not quality but sheer quantity. How will we find anything – and not merely our favourite porn – in the overwhelming cyberbabble of billions of humans and trillions of computers, all chattering simultaneously?

I don't know the answer: and I have a horrible feeling that there may not be one.

November/December 1995

PHILIP FRENCH

No end in sight

Philip French, film critic of the Observer since 1977 and author of The Movie Moguls, Westerns and studies of Louis Malle and Ingmar Bergman's Wild Strawberries, was a founding member of the Society for the Defence of Literature and the Arts. This brief history of film censorship was written to introduce the special issue to mark the centenary of the cinema in 1996.

When the noted UK film critic and scourge of the censors, Alexander Walker, heard that James Ferman, director of the British Board of Film Classification (as the British Board of Film Censors was renamed in 1985), was a member of the committee appointed to celebrate the centenary of cinema, he wrote a letter of protest to the committee's chairman. The reply he received referred to Ferman's probity, his devotion to the cinema and the obvious discourtesy that would be involved in seeking his resignation. A more robust response would have been to say that since its earliest days the movie industry has been in an unholy (though some would say a holy) alliance with the censors, that censorship had shaped the course of movie history and played a part in determining the language of popular cinema. It would thus be as unrealistic and disingenuous to refuse the censor a seat at the centennial feast as it would have been, 40 years ago, to deny the public hangman an invitation to a celebration of British penology.

Even before the first films were projected for a paying audience by the Lumière brothers in December 1895, the police had been intervening in Europe and North America to prevent peep-show machines from showing such innocently erotic items as Dorolita's Passion Dance, which was withdrawn in 1894 from the Kinetoscope Arcade on Atlantic City's Boardwalk. Whether there really was a sequence of flicker-cards or a few dozen feet of film called What The Butler Saw is, I believe, uncertain. But the title has entered the language and for good reason. It suggests

270

three things – voyeurism, class and dangerously illicit activities observed and revealed to an outsider.

In 1896, one year after the Lumière show in Paris, 50 feet of film recording a gentle kiss between May Irwin and John C. Rice, both middle-aged, from the Broadway play The Widow Jones, had US news-papers calling for it to be banned. The following year the moral oppro-brium focused on screen violence as exemplified in a string of films bringing championship boxing matches to the general public. Terry Ramsaye, who lived through the period, wrote in the first comprehen-sive history of American cinema, A Million and One Nights (1926):

One marked effect of the Corbett-Fitzsimmons picture as the out-standing screen production of its day was to bring the odium of pugilism upon the screen all across Puritan America. Until that picture appeared the social status of the screen had been uncertain. It now became definitely lowbrow, an entertainment for the great unwashed commonalty. This likewise made it a mark for uplifters, moralists, reformers and legislators in a degree which would never have obtained if the screen had by specialization reached higher social strata.

Shortly after the turn of the century, a Chicago judge claimed that the cinema was among the chief influences – bad, of course – on the juvenile offenders who appeared before him. His sentiments were echoed over 90 years later when the English judge in the James Bulger murder trial suggested that the juvenile killers had been influenced by the American horror movie Child's Play 3, though the local police could find no evidence that the children had seen it.

What was it that the benign American inventor, Thomas Edison, and his French friends, the photographic manufacturers Louis and Auguste Lumière, had unleashed upon the world, and that had so rapidly led to a demand for its control? The cinema developed during a period of unprecedented social change, and broadly speaking there were seven aspects that made it seem a threatening phenomenon (to which 30 years later was added that of rebarbative language and disturbing sound).

First, there was the very size of the image and the immediacy, the intimacy of the experience. Second, film opened up life socially, geogra-

271

phically, in time and space, transporting audiences to places unknown, hitherto forbidden, invented. Third, the violence and eroticism were palpable, yet they left the audience unscathed. Fourth, the cinema offered an invitation to fantasize, to dream, to revolt, and it is hardly surprising that the Futurists and the Surrealists were among the first to recognize its power. Fifth, the movies rapidly became the most popular leisure activity of the burgeoning urban working classes, feared by the bourgeoisie as a potential source of revolution and by intellectual devotees of eugenics as a threat to the future of Western Civilisation. Sixth, movie-going was a public activity that took place in the dark, offering terrible temptations to innocent boys and girls. Seventh, there were health and safety fears, some real, some imaginary: fear of fire hazards from unsafe buildings and highly inflammable nitrate film; fear that the flickering images might damage eyesight or induce epilepsy; fear that these hot, fetid auditoriums could spread contagious diseases.

Some early opponents of cinema wanted to crush the new medium in the bud. In 1896 Herbert Stone, the eloquent editor of the Chicago literary magazine, *The Chap Book*, wrote: 'I want to smash the Vitascope. The name of the thing is itself a horror. Its manifestations are worse.' Of the notorious Edison clip, universally known as *The Kiss*, Stone fumed:

> When only life size it was pronounced beastly. But that was nothing to the present sight. Magnified to Gargantuan proportions and repeated three times over it is absolutely disgusting. All delicacy or remnant of charm seems gone from Miss Irwin, and the performance comes near to being indecent in its emphasized vulgarity. Such things call for police interference.

Wherever films were made or shown, censorship boards sprang up. Around 1914, American producers united to oppose officially constituted bodies, and the federal government refused to establish film censorship at a national level, though this was precisely what happened in virtually every other country. But a major blow was administered in a crucial judgement by the US Supreme Court in 1915. Delivering the majority opinion following an appeal by the Mutual Film Corporation against censorship boards in Missouri and Ohio, Justice McKenna stated:

It cannot be put out of view that the exhibition of moving pictures is a business pure and simple, originated and conducted for profit, like other spectacles, not to be regarded, nor intended to be regarded by the Ohio constitution, we think, as part of the press of the country or as organs of public opinion. They are mere representations of events, of ideas and sentiments published and known, vivid, useful and entertaining no doubt, but as we have said, capable of evil, having power for it, the greater because of their attractiveness and manner of exhibition.

This decision, denying the cinema the constitutional protection enjoyed by other media, was eventually reversed in 1952. But it set the tone for the way the movies were to be perceived for decades, at least in the Anglo-Saxon world, and continues to do so into the 1990s.

Meanwhile, in the UK, censorship came in through the back door. The 1909 Cinematograph Act was introduced to license cinemas for safety purposes and was extended by the courts to cover the movies shown in them. This led to the creation in 1912 of the British Board of Film Censors, initiated by the Home Office but run as a self-regulating body by the film industry, to license movies for public exhibition. Its second president, the ubiquitous T. P. O'Connor, Conservative MP, author and newspaper editor, served from 1916 until his death in 1929. During his reign, he made the film industry the acquiescent creature of the political establishment, a position from which it has yet to emerge.

Shortly after his appointment, O'Connor told a Cinema Committee of Inquiry that 'there are 43 rules and they cover pretty well all the grounds you can think of.' T. P.'s rules, all of them prohibitions, prevented the production or exhibition of pictures involving 'unnecessary exhibition of underclothing', 'relations of Capital and Labour', 'realistic horrors of warfare', 'executions' and 'subjects dealing with India in which British officers are seen in an odious light'. We must remember that Britain was at war when O'Connor devised this list, but most of the rules remained in force for the next 40-50 years. Alfred Hitchcock turned away from political film-making forever when his plans to make a picture about the 1926 General Strike were rejected by the BBFC.

It was some time before the US industry produced anything as detailed as T. P.'s 43 Rules. But when it came, the Production Code was the most elaborate ever drawn up, and sought to make American movies acceptable and inoffensive to juvenile audiences at home and throughout the world. After World War I, during which US cinema began to establish the worldwide ascendancy that today seems unassailable, the Hollywood studios were coming under attack. Their films and the behaviour of their stars were agents of a changing post-war morality that small-town America found threatening. Anti-Semitism was part of this paranoia, directed towards a new industry largely created and owned by Jewish immigrants fleeing pogroms in Europe. In 1920, newspapers across the country carried an item with a Washington DC dateline that began: 'The lobby of the International Reform Bureau, Dr Wilbur Crafts presiding, voted tonight to rescue the motion pictures from the hands of the Devil and 500 un-Christian Jews.'

The response of the Hollywood moguls was to invite Will H. Hays, a middle-western Presbyterian elder and postmaster-general in Republican President Warren Harding's cabinet, to become president of the newly-constituted Motion Picture Producers of America Inc. The year was 1921, his job to put the industry in order to preserve its leaders' fortunes. He served them well for 43 years, and the present, only the fourth, person to hold this post is another recruit from Washington, President Lyndon Johnson's right-hand man, Jack Valenti, who became MPPA president in 1966.

Hays believed in the 'Ten Commandments, self-discipline, faith in time of trouble, worship, the Bible and the Golden Rule', and at one of his first Hollywood press conferences he declared:

This industry must have towards that sacred thing, the mind of a child, towards that clean, virgin thing, that unmarked slate, the same responsibility, the same care about the impressions made upon it, that the best clergyman or the most inspired teacher would have.

He first introduced a system by which the studios were to submit to the Hays Office the books, scripts and stories they were considering for filming. Subsequently he sent out an informal list of what he called

'Don'ts and Be Carefuls'. The coming of sound with its possibilities for new verbal offence, along with the influx of irreverent new writers, many of them tough ex-journalists from big city newspapers, led to the adoption in 1930 of a Production Code drawn up by two midwestern Catholics, one a Jesuit professor of drama, the other a publisher of trade magazines. This Hays Office Code, made mandatory in 1934, began with three general principles – 'no picture shall be produced that will lower moral standards'; 'correct standards of life, subject only to the requirements of drama and entertainment, shall be presented'; 'law, natural or human, shall not be ridiculed, nor shall sympathy be created for its violation.' This was followed by eight double-column pages of detailed applications, ranging from the demand that 'no film may throw ridicule on any religious faith' to various proscribed words, including 'Fairy (in a vulgar sense)'. The Code was designed to make every film suitable for audiences of any age, and remained in force until 1967 when it was replaced by a system of certificated categories. This change was influenced both by European systems of censorship, and also by European films which, with their greater freedom in the handling of sexual matters, were making serious inroads in the American market.

The Code helped shape the language of Hollywood movies and the cinema worldwide, as writers and directors argued and bargained with the Code's administrators, and invented stratagems to approach forbidden subjects and metaphors to express proscribed acts. Fireworks and crashing waves stood in for sex. Body language could suggest the taboo subject of homosexuality. A woman with shiny lipstick, or chewing gum, or smoking in the streets, was identified as a prostitute. And the public came to take with a pinch of salt the come-uppance that the Code insisted be visited on glamorous villains. Yet there were whole areas of life that were ignored and distorted.

The industry was only opposed to external censorship. It was the major studios themselves who, through their control of production, distribution and exhibition, decided who would make films and whose pictures would be distributed. When Hollywood bowed to the House Un-American Activities Committee (HUAC) and other McCarthyite witch-hunters in the post-World War II years, a group of blacklisted film-makers produced *Salt of the Earth* (1953), an independent film about a miners' strike in New Mexico. They were harassed while on location by local and federal authorities, the leading actress was deported to her native Mexico, and the completed film was denied exhibition in the USA until the 1960s when it became a cult work among student radicals.

While this supposedly voluntary censorship was imposed in the USA, the movie-makers in the newly created Soviet Union were similarly having their talents harnessed to the cause of ideology. During the 1920s, artists were permitted considerable leeway to innovate and Pudovkin, Eisenstein and Dziga Vertov created a cinema that was revolutionary both politically and aesthetically. But with the coming of sound and the replacement of the enlightened Anatoly Lunacharsky by the philistine Stalinist cultural commissar, Andrei Zhdanov, Soviet cinema became rigidly controlled by bureaucrats and the doctrine of socialist realism strenuously imposed on the nation's artists.

Come the 1930s, and the German cinema, formerly among the least circumscribed, was taken over by the Nazis, though relatively few feature films were vehicles for explicit political propaganda. The European dictators of both left and right – Lenin and Stalin, Hitler and Mussolini – were fascinated by the cinema and aware of its power. They therefore sought to exploit it in their own interests. Artists working under them, including French film-makers of the Occupation and Eastern European cineastes of the post-war decades, could subvert censorship and censure by resorting to allegory, making movies with mythical subjects or putting them in historical settings. Likewise in Hollywood in the 1950s, when the studios were reluctant to make political films or touch on matters of race, these issues were dealt with in the guise of westerns or science fiction.

As the first great mass medium, the cinema provided the politicians and guardians of morality with the paradigm for censorship in the twentieth century. And, paradoxically in an era that has seen the democratic urge become central to social progress, there has grown up a culture of censorship, an expectation and acceptance of it. The least censorship – of films, as well as of the other arts and media – is usually found in confidently democratic countries that have recently experienced authoritarian regimes of the left or the right: in Greece and Spain, for instance, or Hungary and the Czech Republic, there is virtually no censorship of movies. But in countries that have not been exposed to such draconian treatment at the hands of the state, movies are subjected to pre-censorship that goes far beyond the methods of certification used to protect children. In Britain, for instance, where the Lord Chamberlain's role in licensing plays was abolished in 1968 and prosecutions of literary works are a thing of the past, the BBFC extends its influence and introduces new criteria. It is true that the situation has become increasingly permissive (despite a lurching, three steps forward, two steps back method of advance). But fashionable feminist sensitivities about possible offences against women, for example, now affect the censors' judgements, and the BBFC's statutory powers to license video cassettes for home use has led to films for domestic viewing being subjected to an elaborate set of rules based on prurient and class-based assumptions about the way people (ie, the proletariat) see and perceive films.

The simple fact is that at every societal level we have been inculcated with the idea that censorship is necessary – to preserve society, to protect people from each other, to save ourselves from our baser instincts. Revolution, personal violence and sex forever lurk to disturb the status quo. And censorship is most evident in the cinema because, unlike books, plays, exhibitions, TV programmes and the radio, every film we see, every video we buy, is prefaced on the screen or on the cassette box by a certificate stating that the work has been examined (the British certificates are signed jointly by the Queen's cousin and the American-born James Ferman) and judged fit for us to see. It isn't in the interest of the film companies to reveal what the censor has excised for cinematic exhibition or video release.

One might suppose that there was enough official supervision. Sadly, the press, both popular and elitist, tabloid and broadsheet, are among the first to demand tighter control of the movies, especially when it claims some gruesome murder has been influenced by a recent film. This isn't confined to editorial writers and sensational columnists. All too often movie critics demand that works that have offended them be cut or banned. The late Dilys Powell, the liberal critic of the *Sunday Times* from 1939 to 1975, gave evidence for the defence when D. H. Lawrence's *Lady Chatterley's Lover* was prosecuted for obscenity in 1960. Yet she claimed in 1948 that the innocuous gangster movie, No Orchids for Miss Blandish, should have been given 'a new certificate of D for Disgusting'. In 1954 she supported the BBFC's total ban on the Marlon Brando biker movie, The Wild One: 'I am bound to say I think the Board was absolutely right.'

Recently we've experienced a new form of censorship as several critics employed by British national daily newspapers have called upon the minister for national heritage to investigate the financing from public funds in Britain and Europe of movies they disapprove of, either on moral or aesthetic grounds (ie, too arty or too sleazy). The films at issue are Michael Winterbottom's harsh road movie, Butterfly Kiss, and Mario Brenta's contemplative Italian picture, Barnabo of the Mountains.

Looking back over a century of movie censorship, like Beaumarchais' Figaro, one laughs for fear that one might cry at the fatuity and foolishness of it all. For 100 years, audiences have been treated like untrustworthy children, artists as enemies of society. The BBFC refusing a certificate for over 30 years to Eisenstein's Battleship Potemkin in case it should ferment mutiny in the Royal Navy. The same board at the height of World War II holding up the distribution of Western Approaches, a documentary tribute to the Merchant Navy, because some torpedoed sailors in mid-Atlantic use the word 'bloody'. The French censors banning Stanley Kubrick's Paths of Glory in 1958 because it casts aspersions on the conduct of French officers in World War I, and Madame De Gaulle, 10 years later, attempting to have a film version of Diderot's La Réligieuse banned because it presented the eighteenth-century Catholic Church in an unfavourable light. The Prince of Wales using his opening speech at the Museum of the Moving Image not to celebrate the cinema but to call for the banning of horror films on cassette – the so-called 'video nasties' – to protect his vulnerable children, and getting applauded by the audience of newspapermen. The Soviet authorities, unable to make any sense of Andrei Tarkovsky's autobiographical film Mirror, banishing it to the cinema circuit that served military bases. The New Zealand censors approving the Joseph Strick version of James Joyce's Ulysses only for exhibition to single-sex audiences. John Huston getting the word 'gunsel', a rare word (possibly of Yiddish origin) for catamite used by Dashiell Hammett in The Maltese Falcon, past the Hays

Office censor, who thought it was underworld slang for a gun-toting gangster, which indeed it became after the film was released. One could go on forever, as indeed film censorship threatens to do.

November/December 1995

KEN LOACH

Market takes all

Ken Loach, Britain's leading radical film-maker on the large and small screens for more than three decades, pointed in this contribution to *The Subversive Eye* (the cinema centenary issue) to the narrowly commercial criteria of the market as the main source of censorship in the contemporary cinema.

Censorship can take many forms. In the cinema decisions about which films are made are usually commercial, which means that many subjects are excluded and the view of the world that is presented – and implicitly endorsed – is usually politically to the right. Americans with guns will solve your problem!

If a film suggests an alternative view of a sensitive subject, it may be attacked before it is seen. Ireland is a case in point. Films that have attempted to tell Irish history from a neutral or Irish perspective are usually vilified in advance. *Michael Collins* is an example. Our film, *Hidden Agenda*, was about the British presence in Ireland and the corrupting effects of this on the British as well as on the Irish. Yet before it had even been shown in Britain it was pilloried in the right-wing press. There was a story in the *Daily Mail*, for instance, in which a Tory MP was quoted as saying it was an IRA film, with absolutely no substantiating evidence. Anything on Ireland seen as critical of the British government's stance was accused of being 'pro-IRA'. As a result, cinemas in the UK chose not to screen the film. It came out about the time of the Gulf War and one cinema owner said she 'preferred not to show anything critical of British troops'.

When *Hidden Agenda* was submitted to the Cannes Film Festival in 1990, a group of right-wing journalists went to Cannes and asked for it to be withdrawn. While the director of the festival refused categorically to withdraw the film, the message that got back to Britain was that 'this is not the sort of film that should be representing our country abroad.'

So-called liberal and democratic societies have their own means of censorship, more insidious than the bureaucrat in his office.

January/February 1996

ANTHONY TUCKER

After Chernobyl: confusion and deceit

Anthony Tucker, former science editor of the *Guardian*, wrote this warning on the tenth anniversary of Chernobyl about how little the world had learned politically or morally from that disaster, and how ill-prepared we were to deal with other Chernobyls that are waiting to happen.

For those unaffected, memory of disaster is short. Who, in the well-heeled West, now recalls that the world first learned of the Chernobyl accident from Swedish scientists and American spy satellites? Or that Gorbachev, promoter of *glasnost*, was, like the world beyond Soviet borders, kept in the dark about the enormity of the accident and the irradiation problems his country faced; or that the period of panic when fallout rained down on western Europe was accompanied by confusion and disinformation, that scientific reports from affected areas were fragmentary, filtered, impossible to validate? Or that, when the brave 'sarcophagus' holding a lid on the grave of the shattered reactor became in serious danger of collapse and Professor Velikov, former chief adviser to Gorbachev, came to a Pugwash meeting at the Royal Society in London to beg for help, there was no response?

Sure, the early silence, confusion and Europe-wide panic led to massive pressure for the speedy international notification of nuclear accidents involving trans-boundary effects, although it is not clear what such an agreement might achieve. Preparedness in the West has barely improved: changes mirror the politically correct message that Chernobyl cannot possibly happen here.

In the Soviet Union the early desperate and often incredibly courageous measures to control the monstrous meltdown, limit damage and evacuate large areas were carried out as a huge military operation amid a morass of technical and political confusion. Tragically for affected civil populations, this confusion was transformed into chaos as the

Soviet Union itself burst apart, fragmenting into the new (or rather old) states whose pride, sensitivities and separate health ministries shattered all immediate hope of co-ordinated follow-up and remedial programmes.

Russia, a nuclear state whose other Chernobyl-type reactors are still essential to power supplies, had a powerful political need to bury the Chernobyl image as quickly as possible. Worldwide cynicism and distrust were inevitable. But the real tragedy of Chernobyl is not that its immediate consequences and immense long-term problems are fading from memory, minimized, played down, obfuscated by the governments and protection agencies of the former Soviet Union and the western world, but that as a disaster it is still growing and that in many ways it is far worse than anyone predicted.

A stark and emotional report by the secretary-general to the fiftieth General Assembly of the United Nations* has revealed that, a decade after the immediate fallout, the humanitarian, health and economic problems entrained by Chernobyl are still emerging and still growing. They are already so huge that they are overwhelming the affected states and threaten to overwhelm the comprehension, the compassion, even the imagination of the world.

The lives and livelihoods of around 10 million people have already been affected. Half a million people have been displaced. Predictably, the abandoned villages and forests of the 30 kilometre exclusion zone around Chernobyl have become a wild, sinister, no-go haunt of criminal and bandit communities. But in Belarus, in the Russian Federation and in the Ukraine, where weather determined fallout would be greatest, agriculture is corrupted by contamination, there is massive social and industrial dislocation, and humanitarian, health and economic problems are of such immensity and complexity that they are far beyond available resources and are perhaps comparable only with the aftermath of civil war.

Ideals are largely pipe-dreams, but even in a world in which we expect only that international responsibilities will be taken seriously, common sense dictates that all nuclear governments should have worked closely in the provision of support, equipment and expertise to investi-

* UN Document A/50/418 of 8 September 1995.

gate and remedy Chernobyl consequences. This is not a matter of generosity or of international aid, but of practicality. Chernobyl offered and still offers the world an opportunity to gain a unique understanding of the effects of nuclear disasters, as essential for critical awareness as to provide a real basis for future emergency responses.

Of course, few countries can afford, like the former Soviet Union, to entomb as radioactive debris a thousand helicopters and the several thousand buses needed to evacuate large populations from contaminated areas. Yet all countries need to know, through independent and openly published investigation and skilled technical interpretation, the true detail of what has happened and what will happen in the decades ahead to the millions of relatively poor and uninformed people whom circumstances force to live amid contamination that will remain for generations.

It hardly matters now that, as it wove its way round Europe and eventually round the world, the Chernobyl plume produced an immediate and powerful amplification of existing public hostility to nuclear power. Official statements were dismissed as deception: the Swedish public demanded an end to nuclear power, the French were evasive, the Americans kept their heads down and the British government quietly delayed the go-ahead for Sizewell B for a few months. Then it was back to business as usual.

The ground for this had already been laid. In the immediate aftermath, amid wild predictions of huge casualties and following correct protocol, the International Atomic Energy Agency (IAEA) – to which nuclear governments belong – produced a large and detailed report. It was based primarily on Russian information and was unexpectedly reassuring, suggesting that overall consequences and long-term effects within the Soviet Union would be much less serious than many feared and, outside the Soviet Union, any effects would be negligible. At the same meeting in Vienna, at which no independent data were presented, the IAEA sought an immediate safety assessment of all Russian reactor designs and proposed guidelines for the assessment of dose, continued monitoring and follow-up of the reactor workers and the emergency teams most directly affected by radiation.

Although it can conjure up design expertise from member states, the

IAEA has little independent money for the support of huge programmes of technical investigation and, in matters of health and epidemiology, plays a specialized but strictly limited industry-focused role. Protocol requires, properly, that the World Health Organization at Geneva (WHO) should be the executive agency for international health programmes, although WHO is itself continually starved of funds. This means that promotion of the vast, specialized and long-term medical programmes of the kind demanded by Chernobyl is largely dependent on dedicated additional finance from member governments, agencies or bodies like the EC. Even then, neither WHO nor the IAEA can act as an independent investigator in the collection and publication of potentially sensitive medical, scientific and technical data.

Neither has the power to enforce collaboration, and participating governments filter their own information. Additionally, in the Chernobyl follow-up, the affected governments chose to channel data only through WHO and the IAEA, thus excluding all normal peer-reviewed routes for scientific and technical publication.

Only SCOPE – the International Union's Scientific Committee on Problems of the Environment – was able to set up an independent programme, and this was limited to monitoring and assessing models of the physical and biological pathways of radioactive elements in different environments.

Thus, although on the face of things it may have seemed that the international community had joined hands to provide the resources, the expertise, the training and the planning needed to cope with and to learn the important lessons the disaster could deliver, the programme was hedged round by crucial limitations. Although expert groups from western Europe and the USA visited their academic and medical colleagues in the seriously affected regions, they did this on their own. The only hard money was a dedicated sum of US$20 million from Japan.

This set WHO's Geneva-based IPHECA (International Programme on Health Effects of the Chernobyl Accident) in motion. After three years, neither acceptable study protocols nor useful data had emerged. The money had vanished in new equipment, mainly in Russian laboratories. Western experts, acutely aware of this failure of management and of the poor lines of communication, advised that IPHECA was itself a disaster. Pressure for reform came, not from WHO HQ at Geneva, but from EC groups collaborating in Belarus and from WHO (Europe) in Rome, whose radiation arm had developed studies alongside the Belarus Ministry of Health.

At this time, little science of western standard was emerging from the affected areas. Worse, the highly prestigious scientific journal *Nature* had been accused of censoring Chernobyl fallout information by accepting papers from western groups and then failing to publish them, and Britain's National Radiological Protection Board stood accused of failing to correct misleading undermeasurement of fallout over Britain, published in its first scientific report. It remains uncorrected. Then, as EC and WHO (Europe) collaborative studies began to pick up evidence of a massive fallout-related increase in the incidence of thyroid cancer among the children of Belarus, their findings came under attack from 'official' Russian-dominated IPHECA scientists (who sought causes other than fallout) and from the United States.

While, in the early stages, the absence of organized studies could be put down to confusion and excused as part of the general cock-up, it was suddenly painfully obvious that western experts collaborating in Belarus and elsewhere could expect obstruction coupled with political and professional attack. Transfer of the essential science and skills in pathology and epidemiology, crucial to the future of large and suffering populations, was being blocked. This was not cock-up: it was cover-up.

Nuclear states, trapped in the same schizophrenic dilemma whatever their colour, sought future safety in all honesty. Yet they also hoped that Chernobyl could be buried in blurred statistics and contradictory arguments, from which its legacy could never be convincingly unravelled. Even though known doses from fallout tellurium and radio-iodine were large and certain to increase the incidence of child thyroid cancer, politics required that studies confirming this increase must be attacked.

The US government had, and still has, powerful political reasons for obfuscating these findings. Its Department of Defense is inundated by civil compensation actions from US citizens seeking damages for thyroid cancer and other health detriments, claimed to result from exposure to radio-iodine and other fallout around the Hanford reactors and from weapons test sites in Nevada and elsewhere. (Over the years Hanford has released almost one million Curies of radio-iodine – about 12 per cent of the Chernobyl release.) Beyond its borders, thyroid cancer excesses had also started to emerge among Pacific islanders affected by fallout from US nuclear tests. On top of this, some parts of the US nuclear medicine profession feared that their profitable freedom to use radio-isotopes might become subject to new restrictions.

Whatever the appalling health consequences emerging among the exposed populations of Belarus, the Ukraine and Russia, the confusion and inadequacy of programmes, as measured by western standards, still acts as a double deterrent in the countries most able to help. In many the internal political position on Chernobyl is best served when scientific and medical reports reaching the West are of such low technical quality that they can be dismissed.

One disgrace is that the world's discredited radiation protection community remained and remains silent. Fortunately, on a narrow front, truth is winning. A Belarus study of thyroid cancer has been taken over by WHO (Europe), new programmes are planned (but not financed) and the latest data are irrefutable. These imply that among the infant group (nought to three years) exposed in the highest fallout areas, up to 25 per cent can be expected to develop thyroid cancer. One in four or five, instead of one in a million.

Even in isolation these figures are horrendous, implying the need for increases in medical resources and surveillance that lie well beyond anything available in the affected states. Worse, they are only a tiny fragment of the huge, interwoven and still emerging humanitarian problem fermenting in the wake of Chernobyl. The importance of the report from the secretary-general of the United Nations is that it cannot be ignored. It signals formal international recognition that the problems entrained by a nuclear accident are vastly greater and cover a far wider range than the health detriment measured in future cancers, still officially seen as the major criterion in assessing the effects of radiation.

It raises some uncontroversial but salutary questions. For example, why has there been no systematic follow-up of the army of Soviet 'liquidators', almost 200,000 strong, each suffering 90 seconds of intense irradiation inside the hulk of the Chernobyl reactor as they saved the world from far worse consequences? They are now dispersed, many untraceable, yet they have become a dramatic source of anecdotal evidence implying very high levels of morbidity and mortality. But what of the future of the huge agricultural populations forced, by economic necessity, to continue to live and work on contaminated land, or those who, as families, chose displacement and desperate poverty as the lesser risk to their children? With agricultural areas in Belarus and the Ukraine the size of England and Wales so heavily contaminated that they cannot be worked until well into the twenty-first century, there is crippling dislocation. International economic and humanitarian aid is needed as urgently by these countries as by any nation stricken by famine or by natural catastrophe.

The Russian Chernobyl Committee figures, seemingly endorsed by UNICEF in the report, suggest that there are around eight million seriously affected victims of the Chernobyl aftermath in these regions alone. This may well be right. It may also be right to point to the observed and often large increases in a wide range of diseases in these areas as a product of stress, an issue judged to be important and real by an expert group at WHO(Europe)* in 1994.

Sadly, the UN report is open to dismissive attack. It quotes such low pre-Chernobyl disease incidence figures that they reveal past under-ascertainment, implying that apparent increases are merely a product of better surveillance. Its reports of stress-related increases in morbidity, birth defects and leukaemia are largely anecdotal and, although possibly real, have no firm statistical base – a weakness already exploited in knock-down comment in the nuclear establishment literature.† Although powerful, the UN document will face the same scientific hostility as the early reports of epidemic child thyroid cancer in Belarus.

Yet this turned out to be real and, since there is increasing evidence that psychological stress adversely affects the immune system,‡ the increases in morbidity may also turn out to be just as real and disastrous as the UN report suggests. In any case, the economic and human disaster is clearly of such proportions that, like famine or catastrophic earthquake, it evidently merits international aid on a massive scale, free

* The author was a member of this group. Its draft report has been circulated but awaits agreement.
† *Journal of Nuclear Medicine* 1995; 36,9, p29N.
‡ eg. *Lancet* 1995; 346: pp1194–96.

of nuclear hostilities and, above all, properly co-ordinated. Is this another pipe-dream?

January/February 1996

MIKHAIL BYCKAU

A liquidator's story

Mikhail Byckau, a physicist at the Sakharov Institute of Radioecology, spent the last nine years before his retirement in April 1995 working on the 'liquidation' and monitoring programmes in the affected areas around Chernobyl. He published in *Index*, for the first time, his personal account of the day following the accident, as radioactive rain was falling in the streets, and the Soviet authorities' immediate response was to bind him and his colleagues to secrecy about every aspect of the plant and its failure.

On the Monday morning, 28 April, at the Nuclear Energy Institute of the Belarusian Academy of Sciences, I switched on the apparatus – the gamma-spectrometer and the dosimeters: everything was (in physicists' slang) 'hot', which meant that there had been a big nuclear accident on the Institute's premises: our dosimetrist ran out of the laboratory, and reported that the level in the yard was about 300 micro-roentgens an hour. Then he was summoned by telephone to monitor the radiation contamination round the nuclear reactor of the Institute of Radioactive Technology; so that was the main source of the accident! But they had their own dosimetrists there, and the dose level was almost the same; the same was true in the vicinity of a third nuclear device . . . Moreover, it was clear that the radiation levels fell the further one went inside the building . . . When the head of the dosimetry service, A. Lineva, telephoned the Central Public Health Station of Minsk, they said, 'This is not your accident.'

We looked at the tall smoke-stack, and then at the map of Europe, and we saw that the wind was blowing radiation towards Sweden. In fact, we learned later, on 1 May the level of radioactive contamination in Stockholm was 17 Curies per square kilometre from Caesium-137, and 87 Curies per square kilometre from Iodine-131.

But in our place, they brought me in a twig from the yard, and I observed that it was emitting radiation . . . the gamma-spectrometer showed Iodine-131 and other 'young' radionuclides . . . Later we tested soil and trees from many regions of Belarus, and the Institute started to measure the specific activity of foodstuffs arriving for the Institute canteen and the crêche.

Meanwhile, the dosimetry service headed by M. V. Bulyha was monitoring the radiation cloud hanging above Minsk.

We started to ring our relatives and friends in Minsk, advising them about safety measures. But this did not last long: at around midday, our telephones were cut off. And a couple of days later we specialists were called into the Secrecy Department, and made to sign a 29-point document forbidding us to divulge secrets connected with the accident at the Chernobyl plant. These included the structure of the RDMK-1000 reactor, the amount of uranium, etc, 'secrets' that had already been published in scientific literature.

And meanwhile out in the street, radioactive rain was falling . . .

We went home from work without looking from side to side; it was painful to see how the children were playing in the radioactive sand, and eating ices.

In our street, I went up to a street vendor and told her to stop selling her sausages, as radioactive rain was falling. But she just said: 'Be off, you drunkard! If there'd been an accident, they'd have announced it on radio and TV.' A naive soul, she believed in the righteousness of the Soviet authorities.

In the evening, on Central TV, Moscow showed us how tractors with great swirls of dust behind them were tilling the soil down in Naroula country, part of which lies in the 30-kilometre zone around the Chernobyl station. Then, on 1 May, as always, children and adults marched in columns through the streets without even guessing at the consequences. So now, today, in Belarus we have some 400 children with thyroid cancer . . . who at that time knew nothing about Iodine-131 . . .

Translated by Vera Rich

January/February 1996

W. L. WEBB

Bosnian diary: Who goes home?

W. L. Webb travelled through Bosnia to Sarajevo in the days after the Dayton meeting in November 1995 to find the villages of the Krajina burning, hamlets deliberately flattened, towns and cities in ruins and the population scattered. 'Obliterating the memory of a place,' he wrote in these reflections, '– making lives and communities as though they had never been – must be one of the ultimate forms of censorship.' How, and to what, were the refugees supposed to return?

Somewhere in *Black Lamb and Grey Falcon*, her epic panorama of Balkan landscape, myth and prejudice, Rebecca West says that she had come to Yugoslavia 'to see what history meant in flesh and blood'. One flinches, reading that 60 years later, following in her footsteps in what must seem to the South Slavs just another such 'low, dishonest decade' as the '30s.

For the moment, their flesh and blood is mostly still safe in its skin, and not, thank God and His improbable agents lately in Dayton, Ohio, splashed around a market-place in Sarajevo, or the little square in Tuzla where boys and girls used to crowd of an evening to drink coffee and hope they were falling in love. Bosnia is still the sovereign place to go for such history lessons. It's also the place in which to contemplate the uses and abuses of cartography. What went on chiefly in the Bob Hope Hotel in Dayton, Ohio, was the endless drawing and tearing up of maps (even the final documents included an annexe of 102 of them), culminating in a session in 'the Nintendo room', the base's map-room, where fancy electronics reproduced the detail of obsessionally fought-over territories down to the last goat path – using, as the Serbs would have been well aware, the very programmes used by the Nato planes that had bombed them back to the conference table. So, as one reporter put it, while the warlords were returning to their strongholds, the resort to virtual reality produced a virtual peace.

Actual reality produces its own gloss on all that. Travellers in the convoy carrying the Helsinki Citizens' Assembly's (hCa) assorted idealists and observers to its annual conference in Tuzla got an insight into the nature of this Balkan war as soon as they reached Pocitelj, the first strategically placed small town on the Neretva river, which was fiercely fought over by all three sides. All the bridges were blown for miles along, including the lovely, springing arch of the sixteenth-century bridge of Mostar, a treasure lost for all Europe.

The pattern Pocitelj showed was to be repeated endlessly in towns and villages between Mostar, Tuzla and Sarajevo in the next fortnight. Yes, look, they *had* once all lived together side by side: here, three intact, ordinary village houses, with chickens and children playing in the yard, were followed immediately by two blackened ruins; another patch of normality – an old man snoozing by a doorstep – then more darkness, half a row this time, and so on; after which village life resumed, men in allotments straightening up to stare at the line of buses and white UNPROFOR jeeps. Further on, the devastation was more comprehensive – whole hamlets wiped out – until, in the Muslim part of Mostar, the coach was silenced by the extent of the wreckage and the improvised cemeteries of lately-dug graves in parks and roadside verges. For the scale of damage, only Sarajevo, at the end of my journey, seemed worse, probably because there it was the modern buildings of its wide, central boulevard – the familiar shapes of tower blocks and shopping centres – that were so broken and ravaged.

The harder part of this history lesson was about the specific character of the destruction. The village houses, especially, were not just ordinary, shell-damaged casualties of war; no, they had been dynamited, bulldozed, systematically razed. It was as though giant goblins had been on the rampage, stamping them flat. What added to the sense of falling into some terrible Balkan *Märchen* was that among these places were alpine villages scarcely touched by the twentieth century, high above the deep wooded valleys of central Bosnia: these archaic pastoral idylls too were blackened with the fierce scorch marks of history. (The nineteenth century dealt with them no less savagely, of course. In despatches for the *Manchester Guardian*, Arthur Evans described the fires of destroyed villages burning just as fiercely in the Balkan Wars of the 1870s; but then, of course, the valiant fighters for Free Bosnia were the Christian–

Serb peasants of the Krajina, struggling against the yoke of the Muslim landlord class, superior in strength and firepower . . .)

It started almost at the beginning of the war, and continued even beyond the end. A week after the ceasefire, Tim Garton Ash and Konstanty Gebert, the Polish journalist and aide to Tadeusz Mazowiecki, who had driven down from Zagreb through the Krajina, arrived in Tuzla half-dazed at the succession of empty, gutted Serb villages, still smouldering, which specially detailed Croatian loot-and-burn detachments had left in the wake of Operation Storm, whose name Franjo Tudjman so loves to pronounce. But weeks after the initialling of the agreement in Dayton, more than a month after the ceasefire, the fires were burning still near the Posavina corridor, where the Croats seem determined to hand back nothing but scorched earth.

These images compose eventually into a comprehensive diagram of the pathology of war, the fact that this is an unusual species of civil war being significant only because civil war is the extreme case, in which the Others who you must drive out, slaughter, eradicate, are people known and seen in desperate close-up: your neighbours, even kin by marriage, made alien and fearful by the exciting madness you have been infected with. Not only must you get rid of them, you must make it impossible for them or theirs ever to return and resume what used to be normal life, for then your madness would be seen for what it is. So while it would have been easier if the goblins could have made the Muslims or the Serbs and their houses simply disappear, one does the best one can with dynamite and bulldozers. Obliterating the memory of a place – making lives and communities as though they had never been – must be one of the ultimate forms of censorship.

There is an actual map which explains better than any narrative the complexity out of which all this came. This ethnographic map of Bosnia from the 1991 census must be one of the most extraordinary exhibits in the history of cartography, just as Bosnia's melting-pot was one of Europe's most curious pieces of nation-making. It shows at a glance the dense and complicated distribution of the Serb, Croat and Muslim mix across all the country's corrugation of mountains and valleys. Compare it with the maps of the ceasefire and what is known of the Dayton maps, and you see almost as quickly how few people are now at home in Bosnia. First, the Muslims of the eastern towns and villages above the Drina, whose centuries-old culture is recreated in the novels of Ivo Andric, were driven west. Then, late in the war, the Krajina (border) Serbs, descendants of those planted by the Habsburgs three centuries ago to stiffen the Croatian frontier against the Turk, were herded east by the US-backed Croat and Bosnian offensives of last May and August in the war's biggest ethnic cleansing – 200,000 or more driven into bulging Banja Luka and its hinterland – or replanted in unwelcoming Kosovo. And everywhere the skilled and educated from the towns had fled abroad, these economically viable ones much less likely to come back, of course, than the several hundred thousand whose permission to stay in makeshift asylum in Germany runs out, with Chancellor Kohl's patience, in March.

It will be some time before it becomes clear whether many displaced Bosnians will be able to go home, or whether the whole notion of restoring Bosnia's communities to their multicultural status quo ante, in which so much liberal hope has been invested, really is the naive illusion some US power brokers were always sure it was. In Sarajevo someone described Richard Holbrooke's explosive reaction to talk about the importance of refugees returning to restore the uniquely mixed character of Bosnian communities: For Chrissake! They've got the whole map just about 90 per cent ethnically cleared. Don't start moving people around now and spoil it all: ie, don't upset this tidy new territorial balance which might get us some sort of settlement of these bloody Balkan quarrels.

Though no-one expects Muslims to return to Serb-held areas for years to come, the Bosniaks are otherwise committed to the return of refugees to their homes, and President Izetbegovic proposes his old city's tradition of tolerance and openness as the very pattern for democracy in Bosnia-Hercegovina: 'We do not see this as difficult. We are used to living like this . . . We were attending classes together with people who had different names, a different religion or nationality. None of this is strange to us.'

But other voices will tell you that that old Sarajevo is gone. Much of the old middle class, I was told, had evacuated itself smartly at the beginning of the war, leaving behind 'a militant mediocrity'. And Kris Janowski, the UNHCR's thoughtful spokesman, calculates that while it was true that 27 per cent of marriages in Bosnia before the war were ethnically mixed, there now remained only about 30 per cent of this original population, the rest being mostly refugees from the villages.

In Tuzla, that other celebrated example of the tradition Izetbegovic invoked, the ethnographic balance has been even more radically disturbed. Before the war, the 1991 census gave the proportion of Muslims to Serbs and Croats as roughly three to one; by 1995, UNHCR estimates showed, the tides of war had altered that proportion to 20 to one. The departure of many Serbs and Croats (though we saw some still in the surrounding villages, their churches undamaged), and the immense influx of Muslim refugees, leaving no billets for the hapless US troops whose headquarters the town has become, had made Tuzla statistically into a Muslim stronghold. In northern and eastern Bosnia-Hercegovina, the position is brutally reversed, the Muslim populations being reduced from 355,956 to 30,000 and 261,000 to 4,000 respectively.

Certainly the city's social democrat-dominated administration remains committed to Tuzla's tradition of tolerant multi-ethnicity. During Hitler's war, this miners' town's militant solidarity prevented the Nazis and their Croat Ustashe allies from taking its Jews to the death camps; and in October it played host for the second time to the hCa, drawing groups from all over Europe, not least a large contingent of opposition liberals from Serbia, who had taken three and a half days, via Hungary and Croatia, to complete a journey that used to take three hours from Belgrade. But survivors of the old Tuzla are well aware of what the changes may bring. Multi-ethnicity was organic to this place, says Sinan Alic, editor of one of the town's two independent newspapers, not some ideology imposed by the authorities; but what the new arrivals from the Muslim villages say to such old Tuzlaners when they question a narrowing of attitudes is: if you don't like the new situation, you can leave.

It's important to remember how much Bosnia was and is a peasant country; only a third of its population lived in the few towns of any size before the war. Revealingly, Karadzic, himself a village boy made good, if that's the word, blames the desire for a strong, multi-ethnic Bosnia he so deplores on 'certain pro-civic circles'. Displaced townsfolk, says a refugee administrator in one of the hCa's workshops, are generally much more confident about trying to return to their former homes, villagers far more scared.

Unsurprisingly the census map was much cited as everyone counted their gains and their losses after Dayton. The Croats used it in arguments especially painful to them over the division (to give the Serbs a viable corridor) of Bosnian Posavina, along the valley of the Sava, and the future allocation of Brcko, postponed for a year when the agreement nearly came unstuck over it. This is one of the most dangerous mine-fields. Another, of course, is the reintegration of Sarajevo into Bosnia-Hercegovina, a question so vexed that President Chirac (Sarajevo is a French area of responsibility under the UN) has written to President Clinton saying that additional guarantees were needed for the 120,000 Serbs involved if the agreement was to be workable. 'The international community has become excessively involved in Sarajevo,' says Karadzic. 'It will have to pay the price, it will have to protect every single Serb house . . . for at least five years.'

Hardly less dangerous is the question of whether President Tudjman can – or cares to – make his Hercegovinian Croats work constructively with the Bosniaks in the Federation, and give up the brutal apartheid they enforced in places like Mostar. There the Muslims who live on the east bank, where 60 per cent of the buildings are damaged, were simply stopped by the Croat police from crossing to the city's administrative offices, installed in a hotel on the western, Croatian bank. In an attempt to make this bitterly divided place into a functioning city again, the European Union installed Hans Koschnick, the tough old ex-Oberbürgermeister of Bremen, as administrator, with a posse of policemen collected from several European countries. But the series of agreements he arduously negotiated, aimed at getting the Croats 'to stop stopping people', were repudiated almost as soon as they were initialled. If the new post-Dayton agreement is still working this month that will be a small miracle, and as good an augury for the Federation's future as anyone can hope for at present.

At least now there are no bodies in the rivers, no more mass graves being dug. For the long uneasy moment, there is peace. 'Cruel but realistic', as Muhamed Sacirbey described it; 'the only possible peace', in the words of his rather more satisfied Croatian opposite number, Mate Granic. Is what has been done a betrayal of Bosnia, as Denis Healey among others has suggested? At Tuzla, Timothy Garton Ash put it to Peter Galbraith, the US ambassador to Zagreb whom unkind persons call 'the tenth member of the Croatian cabinet', that what was in the making in the impending dealings was 'a Yalta for Bosnia'. But it will only be that if 'the international community' – which is to say NATO, which is to say the USA – lacks the will to do what the actual international community failed to do through its common international institution, the United Nations: that is, whatever may be necessary to stop Croatia and Serbia taking Bosnia apart. (All the Balkan leaders, incidentally, and particularly Radovan Karadzic, address 'the international community' ad hominem, as if it were a surly bank manager, or a dodgy landlord who can't be trusted to keep the property in repair; or in the case of Franjo Tudjman, an indulgent rich uncle of whom he still has great expectations.)

If . . . The road ahead, as far as one can see through the snows of a Bosnian winter, is littered with 'ifs'. If implementation proceeds as quickly and firmly as President Izetbegovic insists it must, if it includes enough aid for reconstruction to make people think about the future rather than the past, if the US stays the course, and if no actual or metaphorical landmines blow the peace sky-high, then Bosnia may even manage something a little better than replacing unbearable misery with ordinary, everyday unhappiness, the therapist's traditional goal. But it will be some time yet before we can believe we have really got much further than the moment anticipated in the poem Laura Silber and Allan Little used as envoi to The Death of Yugoslavia:

On that day we'll say to Hell: 'Have you had enough?'
And Hell will answer: 'Is there more?'

January/February 1996

SALMAN RUSHDIE

No room for books

Salman Rushdie sent this message of warning and hope – 'It is perhaps the low-tech nature of the act of writing that will save it' – to *Index*'s supplement on publishing and 'the new censorship' in the spring of 1996.

For those of us who cannot imagine a future without books, it is disturbing to note how many present-day visions have no room for books at all. The view from Bill Gates to *Blade Runner* is distinctly post-literate. For those of us who write books, it sometimes seems that it's open season on writers around the world nowadays, a horrifying state of affairs which this indispensable magazine does so much to record and to protest against. And for those of us who are as concerned about the right to read what we choose as the right to write what we choose, it is alarming that the business of demanding bans on whatever ideas get up people's noses is getting to be respectable. It's getting to be *cool*.

Futurology can be defined as the science of being wrong about the future, and novelists are no better at this kind of speculation than anyone else. Bad news being more glamorous than good, dystopic predictions are far easier to come up with than optimistic ones, and have more apparent credibility. Trapped between indifference and persecution, looking increasingly anachronistic beside the new information technology, what chance of survival does literature have? It's easy to shrug despairingly and start preparing the obituaries.

And yet, I find myself wanting to take issue with this facile despair. It is perhaps the low-tech nature of the act of writing that will save it. Means of artistic expression that require large quantities of finance and sophisticated technology – films, plays, records – become, by virtue of that dependence, easy to censor and to control. But what one writer

299

can make in the solitude of one room is something no power can easily destroy.

March/April 1996

JUAN GOYTISOLO

Urbicides, massacres, common graves

Juan Goytisolo, the widely translated Spanish-Catalan novelist and critic, emigrated to France in 1957 as a political exile, and later held visiting professorships at various American universities. He was a reporter in Cuba in 1965, and wrote these reflections on the long, grim history of Russian-Chechen wars following a journey through devastated Chechnya in June 1996.

On 11 December 1994, the Russian army invaded the Republic of Chechnya 'in order to restore constitutional order' and eliminate a regime of 'bandits and criminals'. According to the ex-minister of defence, Pavel Grachov, the operation was to last a few hours: a simple victory parade. Seventeen months later, the 'parade' has brought some 40,000 civilian victims, including numerous Russians installed in Grozny; the losses of the army of occupation stand at around 13,000 dead and posted missing; and the devastation of the capital, smaller settlements and hamlets can only be compared, in dimension and intensity, to that caused in some Russian and German cities during World War II. In little more than a year and a half of conquest, the army has suffered greater losses than in the 12 years of its disastrous adventure in Afghanistan.

As in Afghanistan, the new Kremlin leaders first tried to cover up the operation as the work of a group of 'patriots' resolved to rid themselves of Dudayev's tyranny and corruption. In November 1994, the tanks entered Grozny for the first time under cloak of 'fraternal help' to honest Chechens, but the incursion ended catastrophically. The armoured cars were destroyed by grenade-throwers and, in spite of official disclaimers from Moscow, attributing the outburst to mysterious mercenaries, the Russian military leaders had to swallow the bitter pill of taking charge of the prisoners generously handed back by Dudayev.

Neither the painful reminder of the defeat in Afghanistan which contributed so much to the fall of the Soviet regime nor the successive wars
against the Chechens from the time of Imam Mansur helped Yeltsin or
Pavel Grachov foresee the likelihood their troops would gradually be
bogged down in a quagmire, sucked into mess they would escape with
difficulty. Hence the pathetic efforts of state television and press to
conceal the wretched truth, to cover up the barbarism, clumsiness and
disorganization of military operations, transmuting disasters into heroic
actions, rehearsing the ritual litany of the 'imminent liquidation of the
last bandit hide-outs'. Despite so much fabrication and self-deception
– a legacy of the defunct regime of the USSR – Shamil Basayev's
incursions in Budennovsk and Raduyev's in Kiliar, with the victorious
return of both to Chechnya in the face of intense army fire that inflicted
more losses in their own ranks than in the enemy's, opened the eyes
of a sector of public opinion and upped the number of citizens opposed
to the war. Few, very few reinforcements of undernourished, badly
paid officers or petty-officers now want to risk their lives and meet a
glorious end on the field of honour. Chechnya, clearly, isn't worth the
candle.

The proclamation of the independence of this autonomous republic of
13,000 square metres on 27 October 1991 by the general of the Soviet
Airforce, Dzhokhar Dudayev, is reminiscent in many ways of that made
by the *naqshbandiya* Nadjmuddin from Gotso in August 1917, then led
militarily by Sheik Uzun Hadji: in both cases their authors took advantage of the opportunities opened up by the collapse of Tsarism and the
foreseeable break-up of the USSR. A significant precursor of Dudayev,
Kaitmas Alichanov, a colonel of Chechen stock in Nicholas II's army,
participated actively in the struggle for independence, first against the
Cossacks and White Russians of Denikin and then against the Bolsheviks.
The war was exceptionally savage and the *murids*, led by Mohammed
of Balkani, whose tomb or *mazar* in Daghestan is the object of pilgrimages
in less harsh times than ours, annihilated a whole brigade of the Red
Army in the valley of Arkhan, very close to the place where on 15
April this year a convoy of the 245th Motorized Infantry Regiment
was wiped out and its complement of tanks burnt. The war ended,
provisionally, in 1925 with the capture of Imam Nadjmuddin and his

lieutenants in their mountain fastnesses in the Caucasus. Both today and in the era of Imam Shamil, the villages of Vedeno and Bamut surrendered after a merciless, bitterly fought siege.

But unlike Imam Shamil and the religious leaders of the Emirate in the Northern Caucasus, Dudayev did not succeed in winning over to his leadership a clear-cut, determined majority of Chechens. His patrimonial concept of the state, the fragmentation of clans and his passivity – some say complicity – in relation to the local Mafia aroused discord and set it at odds with various sectors of the independence movement. During the three years of his presidency, Chechnya was thrown into turmoil: accounts were settled and corruption flourished. As Osman Imaiev, the Republic's former public prosecutor and member of the delegation which discussed with the Russians the ceasefire of 30 July 1995, admitted to me, a number of files passed through his hands of those 'disappeared' in confrontations between rival clans. The laying of the oil pipeline from the Caspian to the Black Sea through Chechen territory equally aroused the greed and latent war of conflicting interests. But what Dudayev failed to achieve via personal manoeuvring and weakness, the Russians created in a few days by their brutal intervention in December and devastation of the capital: almost total Chechen unity in defence of their independence.

It is not at all exaggerated to speak of Leningrad or Dresden, and those black and white images of desolation etched in the memory for ever. The centre of Grozny was literally flattened by the joint action of heavy artillery and tank-fire, missiles and bombs launched from aeroplanes and helicopters. The Presidential Palace from whose cellars Dudayev resisted, Parliament, the Institute of Pedagogical Sciences, National Bank of the Republic, Higher Institute for Oil Studies, Abdelrrahman Avturkhanov Museum, Lermontov Theatre, Fine Arts Museum, Caucasus Hotel etc all vanished from the face of the earth. To conceal the magnitude of the urbicide, mountains of debris were heaped up and thrown on rubbish tips and pits around Grozny. The infill work proceeds and the authors of the 'feat' have cast a veil of metal fences around the affected area to ward off prying eyes. Through cracks and holes one can glimpse even today the incessant activity of bulldozers and crushers. Only a handful of wild shrubs and small trees survive the devastation. On the horizon, two plumes of black smoke atop the blazing oil wells on the outskirts: their burning still darkens the gloomy atmosphere and, now and then, the voracious, blazing flames reach up as a living symbol of the hell which descended on the city like a bird of prey.

In neighbouring areas, the spectacle is, if possible, more desolate: hollowed-out buildings, blackened eye-sockets, toothless mouths; wrinkled, half-melted houses, facades pitted by smallpox; derisory traffic signals; ghostly cranes suspended in the void. A pink block of flats, once occupied by the local nomenclatura, shows off slightly twisted Doric, Ionic and Corinthian columns, balconies with singed balustrades, small opera-boxish balconies mushy as meringues. My companion tells me a Russian family survives, crouched in one of the back cellars. We go to have a look: a half-crippled man with disturbed mother and 19-year-old daughter live in a dingy room exposed to the elements: no work, no wages, no help. They subsist like many old and infirm Russians on Chechen charity. Whilst the Caucasians keep alive the bonds of family and clan solidarity, the Russians suffer a more tragic destiny, abandoned by the indifference of their compatriots responsible for their plight. The old women begging in the area of the market show that the invaders' destructive fury didn't even spare their compatriots.

In a park by the fenced-off area, among trees and rose borders, I discover the incongruous statue of a bear on a bicycle in what two years ago must have been a children's park. The small monument had had better luck than the one erected to Lenin a hundred metres further on, which only preserves its pedestal. (Days later, in an abandoned plot by the battered railway station, I found the leader of the Soviets' enormous statue, hidden under thick undergrowth. Vladimir Illich Ulyanov seemed to be preaching fiercely and energetically at the leafy vegetation on behalf of new, equally implacable ecological revolution.)

The rest of the city offers the same scenario of rage and decrepitude: ruined buildings, burnt-out tanks, skeleton roofs, hanging beams, entire districts abandoned by their inhabitants. Sometimes, in the remnant of a building, a sign warns off possible marauders: 'People living here', or even more laconically, 'People alive'. The new city centre, with the pro-Russian presidency building and army barracks, is a veritable entrenched battleground: fortified posts, tanks at every corner, nests of machine-guns on the roofs of main buildings, endless soldiers and policemen on a war footing. All the places I have visited – the press centre, the offices where I obtained first my Russian press credentials and, second, those from Zavgaiev's puppet administration – are protected by sandbags and guards with machine-guns. Despite such an imposing array of firepower, the capital conquered in two months of blood and fire fell in a few hours on 6 March to several hundred independence fighters armed with grenade-throwers. As the success of their lightning incursion demonstrates, the much heralded Russian pacification is quite illusory. As I saw for myself days later, night belongs to the Chechens and the innumerable control posts and military bases set up in the theoretically pacified zone are frequently transformed into besieged islets, exposed to sudden thrusts from an invisible enemy force.

To the indeterminate number of civilian deaths caused by the war – Russian and Chechen commentators and experts estimate a figure of 40,000 – must be added the number of people who disappear in regular round-ups and are sent to the sinister filter points. Together with Ricardo Ortega, Antena 3's Moscow correspondent, I interviewed the Red Cross president in Grozny, Hussein Khamidov. This civil aviation pilot's life abruptly changed direction the day he found the corpses of two of his children in a common grave, a few weeks after they 'vanished' at the end of January 1995. Since then, Khamidov, elegantly dressed in grey suit and tie, has devoted himself entirely to the task of uncovering the slaughter-houses and ossuaries scattered throughout Chechen territory and to photographing the victims. Seated in his tiny office, he shows us sheaves of cards with carefully appended photographs. Each dead person appears marked with a number to the provisional figure of 1313. Four hundred and twenty-six have been identified and numerous people come to his office to search out and identify their relatives. As we talk, a man appears who has 11 disappeared in his family: he comes daily, hopeful new 'finds' will allow him to bury one of them.

Identification is difficult: in many cases, they are skulls scalped or incinerated by flame-throwers, corpses stacked in munitions boxes in foetal position. Almost all bear signs of torture and summary execution:

shot at close range in eyes, forehead, neck, hands tied by rope or wire. In a pitiless succession of horror prints, I gaze at victims with empty eye-sockets, hollow nasal orifices, skulls set in a cast howling, gasping from asphyxiation, protesting indignation, signs of shock, unspeakable pain, sometimes surprised innocence, rarely serenity. Despite the insistence of the Red Cross, the Russian military authorities have opened no investigation of the wells and ditches replete with corpses. No court will judge the architects of such slaughter.

While we were at the Red Cross, a Chechen cameraman showed us a video of images of the bombing of Kadir Yurt on 28 March: 12 children were killed. The Russian High Command denied the attack occurred and blamed the disinformation on a propagandistic manoeuvre by the 'bandits'.

Although the majority of the executions date back to March and April 1995, the round-ups and arbitrary arrests continue. At the filter point in the Staro-Promislovi district, dependent on the Russian Federation Ministry of the Interior in Chechnya, hundreds of detainees were interned at the beginning of June and each barracks is provided with dungeons for interrogation and torture. A youth called Salman related before the camera his journey and stay in one of them. In the lorry which carried him packed with dozens of suspects, the Russian soldiers killed eight of his companions who had protested against the conditions of their transportation and they then drank vodka sitting on the corpses. The Military Command issued a communiqué to the effect that the murdered were victims of bullets from independence guerrilla fighters.

The second protocol of the agreements signed on 10 June in Nazran stipulates the creation of a commission comprising six Russians and six Chechens to search out and identify those who have disappeared or been arrested in the 17 months of war. Another clause indicates the definitive closure of the filter points. But after so many broken promises and unkept pacts, the Chechens awaited the results of the Russian elections without forging too many illusions as to Zyuganov and Yeltsin's real intentions. Everything may continue as before and the desire for revenge on the part of military commanders like Vladimir Shamanov and Viachesvav Tikomirov, humiliated by the failure of their brutal pacification and the disorganization and low morale of their troops, inevitably augurs nothing different. 'The war,' one of the leaders of the independence struggle later interviewed by me said without boasting, 'has lasted for two centuries. Who knows whether it will last another 40 or 50 years?'

Translated by Peter Bush

September/October 1996

VICTOR PELEVIN

Astrakhan on the Kremlin towers

Victor Pelevin is one of the darkest comedians among Russia's new writers. This story provides a characteristically ironic view of Russian society and politics, and in particular of the effects of the intervention in Chechnya, in the run-up to the 1996 presidential elections.

Since the age of Homer there has been an extraordinary persistence about his theme of one group of heroes defending a fortress while another is trying to storm it. Embarrassingly inappropriate examples can be found by opening any newspaper and reading, say, about 'the storming of the cosmos'. Let us not be thrown by the fact that what is being stormed in this instance is a void, but rather see it as further confirmation of the thesis of the philosopher Ilyin that Russian thought evolves inexorably to an instinctive Buddhism.

It is interesting, and indeed instructive, that the identity of the defenders seems never to be very clear, perhaps because the assaults seem never to succeed fully. Even more interesting is the fact that where an event in real life fits perfectly into Homer's framework, our consciousness will refuse categorically to acknowledge any resemblance. The defenders themselves are rarely even aware that they have defended a fortress, as our story will demonstrate.

For some reason, that memorable August day when the Kremlin was stormed by the Chechen leader Shamil Basayev, news of its fall proved strangely reluctant to cross the boundary of Moscow's inner ring road. Perhaps talk of its 'fall' seemed incongruous when the operation had been accomplished without bloodshed (if we overlook the wasting of the traffic policeman perched in a glass tumbler at the entrance to the Kremlin. Even there, as was later established, he was shot only because the female Ukrainian sniper in one of the leading vehicles overreacted to the suspiciously large black telephone into which he was talking.)

The lightning success of the operation was doubtless due primarily to meticulous planning, and to lessons having been learnt from the Budennovsk raid.

This time there were no trucks and no camouflage. Two hundred men of Basayev's assault and sabotage battalion travelled up to Moscow in 40 Mercedes 600s requisitioned from inhabitants of the mountainous regions of Chechnya. The successful outcome was due in part to the fact that most of the vehicles were equipped, in accordance with the mountain-dwellers' etiquette, with emergency vehicle flashing lights. Each of the battalion's fighters was clean shaven and wore a cheerful maroon blazer (hastily fashioned from sacks dyed with beetroot juice), and around their necks a heavy gold(-painted toilet) chain. These, as the subsequent commission of enquiry was to establish, had been put through as a rush order by one of the Grozny funeral parlours.

In accordance with the initial operational plan all the Kremlin's entrances and exits were immediately barricaded. Weapons stockpiled in advance were retrieved from the cellars of the Palace of Congresses, the fighters changed back into their traditional combat jackets, and the telescopic sights of Basayev's snipers were soon glinting from the Kremlin battlements. The assault had been a complete success, except that not a single member of the government, or even a civil servant of any distinction, had been seized. In all, Basayev's men had taken some 20 hostages, mostly employees of the casino in the Palace of Congresses, along with a few fitters engaged in maintenance work despite its being a Sunday. Basayev was not in the least put out by this modest haul.

'They come by themselves tomorrow, trust me,' he said to his distraught Pakistani adviser. 'So many we can't keep them all in prison.'

The terrorist leader's intuition did not fail him, but of this more anon. Immediately after occupying the Kremlin and organizing defensive positions on the three main axes along which counter-attacks were to be expected, Shamil Basayev proceeded to implement the second part of his plan. This related directly to a phenomenon which might at first sight seem remote from terrorism, namely the steep rise in the price of Astrakhan fleeces on the Moscow fur exchange. Picking up the telephone, Basayev dialled a number which he knew by heart, uttered a single codeword, and rang off.

Nowadays we all know that behind bloodshed there is always somebody's money. Shamil Basayev's activities were no exception. It has now been established beyond doubt that Basayev's principal sponsor and ally in Moscow was the chairman of the Aenea Bank, Kim Polkanov. He it was who a good two months before the events described had engaged in intensive speculative buying of Astrakhan fleeces which, in consequence, almost trebled in price.

The Aenea Bank took its name from Polkanov's method of accumulating his start-up capital. He would hang a sign bearing the legend 'Bureau de Change' at the entrance to a dark alleyway and when a customer appeared asking where the bank was he would reply 'In 'ere' and strike him a sharp blow with a hammer kept for the purpose.

Immediately after the phone call two covered trucks drove out from Polkanov's dacha and headed for the Kremlin, which they entered unhindered. The gates were at once closed behind them, and a few hours later the red stars on the towers of the Kremlin disappeared beneath gigantic Astrakhan fur hats.

Basayev's men who carried out this operation had undergone a lengthy period of training in the mountains of Chechnya. Ordering the sentries to redouble their vigilance, Basayev said *namaz* and awaited the appearance of mediators.

His wait was a lengthy one. As we have already noted, for a considerable time rumours that the Kremlin had been seized circulated only within the confines of the inner ring road, spread in the main by taxi-drivers who refused to carry passengers through the city centre, or demanded improbably high fares to do so. The Federal Security Service (FSS) first heard of the terrorists' success from one of their employees who had tried to take a taxi to work. They didn't take it seriously at first, but decided to check it out with the Moscow office of CNN, who advised that nothing had been synchronized with them, from which the FSS concluded that the whole thing was a hoax.

The situation was further complicated by the fact that all the top FSS brass were away accompanying the president, who was inflicting an official visit on Greenland, which left nobody at home with authority to take rapid decisions. No credence should be given to assertions that the president's bodyguards had been tipped off and simply carted their meal ticket as far as possible out of harm's way. This is manifestly scabrous pre-election rumour-mongering. Neither do we consider it necessary to refute the allegation that the remote location chosen for the presidential visit had anything to do with the terrorists' having picked up an atomic warhead on the cheap during their progress through the Ukraine.

When, however, the authorities were finally persuaded that Basayev had indeed seized the Kremlin, the analysts of the FSS were instructed to propose appropriate counter-measures. As a first priority it was deemed essential to give the inhabitants of the capital an explanation for the appearance of the enormous Astrakhan fur hats on the towers of the Kremlin (although, if we are to be entirely honest, very few people had actually noticed them). To this end disinformation was spread through the city and over a number of subordinate television channels to the effect that a concert would be taking place in Red Square at which Makhmud Esembayev would be accompanied by a group of Sufi musicians who were flying in from Pakistan. It was even claimed that the event was being sponsored by Peter Gabriel, and that Nushrat Fatekh Ali-Khan would be singing with Esembayev. Immediately after this announcement a huge quantity of undated tickets were printed and sold in Moscow by persons unknown.

The Kremlin was cordoned off and closed to visitors, but this evoked no surprise. The Russian people continued, as it had since Pushkin penned the last scene of *Boris Godunov*, to keep its counsel. Negotiations were conducted with Basayev over police frequencies. He had settled into the bunker under the Palace of Congresses and his demands which, according to confidential information, related to the granting of vast loans to revive farming in Chechnya, had already virtually been conceded. It might have been possible to conceal the seizure of the Kremlin entirely had not a number of Basayev's men started trading grenade launchers and ammunition in Alexander Park right next to the Kremlin walls. When rival arms traders from a certain location on Kotelnicheskaya Embankment heard of this and sent round their heavies to sort them out, Basayev's men simply locked themselves in the Kremlin. The incident came to the attention of journalists, and ended all further possibility of concealing the occupation.

The FSS now decided to resort to force, but the Alpha special forces group's reaction to the suggestion that they should storm the Kremlin while taking care not to cause any damage was extremely rude, and it

VICTOR PELEVIN

was decided instead to pressure the terrorists indirectly by cutting off
their water, light, and sanitation. However, after several grenades were
launched from behind the walls and a caustic remark was made in a
newspaper controlled by Polkanov's bank that only the present Russian
government was capable of treating unknown bandits the same way as
it treated legitimately elected members of parliament, mains water and
sanitation were restored.

Press reaction was varied, but some of the more intellectual newspapers remarked coyly on a certain resemblance of the Astrakhan caps
to condoms and wrote about the inevitability in the post-imperial era
of a demasculinisation of the Kremlin, an Oedipus complex among the
newly independent former Soviet republics with regard to their former
mother country, and much else besides. Indeed, the level of insight in
such articles was of such a high order that one could scarcely imagine
how an event like the seizing of the Kremlin was possible in a country
inhabited by such clever people. The ultra-patriotic press achieved a
rare degree of unanimity. Since, they contended, it is indisputable that
the Kremlin is controlled by Jews, and since Basayev has occupied the
Kremlin and consequently controls it, no further doubt can remain as
to his racial origins. Basayev was simply a run-of-the-mill agent of
international Zionism and was acting on the orders of its world government. A number of intriguing facts about his biography were made
public, including a dozen or so variants of his real surname, which
ranged from Basaiman to Gorgonzoller. Some sources claim that the
latter surname was not unrelated to an inferior pizza served to the
patriotic journalist concerned in the Chechen pizzeria on Gorky Street.
The ultra-right journalists were, however, all agreed that his real first
name was Schlemihl.

Meanwhile Basayev's prediction about volunteer hostages began to
be realized. The Borovitsky Gate was opened to admit them. In the first
two days the influx was so large that the terrorists guarding the entrance
had to arrange a small vetting station by the gate, allowing into the
Kremlin only television reporters and celebrities of one kind or another:
society gurus, variety artistes, members of parliament, television presen-
ters, and anyone else who might add to the publicity value of Basayev's
performance.

The opening of the Borovitsky Gate for the admission of hostages and television crews was, however, the moment when the first crack, as yet invisible, opened in the ground beneath Basayev's feet. This, to paraphrase the immortal words of Winston Churchill, was the beginning of the end.

It would be unfair to say that Basayev had committed an error which was to wreck the entire operation. It was later claimed in numerous interviews that he had been defeated by Operation Trojan Horse, but in fact at the moment when the mass inflow of hostages to the Kremlin began the FSS was in a state of total paralysis. Virtually the entire beau monde of the capital had presented itself. A demonstration on Manège Square by several dozen patriots waving banners reading 'Arrest the Gorgonzoller Gang' had to be dispersed because it was interfering with the televising of the arrival of more and more celebrity hostages. Many came with a variety of home comforts, sandwiches and thermos flasks, and regaled the ravenous fighters, so that the Kremlin events began to take on the aspect of an enormous family picnic.

But then, taking advantage of the attentive television lenses glinting from every corner, the hostages assembled in the Kremlin gradually proceeded to what it was they had actually come for.

It all started when the renowned vocalist Polyp Pigdick succeeded in becoming the centre of attention. Disporting himself in front of the cameras for some time in his saffron cloak and green turban, he suddenly pointed skywards in amazement and collapsed in what appeared to be a fainting fit. When those around him looked up they discovered that a trapeze had been suspended at a dizzying height between the towers on which his celebrated friend Stepanida Razina was flying back and forth illuminated by spotlights. A microphone materialized in Pigdick's hands and, with much expressive play of the eyebrows, he began to sing:

'Do not believe them when they say
The Kremlin path is one of ease!'

As he sang, he gazed in an agony of plaintive languor at the corpulent Stepanida cleaving the night sky high above and stretched out his hand to her, clearly giving those present to understand that he was singing for her alone.

This had the effect of a starting pistol on all those assembled. Almost immediately in another corner of the Kremlin dazzling arc lights came on and a twisted figure with a red beard and close-set beady eyes who had been one of the first to volunteer himself as a hostage began filming an advertising video for Adidas trainers, with the participation of a number of Chechens hired for very large fees. The concept was unsophisticated: gunfire in the night, tracer bullets, a glimpse of masked faces, soft cat-like leaping in the dark. Somebody stumbles and does not rise, and the last shot shows feet in Adidas trainers, lit by a flare, the bearded face of a vanquished foe and the smoking barrel of a semi-automatic rifle. There followed a niftily edited sequence: three rifle muzzles bound with insulating tape, the three stripes on the trainers, three flares in the sky. This was the first video to use the new slogan, specially devised for the countries of the CIS: 'Adidas. The bitter joy of victory!' (later superseded by: 'Adidas. Three on the side and you're dead.')

At the same time another film crew were rolling the first trials for a change of image for the smoker of Winston high tar cigarettes to determine whether the whiskered outdoor hero should be replaced by a bearded figure in combat kit, and the ember from the campfire by a lit Molotov cocktail.

In short order Basayev found himself and his thugs sidelined, and when he tried to put a stop to what he called debauchery and immortality, giving orders that all filming was to stop and that the hostages and television crews were to be locked up in the Kremlin Palace of Congresses, he was unexpectedly detached from the handful of fighters not yet employed by film crews and politely advised that he wasn't in Budennovsk now and he'd better cool it if he didn't want to find himself wearing concrete boots at the bottom of the Moscow River.

Shocked by such unprecedented disrespect, Basayev turned to his Pakistani advisers, who contacted their Moscow residency using the secure Kremlin telephone system. Basayev was horrified to discover that advertising slots between reports from the Kremlin were running at a full US$250,000 a minute. An hour-long news programme titled *Astrakhan on the Kremlin Towers* was scheduled for broadcast every evening, and had been written into the Ostankino broadcasting schedules for a month ahead. Thirty minutes of the hour were allocated to advertising.

Basayev soon recognized that while his assault and sabotage battalion might successfully resist a couple of armoured tank divisions of the Russian army, it was certainly no match for that kind of money. The moral fibre of his fighters was being undermined at a phenomenal rate. Many had succumbed, and begun drinking and consorting with women, a great many of whom were now gathered in the Kremlin in anticipation of the 'Legs and Smoke' beauty contest. When Basayev tried to find out how all these people had got in, he discovered that control of admissions through the Borovitsky Gate had gradually and in a wholly opaque manner passed from his deputy for religious matters, Khodzhi Akhundov, to an Armenian called Eddie Simonyan, and that quite apart from group bookings like the beauty contest, anybody with US$5,000 to spare was free to enter.

Working out that the admission price for an assault on the Kremlin would be well beyond the means of the Russian army, Basayev was somewhat reassured. The following morning, however, he was approached by a major television producer who glanced anxiously at the two grenade launchers Shamil, who happened to be in a bad mood that day, had hung about his person, and said,

'Mr er – em Basayev, forgive my troubling you, I know you are a busy man, but you will understand, we have put big, very big money in here, and there are some very odd characters sloping around. Could you tighten up admissions procedures, do you think? We have the élite of Russian culture here. Imagine what might happen if a group of terrorists were to get in . . .'

This was the moment when Shamil was forced to recognize that the situation was out of control. It was not only the nightly programme *Astrakhan on the Kremlin Towers*. Advertising rates for all news programmes had doubled. He decided to withdraw in total secrecy. He therefore contacted the FSS and demanded two trucks and five million dollars, calculating that this should be sufficient to bribe the traffic police all the way back to the northern Caucasus.

The forces loyal to Basayev were by now down to eight or nine diehards. One night he and his remaining fighters piled into two Mercedes and, under the pretext of inspecting his guards, slipped out of the Kremlin. The terrorists' last victim was that well-known avant-gardiste Shura Brenny who, in the presence of a large crowd, was masturbating with the aid of a grenade launcher directly in the path of the fighters. The female Ukrainian sniper who shot him had over-reacted to the suspiciously large black telephone on which Shura was about to ejaculate in the cause of art. If this minor incident is ignored, the evacuation took place without incident. Basayev was silent the whole way, but when his vehicle stopped at the ring road where he and his people were to transfer to the trucks he turned, as the few people present later recalled, to face Moscow, raised his fist to the firmament (which was turning pink in the first rays of dawn), shook it and shouted:

'Woe to thee, Babylon, that great city!'

They say tears started to his eyes. Need we add that in Basayev's last words, which very soon became public knowledge, the patriotic press found final, incontrovertible proof of his Jewish origins.

If at the end of our brief narrative we return to where we began, namely the mythical storming of a fortress, then the position of those doing the storming seems straightforward enough. What is less clear is who was defending it. Are we really to say that Moscow was saved by Polyp Pigdick? And yet, to the unbiased eye, that would seem to have been the case. The events taking place in Russia seem explicable only in terms of Lobachevskian logic, and their meaning, if there is one, only discoverable from a great distance in time.

Or to put it another way: Russia's history is a kind of fourth dimension of its chronology, and only when you look out from this fourth dimension do all the inexplicably monstrous shifts and zigzags and shudders of her day-to-day existence merge into a clear, distinct line, straight as an arrow.

Translated by Arch Tait

September/October 1996

PIETER-DIRK UYS

The truth, the whole truth and nothing but . . .

Pieter-Dirk Uys, playwright, producer and performer, has contributed several satirical accounts of life in South Africa under apartheid, including this comment on the setting up of the Truth and Reconciliation Commission.

Fifty years after the Nuremberg Trials, South Africans stand on the eve of their Truth and Reconciliation Commission. The search for the truth about the past. The demand for the guilty to step forward. To be forgiven? To be punished? A former apartheid minister takes the stand. He peers at the watching Commissioners.

'Comrades,' he says, his moustache twitching. 'I have a clear conscience. I have never used it!'

On the other side of the political spectrum, the former terrorists and tired ANC rebels who now rest in the armchairs of power seek the truth with all their might. Just to hide it deeper?

A Truth and Reconciliation Commission sounds as silly as John Cleese's Ministry for Funny Walks! Of course it's not; it's probably the only way that some of our people will find out what happened to them and their loved ones during a time of great darkness and fear. So there's nothing funny about having a Truth Commission.

Happily we have a man with a great sense of humour leading it. And knowing that Archbishop Desmond Tutu is the only person in the land who can sit in a glass house and throw stones, one also hopes that if he thinks the dirty washing of the past will damage our fragile reconciliation, he'll pull the plug and let it all gurgle away down the drain.

What is funny about a Truth Commission are the people now accused of crimes against humanity, who are all determined to be seen telling the truth their way! They're queuing up to get into the stand, where they can passionately admit to pulling triggers, hiding bombs, cutting up bodies. But only because someone else told them to.

'We were only obeying orders!' they will mutter, sounding like a Mel Brooks comedy. There are just too many clever people around, those jackbooted survivors of the shadowlands of apartheid, who now toyi-toyi with clenched fists in the air. They all have blood up to their elbows, but keep referring to it as 'long red gloves'. And we believe them for the sake of peace.

Of course they'll not be packed off in disgrace with the facts of their folly branded across their faces. They'll get away with murder, like so many of their bloody brothers have done all over the world. It's the poor clerk who pushed a pen for 46 years, doing his dreary job without question, who'll get the finger.

'You are responsible!' the Commission will thunder. That's us, the people. The 'you'. And they're probably right. And yet, how can we whites be guilty of anything, if we were all anti-apartheid? I haven't met anyone in South Africa lately who had anything to do with those years of oppression. The white policeman says he fought the System secretly. The black teacher insists he subverted the bad policies with a smile. The Indian doctor swears he sewed up broken terrorists with love. The mixed-race, coloured journalist admits to quoting banned words with guts. The parents all told their children the truth.

Of course they did. After all, we were all in the Struggle! So how can a Truth Commission find any truth, when we have no-one who admits to the lies? How can we find guilt when all the evidence has been destroyed? Files have been shredded, names have been changed. A past has been forgotten. A nation stares into the future, lobotomized by soccer fever and embracing amnesia like a child a fluffy toy.

There will be much anger and many tears during the sessions of the Truth Commission. Terrible realities will take the place of the frightful rumours. But I think there will also be much bitter laughter, as we see those who parade their designer innocence trip over their own nooses of deception. Every generation has its fools who will speak the truth as they see it. If we have 11 official languages, surely we can also find 11 million official truthsayers.

When we look back to those bad years when the lights of our civilization seemed to be out forever, one can see how Truth, as we think we know it today, passed through three stages. First it was ridiculed, and as a result the bearers of that truth were imprisoned, banned and killed. Then it was opposed as being the Lie, the subversion of goodness, the Satan! And now it is regarded as self-evident!

It is said the man who fears no truths has nothing to fear from lies. But then it also takes two to speak the truth. One to utter it and one to hear. A sinister minister of police during the 1980s said it all, as only they could: 'The public is entitled to know what is happening around it. But at the same time, it is equally entitled to the Truth.' We look forward to seeing this man on the stand, eyes filled with crocodile-tears as he repeats again and again: 'This is the pure and simple truth, Your Honour. I just didn't know what was going on!'

Same old story. Truth is rarely pure and never simple! And 50 years after the Nuremberg Trials, will we see history not just repeating itself, but taking tragedy and turning it into farce?

September/October 1996

MICHAEL IGNATIEFF

Articles of faith

Michael Ignatieff, writer, broadcaster and journalist, and author of *The Needs of Strangers*, *The Russian Album* and the novel *Asya*, has recently finished a biography of Isaiah Berlin. With this article he introduced *Index*'s examination of the broader issues involved in the setting up of truth commissions and war tribunals in the wake of the new South Africa and the end of the Yugoslav conflict.

What does it mean for a nation to come to terms with its past? Do nations, like individuals, have psyches? Can a nation's past make a people ill as we know repressed memories sometimes make individuals ill? Conversely, can a nation or contending parts of it be reconciled to their past, as individuals can, by replacing myth with fact and lies with truth? Can we speak of nations 'working through' a civil war or an atrocity as we speak of individuals working through a traumatic memory or event?

These are mysterious questions and they are not made any easier to answer by the ways our metaphors lead us on. We do vest our nations with consciences, identities and memories as if they were individuals. But if it is problematic to vest an individual with a single identity, it is even more so in the case of a nation.

These are mysterious questions, but they are urgent and practical ones too. The War Crimes Tribunal in The Hague is collecting evidence about atrocities in the former Yugoslavia. It is doing so not simply because such crimes against humanity must be punished – otherwise international humanitarian law means nothing – but also because establishing the truth about such crimes through the judicial process is held to be crucial to the eventual reconciliation of the people of the Balkans. In the African city of Arusha, a similar tribunal is collecting evidence about the genocide in Rwanda, believing likewise that truth, justice and reconciliation are indissolubly linked in the rebuilding of shattered societies. In both these instances – Yugoslavia and Rwanda – the rhetoric is noble but the rationale unclear. Justice in itself is not a problematic objective, but whether the attainment of justice always contributes to reconciliation is anything but evident. Truth, too, is a good thing; but as the African proverb reminds us, 'truth is not always good to say'.

In South Africa, Archbishop Tutu's Truth Commission is collecting testimony from the victims and perpetrators of apartheid. In Tutu's own words, the aim is 'the promotion of national unity and reconciliation' . . . 'the healing of a traumatized, divided, wounded, polarized people'. Laudable aims, but are they coherent? Look at the assumptions he makes: that a nation has one psyche, not many; that the truth is one, not many; that the truth is certain, not contestable; and that when it is known by all, it has the capacity to heal and reconcile. These are not so much assumptions of epistemology as articles of faith about human nature: the truth is one and if we know it, it will make us free.

Such articles of faith inspired the truth commissions in Chile, Argentina, Brazil that sought to find out what had happened to the thousands of innocent people killed or tortured by the military juntas during the 1960s and 1970s. All these commissions believed that if the truth were known, a people made sick by terror and lies would be made well again. In all cases, the results were ambiguous. First, as Pilate said when washing his hands, what is truth? One should distinguish between factual truth and moral truth, between narratives that tell what happened and narratives that attempt to explain why things happened and who is responsible. The truth commissions had more success in establishing the first than in promoting the second. They did succeed in establishing the facts about the disappearance, torture and death of thousands of persons and this allowed relatives and friends the consolation of knowing how the disappeared had met their fate. It says much for the human need for truth that the relatives of victims preferred the facts to the false consolations of ignorance. It also says a great deal for the moral appeal of magnanimity that so many of them should have preferred the truth to vengeance or even justice. It was sufficient for most of them to know what happened: they did not need to punish the transgressors in order to put the past behind them.

The truth commissions closed many individual dossiers in the painful histories of their nations' past. At this molecular, individual level, they did a power of good. But they were also charged with the production of public truth and the re-making of public discourse. They were told to generate a moral narrative – explaining the genesis of evil regimes and apportioning moral responsibility for their deeds.

The military, security and police establishments were prepared to let the truth come out about individual cases of disappearance. But they fought tenaciously against prosecutions of their own people and against shouldering responsibility for their crimes. To have conceded responsibility would have weakened their legitimacy as institutions. Such was the resistance of the military in Argentina and Chile that the elected governments which had created the commissions had to choose between justice and their own survival: between prosecuting the criminals and risking a military coup, or letting them go and allowing a democratic succession to consolidate itself.

The record of the truth commissions in Latin America has disillusioned many of those who believed that shared truth was a precondition of social reconciliation. The military and police apparatus survived the inquisition with their legitimacy undermined but their power intact. The societies in question used the truth commissions to indulge in the illusion that they had put the past behind them. The truth commissions allowed exactly the kind of false reconciliation with the past they had been expressly created to forestall.

The German writer and thinker Theodor Adorno observed this false reconciliation at work in his native Germany after the war:

'"Coming to terms with the past" does not imply a serious working through of the past, the breaking of its spell through an act of clear consciousness. It suggests, rather, wishing to turn the page and, if possible, wiping it from memory. The attitude that it would be proper for everything to be forgiven and forgotten by those who were wronged is expressed by the party that committed the injustice.'

The dangers of this false reconciliation are real enough but it is possible that disillusion with the truth commissions of Latin America goes too far. It was never in their mandate to transform the military and security apparatus any more than it is in Archbishop Tutu's power to do the same in South Africa. Truth is truth; it is not social nor institutional reform.

Nor is it realistic to expect that when truth is proclaimed by an official commission it is likely to be accepted by those against whom it is directed. The police and military have their truth – and its continuing hold consists precisely in the fact that it is not a tissue of lies. It is unreasonable to expect those who believed they were putting down a terrorist or insurgent threat to disown this idea simply because a truth commission exposes this threat as having been without foundation. People, especially people in uniform, do not easily or readily surrender the premises upon which their lives are based. Repentance, if it ever occurs, is an individual matter. It is too much to expect an institutional order to engage in collective repentance. All that a truth commission can achieve is to reduce the number of lies that can be circulated unchallenged in public discourse. In Argentina, its work has made it impossible to claim, for example, that the military did not throw half-dead victims into the sea from helicopters. In Chile, it is no longer permissible to assert in public that the Pinochet regime did not dispatch thousands of entirely innocent people. Truth commissions can and do change the frame of public discourse and public memory. But they cannot be judged a failure because they fail to change behaviour and institutions. That is not their function.

A truth commission cannot overcome a society's divisions. It can only winnow out the solid core of facts upon which society's arguments with itself should be conducted. But it cannot bring these arguments to a conclusion. Critics of truth commissions argue as if the past were a sacred text which has been stolen and vandalized by evil men and which can be recovered and returned to a well-lit glass case in some grand public rotunda like the US Constitution or the Bill of Rights. But the past has none of the fixed and stable identity of a document. The past is an argument, and the function of truth commissions, like the function of honest historians, is simply to purify the argument, to narrow the range of permissible lies.

Truth commissions have the greatest chance of success in societies that have already created a powerful political consensus behind reconciliation, such as in South Africa. In such a context, Tutu's commission has the chance to create a virtuous upward spiral between the disclosure of painful truth and the consolidation of the political consensus that created his commission in the first place.

*   *   *

In places like Yugoslavia where the parties have murdered and tortured each other for years, the prospects for truth, reconciliation and justice are much bleaker. These contexts, however bleak, are instructive because they illustrate everything that is problematic in the relation between truth and reconciliation.

The idea that reconciliation depends on shared truth presumes that shared truth about the past is possible. But truth is related to identity. What you believe to be true depends, in some measure, on who you believe yourself to be. And who you believe yourself to be is mostly defined in terms of who you are not. To be a Serb is first and foremost not to be a Croat or a Muslim. If a Serb is someone who believes Croats have a historical tendency towards fascism and a Croat is someone who believes Serbs have a penchant for genocide, then to discard these myths is to give up a defining element of their own identities.

Obviously, identity is composed of much more than negative images of the other. Many Croats and Serbs opposed these negative stereotypes and the nationalist madness that overtook their countries. There were many who fought to maintain a moral space between their personal and national identities. Yet even such people are now unable to conceive that one day Zagreb, Belgrade and Sarajevo might share a common version of the history of the conflict. Agreement on a shared chronology of events might be possible though even this would be contentious; but it is impossible to imagine the three sides ever agreeing on how to apportion responsibility and moral blame. The truth that matters to people is not factual nor narrative truth but moral or interpretive truth. And this will always be an object of dispute in the Balkans.

It is also an illusion to suppose that 'impartial' or 'objective' outsiders would ever succeed in getting their moral and interpretive account of the catastrophe accepted by the parties to the conflict. The very fact of being an outsider discredits rather than reinforces one's legitimacy. For there is always a truth which can only be known by those on the inside. Or if not a truth – since facts are facts – then a moral significance for these facts that only an insider can fully appreciate. The truth, if it is to be believed, must be authored by those who have suffered its consequences.

The problem of a shared truth is also that it does not lie 'in between'. It is not a compromise between two competing versions. Either the siege of Sarajevo was a deliberate attempt to terrorize and subvert a legitimately elected government of an internationally recognized state, or it was legitimate pre-emptive defence by the Serbs of their homeland from Muslim attack. It cannot be both. Outside attempts to write a version of the truth which does 'justice' to the truth held by both sides are unlikely to be credible to either.

Nor is an acknowledgement of shared suffering equivalent to shared truth. It is relatively easy for both sides to acknowledge each other's pain. Much more difficult, usually impossible in fact, is shared acknowledgement of who bears the lion's share of responsibility.

Atrocity myths about the other side are an important part of the identities in question. Hill-country Serbs in the Foca region of Bosnia told British journalists in the summer of 1992 that their ethnic militias were obliged to cleanse the area of Muslims because it was a well-known fact that Muslims crucified Serbian children and floated their bodies down the river past Serbian settlements. Since such myths do not need factual corroboration in order to reproduce themselves, they are not likely to be dispelled by the patient assembly of evidence to the contrary. This particular atrocity myth used to be spread about the Jews in mediaeval times. The myth was not true about the Jews and it is not true about Muslims, but that is not the point. The point is that myth is strangely impervious to facts.

Aggressors have their own defence against truth, but so do victims. Peoples who believe themselves to be victims of aggression have an understandable incapacity to believe that they also committed atrocities. Myths of innocence and victimhood are a powerful obstacle in the way of confronting unwelcome facts.

To call them myths is not to dispute that one side may be more of a victim than the other; nor to question that atrocities do happen. What is mythic is that the atrocities are held to reveal the essential identity of the peoples in whose name they were committed. The atrocity myth implies an idea of a people having some essential genocidal propensity toward the other side. All the members of the group are held to have such a propensity even though atrocity can only be committed by specific individuals. The idea of collective guilt depends on the idea of national psyche or racial identity. The fiction at work here is akin to

325

the nationalist delusion that the identities of individuals are or should be subsumed into their national identities.

But nations are not like individuals: they do not have a single identity, conscience or responsibility. National identity is a site of conflict and argument, not a silent shrine for collective worship. Even authoritarian populist democracies like Serbia and Croatia never speak with one voice or remember the past with a single memory.

The essential function of justice in the dialogue between truth and reconciliation is to disaggregate individual and nation; to disassemble the fiction that nations are responsible like individuals for the crimes committed in their name.

The most important function of war crimes trials is to 'individualize' guilt, to relocate it from the collectivity to the individuals responsible. As Karl Jaspers said of the Nuremberg trial in 1946, 'For us Germans this trial has the advantage that it distinguishes between the particular crimes of the leaders and that it does not condemn the Germans collectively.'

By analogy with Nuremberg, therefore, The Hague trials are not supposed to put the Serbian, Muslim or Croatian peoples in the dock but to separate the criminals from the nation and to lay the guilt where it belongs, on the shoulders of individuals. Yet trials inevitably fail to apportion all the guilt to all those responsible. Small fry pay the price for the crimes of the big fish and this reinforces the sense that justice is not definitive but arbitrary. Nor do such trials break the link between individual and nation. Nuremberg failed to do this: the rest of the world still holds the Germans responsible collectively and the Germans themselves still accept this responsibility. The most that can be said is that war crimes trials do something to unburden a people of the fiction of collective guilt, by helping them to transform guilt into shame. This appears to have happened in Germany. The German novelist Martin Walser once wrote that when a Frenchman or an American sees pictures of Auschwitz, 'he doesn't have to think: we human beings! He can think: those Germans! Can we think: those Nazis! I for one cannot . . .' This is to say that most West Germans accept the same version of the truth about their past; they take responsibility for it in the sense that they believe it was shameful; and to this degree, therefore, believe the past will not return.

Again, however, it is not clear that Nuremberg itself accomplished this transformation of German attitudes. As Ian Buruma has pointed out in *The Wages of Guilt*, many Germans dismissed the Nuremberg trials as nothing more than 'victor's justice'. It was not Nuremberg but the strictly German war crimes trials of the 1960s that forced Germans to confront their part in the Holocaust. Verdicts reached in a German courtroom benefited from a legitimacy the Nuremberg process never enjoyed.

Nor was coming to terms with the past confined to war crimes trials. It was an accumulation of a million school visits to concentration camps, a thousand books, the Hollywood television series *Holocaust* – a vast molecular reckoning between generations that is still going on.

The German example suggests that it is best to be modest about what war crimes trials can accomplish. The great virtue of legal proceedings is that its evidentiary rules confer legitimacy on otherwise contestable facts. In this sense, war crimes trials make it more difficult for societies to take refuge in denial: the trials do assist the process of uncovering the truth. It is more doubtful whether they assist the process of reconciliation. The purgative function of justice tends to operate on the victims' side only and not on the perpetrators. While it leaves victims feeling justice has been done, the community from which the perpetrators come may feel only that they have been made scapegoats. All one can say is that leaving war crimes unpunished is worse: it leaves the cycle of impunity unbroken and permits societies to indulge their fantasies of denial.

It is open to question whether justice or truth actually heals. While it is an article of faith with us that knowledge, particularly self-knowledge, is a condition of psychic health, all societies, including our own, manage to function with only the most precarious purchase on the truth of their own past. Individuals may be made ill by repression of their own past but it is less clear that what holds true for individuals must also hold true for societies. A society like Serbia, which allows well-established war criminals to hold public office and prevents them from being extradited to face international tribunals, may be a distasteful place to visit but it is not necessarily a sick society. For such societies will not see themselves as sick but as healthy, refusing the outside world's iniquitous attempt to turn their heroes into criminals. All societies have a substantial psychological investment in their heroes. To discover that their heroes were guilty of war crimes is to admit that the identities they defended were themselves tarnished. Which is why societies are often so reluctant to surrender their own to war crimes tribunals, why societies are so vehemently 'in denial' about facts evident to everyone outside the society. War crimes challenge collective moral identities, and when these identities are threatened, denial is actually a defence of everything one holds dear.

There are many forms of denial, ranging from outright refusal to accept facts as facts to complex strategies of relativization. Here one accepts the facts but argues that the enemy was equally culpable or that the accusing party is also to blame or that such 'excesses' are regrettable necessities in time of war. To relativize is to have it both ways: to admit the facts while denying full responsibility for them.

Resistance to historical truth is a function of group identity: nations and peoples tie their sense of themselves into narcissistic narratives which strenuously resist correction. Regimes also depend for their legitimacy on historical myths which are armoured against the truth. The legitimacy of Tito's regime in Yugoslavia depended on the myth that his partisans led a movement of national resistance against the German and Italian occupations. In reality, the partisans fought fellow Yugoslavs as much as they fought the occupiers and even made deals with the Germans if it could strengthen their hand against domestic opponents. Since this was common knowledge to any Yugoslav of that generation, the myth of brotherhood and unity required the constant reinforcement of propaganda. What is one to conclude, though, from this case? That regimes founded on historical myth are bound to crumble when the truth comes out? Or that the Titoist myth was a necessary fiction, the only lie that stood a chance of holding the separate ethnic traditions of Yugoslavia together in one state? How much truth could the immediate post-war Yugoslavia have stood before it fractured into civil war? The tragedy of Yugoslavia might not be that its ruling myth of brotherhood and unity was false to the history of the civil war in 1941-5, but that this myth was propagated by a Communist party – by one incapable of eventually ensuring a peaceful democratic transition. Democracy is a pre-condition for that free access to historical data and free debate about its meaning on which the creation of public truth depends. The

Balkan War of 1991-5 was a continuation of the civil war of 1941-5. Competing versions of historical truth – Serb, Croat and Muslim – which had no peaceful, democratic means of making themselves heard in Tito's Yugoslavia took to the battlefield to make their truth prevail. The result of five years of war is that a shared truth is now inconceivable. In the conditions of ethnic separation and authoritarian populism prevailing in all the major successor republics to Tito's Yugoslavia, a shared truth – and hence a path from truth to reconciliation – is barred, not just by hatreds but by institutions too undemocratic to allow countervailing truth to circulate. It is not undermining the war crimes tribunal process to maintain that the message of its truth is unlikely to penetrate the bell jars of the successor states of the former Yugoslavia. The point is merely that one must keep justice separate from reconciliation. Justice is justice, and within the strict limits of what is possible, it should be done. Justice will also serve the interests of truth. But the truth will not necessarily be believed and it is putting too much faith in truth to believe that it can heal.

When it comes to healing, one is faced with the most mysterious process of all. For what seems apparent in the former Yugoslavia, in Rwanda and in South Africa is that the past continues to torment because it is not past. These places are not living in a serial order of time, but in a simultaneous one, in which the past and present are a continuous, agglutinated mass of fantasies, distortions, myths and lies. Reporters in the Balkan wars often reported that when they were told atrocity stories they were occasionally uncertain whether these stories had occurred yesterday or in 1941 or 1841 or 1441. For the tellers of the tale, yesterday and today were the same. When Joyce had Stephen Daedalus say, in the opening pages of *Ulysses*, that the past was a nightmare from which the Irish people were struggling to awake, this is what he meant: as in nightmare, time past and time present were indistinguishable. This, it should be added, is the dream-time of vengeance. Crimes can never be safely fixed in the historical past; they remain locked in the eternal present, crying out for vengeance. Joyce saw that in the identities of both Irish Nationalism and Ulster Protestantism, the past was never safely past; its bodies were never safely buried; they were always roaming through the sleep of the living, calling out for retribution. What is mythic – and hence what is poisonous – about the past in societies torn apart by civil war or racial conflict is that it is not past at all.

This makes the process of coming to terms with the past, and of being reconciled to its painfulness, much more complicated than simply sifting fact from fiction, lies from truth. It means working it through the inner recesses of the psychic system so that a serial sense of time eventually replaces the nightmare of pure simultaneity. We know from victims of trauma that this mysterious inner work of the psyche is arduous. At first, the memory of the trauma in question – a car crash, the death of a child or a parent – returns so frequently to the mind that it literally drives the present out of the frame of consciousness. The victim lives in the past and suffers its pain over and over again. With time and reflection and talk, trauma leaves the order of the present and takes its place in the past. As it does so, the pain begins to diminish and what had become a nightmare, becomes only a memory. In this slow reinstatement of the order of serial time, the sufferer can be said to come awake and recover the momentum of living.

It is perilous to extrapolate from traumatized individuals to whole societies. It is simply an extravagant metaphor to think of societies coming awake from nightmare. The only coming awake that makes sense to speak of is one by one, individual by individual, in the recesses of their own identities. Nations, properly speaking, cannot be reconciled to other nations, only individuals to individuals. Nonetheless, individuals can be helped to heal and to reconcile by public rituals of atonement. When Chilean President Patricio Alwyn appeared on television to apologize to the victims of Pinochet's repression, he created the public climate in which a thousand acts of private repentance and apology became possible. He also symbolically cleansed the Chilean state of its association with these crimes. German Chancellor Willy Brandt's gesture of going down on his knees at a death camp had a similarly cathartic effect by officially associating the German state with the process of atonement. These acts compare strikingly with the behaviour of the political figures responsible for the war in the Balkans. If, instead of writing books niggling at the numbers exterminated at Jasenovac, President Franjo Tudjman of Croatia had gone to the site of the most notorious of the Croatian extermination camps and publicly apologized for the crimes committed by the Croatian *Ustashe* against Serbs, gypsies, Jews and partisans, he would have liberated the Croatian present from the hold of the *Ustashe* past. He would also have increased dramatically the chances of the Serbian minority accepting the legitimacy of an independent Croatian state. Had he lanced the boil of the past, the war of 1991 might not have occurred. He chose not to, of course, because he believed Serbs as guilty of crimes against the Croats. But sometimes, a gesture of atonement is effective precisely because it rises above the crimes done to your own side.

Societies and nations are not like individuals, but the individuals who have political authority within societies can have an enormous impact on the mysterious process by which individuals come to terms with the painfulness of their society's past.

The experience of the war in Yugoslavia makes it difficult to conceive of reconciliation, if it were ever possible, in terms of those clichés – 'forgiving and forgetting', 'turning the page', 'putting the past behind us' and so on. The intractable ferocity and scale of the war shows up the hollowness of these clichés for what they are. But reconciliation might eventually be founded on something starker: the democracy of the dead, the equality of all victims, the drastic nullity of all struggles that end in killing and the demonstrable futility of avenging the past in the present.

September/October 1996

JOHN GITTINGS

Cost of a miracle

John Gittings, the *Guardian's* chief foreign leader-writer, has travelled to China many times since his first visit in 1971. His latest book, *Real China: from Cannibalism to Karaoke,* based on his journeys in the little-visited central provinces, was published in 1996. In this article he set the scene for the file *Index* published on China and Hong Kong before the handover on 1 July 1997, showing that the repression of dissidents is as harsh as ever, while Deng Xiaoping's economic reforms have left a growing gap between rich and poor, town and country.

The long march of Chinese society has been under way since Mao Zedong died 20 years ago. It had already started, beneath the surface of the 'Cultural Revolution' (1966-76), while he was still alive. It is as stupendous an epic as the original Long March in the mid-1930s when Mao led the Communists across China to a new revolutionary base. To adapt Marx, it is a journey from the realm of necessity to the realm of freedom, but it still has a very long way to go.

The world outside China has paid only intermittent attention to this difficult and painful process which involves 1.1 billion people on a scale almost too huge to comprehend. Only the moments of drama attract headlines: those in China who struggle for reform and democracy do so mostly in silence, with far less encouragement than was given in the past to those making a similar effort in the Soviet Union and Eastern Europe. By joining the world market, Deng Xiaoping has earned a large measure of international immunity.

On 30 June this year the 'return to the motherland' of another six and a half million, in Hong Kong, should focus our attention more acutely. They are about to become part of the story which till now they have witnessed at close hand but apart. They do so from a unique position, already enjoying most of the freedoms which are much harder to secure across the border. They have the advantage that these benefits are still guaranteed to them under international treaty – but only if the outside world (and particularly Britain) chooses to monitor what happens to them and protest if it is needed.

China has made vast progress in the last two decades. In economic policy, the results have already been breathtaking. When weeping crowds filled Tiananmen Square two decades ago, no-one could have imagined that China would jettison within a few years the whole model of alternative development – from people's communes to national self-reliance – which underpinned Mao's 'socialist road'. China has joined the global market and offers an entirely different model of participation in the 'international division of labour'.

Yet the transformation of China's economic base has not been matched in the superstructure of Chinese politics. Those cracks which did emerge have been arrested – often in a literal sense. The first fissure was seen even before Mao's death, in April 1976, when thousands of Beijing residents gathered on Tiananmen Square in a huge wave of grief for the earlier death of Premier Zhou Enlai: a pretext to demonstrate against the ultra-left clique (the Gang of Four led by Mao's wife Jiang Qing) which had usurped power.

Their poems and manifestos, written in chalk – or blood – on the pavement, were washed out of sight by Beijing's entire fleet of water carts. A furious Communist Party leadership forced half of Beijing to parade through the streets with limp flags in denunciation. Three years later, in the street newspapers and posters of Beijing's Democracy Wall (1979-80) – briefly approved by the new leadership of Deng Xiaoping – this new movement for social justice and democracy, at first still socialist democracy, seemed to gather strength. Yet the decade and a half since then has seen an increasingly unequal struggle between the voices of reform and the instruments of repression.

This winter Wei Jingsheng, China's most-imprisoned dissident, settles to the second year of his second jail term of 14 years, in a prison camp on a north Chinese salt marsh, sharing an unheated cell with other hostile inmates. As a young Red Guard 30 years ago, Wei had been shaken by the poverty and oppression that he witnessed while roaming China to 'make revolution'. Once he saw a young woman begging for food by the railway track: she had no clothes so had

JOHN GITTINGS

daubed her body with mud and ashes. Such sights were the start of
real 're-education' for many young Chinese. Wei's uncompromising
call for democracy – on Democracy Wall – led to his first long prison
sentence in 1979.

Another veteran dissident, Wang Xizhe – who fled to the US in
October 1996 – has been active for even longer. Sent down to the
countryside by Chairman Mao, Wang and other idealistic youth worked
all day for one or two 'workpoints' – just enough to buy a tube of
toothpaste. Seeing rural poverty at first hand, they became sceptical of
the official doctrine that 'China's future lies with the peasants'. Wang
co-authored the first dissident manifesto 'On socialist democracy and
legality' in 1973. It argued that the Communist Party had been hijacked
by a 'privileged stratum' which maintained the old Chinese tradition
of feudal autocracy under a different name.

Many feudal habits have been discarded, but a regime which decrees
that political dissent should be treated as a counter-revolutionary threat
is still profoundly autocratic. This mismatch between the pace of economic and political reform in post-Mao China remains a fundamental
though largely hidden flaw in Chinese society. Any attempt to reach a
conclusion on this period, or to predict where China is heading, must
acknowledge both the magnitude of what has been achieved in changing
the face of China, and the extent to which many deeper features remain
largely unaltered.

The Gang of Four was arrested within a month of Mao's death:
everyone agreed that their 'ultra-left excesses' would have to be purged
from the system. But when I visited China again in 1978, only one
far-sighted Chinese scholar predicted that the Cultural Revolution – not
just the Gang – would be repudiated. Many people were shocked to learn
about the emergence of a system of elite schools for clever children, and
to discover that bonuses were being offered to factory managers and
workers.

China had struggled to survive for 25 years against a subtle combination of US and Soviet hostility – hence the strategic need for 'self-
reliance'. Though Richard Nixon opened the door in 1972, while Mao
was still alive, China was still remote and the outside world was
unknown. In the whole of the capital city, there was only one set of
automatic doors – at the entrance to the Beijing Hotel. Large crowds

334

gathered on the pavement to see them in operation. In 1978, foreign beverages — alcoholic and soft drinks — were served for the first time in this and other hotels (which were barred to Chinese). For a few glorious months, whisky was on sale in full glasses for the same price as Coca Cola. Beijing shut down early: it was impossible to buy a meal after seven in the evening.

Beijing today is unrecognizable to anyone who remembers the 1970s. There is a surplus of five-star hotels, three separate ring-roads, scores of high-rise office blocks, dozens of department stores selling more foreign than Chinese goods, hundreds of restaurants open till late with strings of fairy lights outside — and endless traffic jams. Out of sight in the suburbs, there are encampments of migrant workers on whose cheap labour the building boom depends.

Progress across China is more uneven, but even in the deep interior, every medium-sized town will have a pocket of Hong Kong-style shops and housing. Small towns, even villages, have their own karaoke bars. And from Beijing to the countryside, the lone traveller will receive advice which would have once been unthinkable: 'Don't go out alone late at night.' 'Watch out for highwaymen on the long-distance buses!'

Modernization has occurred in three great overlapping waves, with the impetus coming both from within and from outside China. First, in the early 1980s, Deng Xiaoping's reforms liberated a huge pent-up torrent of human and material resources. In the countryside, production soared as peasants were given responsibility for farming the land household by household instead of in groups or teams. But they also benefited from the vast capital investment (irrigation works, land enrichment and so on) which had been made during the collective years. In 1983 I visited former communes in central Anhui province whose population had scattered during the Great Leap Forward (1958-60) to beg for food. Each family proudly displayed their 'household contract' book with the state. They were buying their first bicycles and sewing machines. Rural markets, foolishly restricted in the Maoist years, quickly regained their traditional place as centres of craft and commerce.

The New Way of Deng Xiaoping still stressed the goal of socialism but Deng stressed that 'poverty is not socialism'. The battle with capitalism continued, he said, but its outcome would depend on which system could satisfy the needs of more people. At this stage, many Chinese still hoped to return to the collective path once higher living standards had been achieved. They shared the official verdict on the past: Mao had tried to build socialism too fast and had committed too many 'mistakes'.

The second great wave of modernization came from outside, with Deng's encouragement, and gathered pace in the second half of the 1980s. Deng insisted, against the objections of conservative critics, that 'the world today is an open world' and that China's 'closed-door policy' had led to a state of 'backwardness'. This was essentially correct. He also argued (like the modernizers in the late years of Imperial China) that western techniques could be imported without undermining Chinese values. This proved to be a much more dubious argument.

The new Special Economic Zones on the coast became magnets for development, attracting ambitious young Chinese from all over the mainland. Crucially, they also attracted investment from the wealthy and widespread overseas Chinese community. Foreign cultural and consumption models were copied throughout China. Nine out of 10 popular magazines portrayed foreign fashion, films, sport, food and technology. In the early 1980s, young urban Chinese saved to buy a three-piece suite of furniture. By the end of the decade, they were aiming for a video player.

This opening up coincided with, and sought to take advantage of, the emerging global economy and the revolution in global communications. Hong Kong and other foreign manufacturers transferred production to China to exploit the cheap labour. The zones also fostered criminality, prostitution and large-scale fraud involving senior Chinese officials. In the biggest scam, cadres on Hainan Island, led by the governor himself, imported more than 80,000 cars in less than a year for illegal resale to the mainland.

The giant modernization of the economy and society was not paralleled in political life. After briefly encouraging the protesters on Beijing's Democracy Wall (1979-80), Deng Xiaoping clamped down, personally approving long jail sentences on Wei Jingsheng and other ex-Red Guard dissidents. Reform-minded intellectuals and progressive Party cadres sought in the mid-1980s to push forward the boundaries of political debate. They called for separation of power between Party and state, for democratic debate and even a free press. In 1989 their efforts combined with a new outburst of protest by students and an emerging workers' movement against Party despotism and corruption. This triple combination – intellectuals, students and workers (backed by millions of ordinary citizens) – terrified the elders of the old guard. The result was the Beijing Massacre on 3-4 June.

A few days before the massacre, I studied a poem pasted on a lamp-post in Tiananmen Square. 'Deng Xiaoping suffered criticism (in the Cultural Revolution)', it began, 'and the people raised him up. Now the country does not want him, and the people do not want him. The officials eat the food, the common people labour all year. A small handful get fat, a billion are poor.' This was the authentic voice of millenarian protest in China, heard in the peasant revolts of the imperial past. By now the initial gains of economic reform had become obscured – especially in the countryside – by inflation, corruption and the uneven pace of development between rich and poor areas.

Having suppressed political protest, Deng knew that he had to offer another 'way out' for the majority of Chinese people. The third and current great wave of change was launched by him in 1992 after two years of stagnation. Making his famous 'southern expedition' to the Special Economic Zones adjacent to Hong Kong, he proclaimed a new drive to 'catch up' with the other expanding economies of east Asia. Most of China was now allowed to seek foreign investment and set up its development zones. The state in Beijing still retained control over the levers of macro-economic power, but far more autonomy was granted to the provinces and the market was permitted to overtake the planned sector. Socialism merely meant that the Party remained in charge. The road to prosperity no longer lay through collective struggle: it was to be achieved by individual enterprise. Local newspapers published eulogies not to labour heroes but to model entrepreneurs.

Deng's Great Leap of the 1990s has changed the face of China irrevocably. Western business and media hailed it uncritically as an 'economic miracle': the butcher of Beijing became Time magazine's Man of the Year. It has produced enough new wealth – or expectations of wealth – to bury the political protest of the 1980s. (More long jail sentences, including the vicious re-sentencing of Wei Jingsheng, and, most recently in October 1996, student leader Wang Dan, have also deterred dissent.) But if it is a miracle, it is a flawed one. Travelling widely in

337

provincial China over the past five years, I have seen many of its limitations.

In many areas the gains of agriculture have slowed down or been reversed, while local Party cadres increase their extortion, levying illegal taxes and fines. Millions of peasants flock to the cities creating the sort of underclass long found in other Third World countries. Rural health and education have suffered as the collective structures which support them have been weakened. The current policy is also familiar elsewhere: urban wealth is accumulated on the basis of peasant blood and sweat, and on the theory that some of the proceeds will trickle down to the rural areas.

Urban growth has been phenomenal but wasteful of resources. New 'development zones' are often idle, taking up valuable arable land. The intense struggle for profitable business opportunities encourages more corruption. The successful aspire to a Hong Kong lifestyle which is openly displayed with elite housing precincts, luxury automobiles, exclusive golf and business clubs. Benefits are not confined to the few: a sizeable new middle class has emerged forming the basis of an incipient civil society which China has never known before. But there is also a new urban underclass of the unemployed, the very poor and the rapidly expanding criminal world.

The biggest casualty of the 'economic miracle' has been the environment, already under severe pressure for many decades as population expanded. The pollution of air and water, the lack of safety at work, the despoiling of the countryside, the illegal mining for gold (which has killed hundreds of prospectors), is reminiscent of the early industrial revolution in the West. These problems are compounded by a late twentieth-century phenomenon: China now plans to become a 'great car economy', producing millions of new private automobiles in the next decade.

In 20 years China has shifted from one extreme to the other in its development strategy: a middle way was briefly contemplated but soon swept aside. Now the big question – which some in Beijing are beginning to understand – is whether China can learn from the failures as well as the successes of the western capitalist system. China's political culture has changed much less. Young Chinese are either extremely cynical about their own society or intensely patriotic – sometimes the two together. Politics, they say, is less interesting than making money. The mood is sustained by the outside world's continued eagerness to invest in China and employ its cheap labour: China's wealthy diaspora of overseas Chinese confers a special advantage. But the mismatch between political and economic change remains: a crisis in the Party after Deng's death, or an economic downturn (or a combination of both) could revive popular demands for a more just and democratic society. Then the crowds might even return to Tiananmen Square.

January/February 1997

IRENA MARYNIAK

Whatever happened to Soviet childhood?

Irena Maryniak, Index's eastern Europe editor, who is now based in Budapest, visited Moscow in 1996. Her moving report on the wretched condition of hundreds of thousands of children there provides a painful metaphor for the collapse of the Soviet dream, and with eight out of ten families living below the poverty line, casts a black shadow over the new Russian capitalism.

'We shall prove to them that they are mere pitiable children, but that the happiness of a child is the sweetest of all. We shall make their life like a children's game, with children's songs, in chorus, and with innocent dances . . . it will relieve them of their present terrible torments of coming to a free decision themselves. And they will all be happy . . . thousands of millions of happy infants . . .' Fyodor Dostoyevsky, The Brothers Karamazov, 1880

Once upon a time, there was a boy, and his name was Vitya. He had short spiky hair, bright little eyes and a cheeky grin and he was just 13. Vitya lived in a sprawling, troubled metropolis about 1,000 miles west of the Urals. Every morning he would get up and hurry off to the Dinamo metro station where, in between mooching and pilfering and very possibly other things, he did odd jobs carting boxes for the equivalent of about a dollar a day. And every night he would scramble up to the sixth floor of one of those looming grey apartment blocks to see his brothers and sisters and, of course, his mother and give her what he had earned: which was nice for her because she badly needed a tipple every now and again. After that he would go home. Vitya lived in a kennel. This wasn't too bad because there was a dog in the kennel who got a fistful of scraps every day which he shared with Vitya. But then it was December and Vitya's feet froze.

One day a beer-cart driver called Anatoly saw Vitya at the Dinamo station and stopped off for a chinwag. He wanted to know Vitya's name and where he lived and why he was having such trouble shifting those boxes. The next day Anatoly brought some friends and they examined Vitya's feet. And because this is a tale for those who long for happy ends, they all turned out to be from the Leopold Union for the Protection of Orphans, and they drove Vitya off to a sanatorium where his feet could be treated. Anatoly took Vitya home to his wife and three children, and they fostered him for a year. They also tried to teach him to read. After that, the Leopold Union arranged for Vitya and his four brothers and sisters to be placed in a children's home on Garibaldi Street in the southwest corner of the city. And they all lived happily ever after.

If statistics and press reports are any more a reflection of the true state of things than stories told over a glass of Pickwick tea in a Moscow bar, Vitya could have known worse. He might have been picked up for slave labour in Azerbaijan where, *Argumenty i Fakty* reports, children are kept as unpaid house servants by well-heeled families with an image to think about. He might have slipped into drug smuggling or prostitution, or ended up fruit-picking in an isolated settlement in the central Asian outback where children are said to work for 14-16 hours a day under armed guard. Or he might have been sold to the West, either for adoption or, as lurid Moscow tabloids claim, as an organ donor.

In fact, Vitya was taken into care by one of those private child-welfare charities which have been springing up in Russia over the past five years, in response to the soaring numbers of children on the streets and to the harsh reputation of overcrowded state orphanages remaining from Soviet times. With their impenetrable concrete walls, collective regimentation and corrupt administrations, supporters of the new voluntary sector say they leave their inmates dependent, stultified and spectacularly unprepared for assimilation into a market community. But of the more than 300 independent children's charities active in Moscow now, many are run on enthusiasm rather than professional skill and some operate well outside the law. Others are downright nefarious.

One of the most reputable is NAN (No to Alcoholism and Drugs), which runs a children's shelter in a northern Moscow suburb, encased by apartment blocks and a small patch of woodland. It's called 'The Way

Home'. I approached it after dark, guided only by a neon searchlight dazzlingly poised on the roof. The compound had thick metal railings and, as it turned out, two very locked gates. Hard to tell whether this was intended to keep strangers out or children in. I circled the grounds, tramping through viscous mud and peering anxiously for a footpath through the trees. There was none. In daylight, doubtless, it would have been innocuous enough. After an oddly timeless space I caught sight of a stooped figure shuffling between the birches a little way ahead.

The old woman (Russia breeds old and young, with little in between) was unperturbed to be approached by a breathless and visibly unsettled foreigner. She explained insistently and at length that this really wasn't the way things used to be. Only a year or two ago *anyone* could get in. But now we were back at the main gate and, somehow, somebody from inside the building must have seen us. An anonymous-looking figure in plain clothes emerged and, once assured that I had an appointment, opened up. My guide was left waving on the other side of the barrier.

Inside it was warm, kindly and very clean. Before visiting the children's dormitories I was asked, in the nicest possible way, to remove those mud-caked boots. Here, Sapar Koulyanov, the director, is surrogate father to about 30 children aged three to 13. It was 8pm on a Wednesday; party-time in the director's study. There was tea and biscuits and music and dancing, and as a special treat Sapar took photographs of everyone with his Polaroid camera. It was all very reassuringly normal. Each child had a history a bit like Vitya's, but here everyone was fed and clothed and out of danger, at least for the moment. The regime was relaxed and benignly paternalistic.

Sapar Mullaevich talks about the present with a kind of suppressed horror and about the past with ill-concealed nostalgia: cosy little backyards between apartment blocks where children could play in safety; Palaces of Culture where any hobby was catered for after school hours – athletics, drama, music, airplane modelling; secure schooling with the certainty of work at the other end; those long sun-splashed summers in Pioneer camps and the neatly coiffed little girls with huge bows in their hair.

'It all seems to be about money and prestige these days,' he says tentatively and his voice is an unbroken sigh. 'There may seem to be a bubbling universal freedom, in which everything is permitted but then, on the other hand, one has to pause. One may even be tempted to think that this is wrong, that there should, after all, be a collective morality.'

In a sense 'The Way Home', so pristine, easygoing and cheerful, was like a projection of the world many former Soviet citizens must hanker for. Barred, protected from the outside, warm and welcoming within; a place where immediate needs are met and socialising codes of conduct taught. Here, if anywhere in modern Russia, children will learn something of the old Soviet values instilled in their carers by the Pioneer movement and the Komsomol: respect for authority, diligence, obedience, good manners, helpfulness and, by extension, docility, conformity and an ambition confined to a diploma, an apartment, a job, a family, perhaps a car. All costly commodities these days. Perhaps by some kind of osmosis they will get a whiff, too, of those golden days when morality meant devotion to the Spiritual Father of the Nation (as Stalin liked to be known) before loyalty to blood kinship. And that may be something that *these* young people – neglected or abandoned by their closest kith and kin – will more easily understand than most.

There was a Pioneer in those golden days whose name was Pavlik Morozov. He lived in a village in the Urals and he wore a white shirt and a blazing red scarf. When he was 13 he stood up under Lenin's portrait before the local governing council and denounced his father for collaboration with the *kulaks*. It was 1932. His story became the myth on which all Soviet children were raised because, shortly afterwards, he was murdered. He became the model to which all Pioneers were to aspire, the archetype they were to reflect as they performed their countless salutes, their missions and assignments, received badges and prizes for good behaviour, celebrated feast-days in memory of Soviet heroes, and sang in unison around the camp fire:

Let the sun shine forever
Let the sky always be
Let there always be mama
Let there always be me.

Later there would be the Komsomol, harvesting brigades, summer construction camps: the Komsomol City-on-the-Amur, Magnet City in the Urals, the Baikal-Amur Railway ... Trailblazing projects all, built by Communist Youth, their tents pitched on mountains and steppes and riversides. No sex, fights or drugs, just the power of faith, enthusiasm and hard work – or so the subsidized hoopla which surrounded them would have had us believe.

That was before jazz, gays, drugs and bourgeois eroticism came muscling in. The only discordant notes in this glorious chorale were the itinerant kids who would appear in well-heeled resorts, sometimes armed, and claim to be implementing social justice by fleecing the better off. They were the neglected children of the post-revolutionary decades – victims of combat, hunger and relocation – who poured into cities, flooded train stations and markets and derelict houses and could be found packed into the undercarriages of trains on the way to holiday resorts in the Crimea. They terrorized their peers, dismayed or infuriated adults and deeply embarrassed successive regimes by surviving burrowed into woodpiles, haystacks, coal reserves, drainage pipes, garbage dumps and cemetery burial vaults.

The summer of 1917 left 150,000 children destitute in Petrograd alone. But the economic and political transition of the 1990s, war in the former republics, the migration of refugees and the relocation of the military have deposited a legacy hardly less devastating. What statistics there are indicate that in democratic Russia up to 700,000 children are on the streets; over 400,000 are known to be orphaned; around 30,000 are listed as disappeared; and 150,000 run away from home every year. None of these figures take account of the war in Chechnya.

According to *Moscow News* correspondent Galina Mashtakova, countless children now fend for themselves in the cellars and shattered apartment blocks of Grozny. They dart about in oversize ladies' sweaters and newly acquired green velvet berets begging, pilfering and sniffing glue. During the war they had the job of cycling round the city to check out the numbers of Russian Federal troops, their position and ammunition stores. These days they rummage for unused shells in the cellars and snowdrifts of Grozny and sell them to Chechen fighters for the equivalent of US$6 apiece. Those living alone in relatively undamaged property are exposed to danger from racketeers, and from the desperate, on the prowl for living space. Two adolescent orphans Mashtakova befriended last October were murdered a month later in exactly these circumstances.

But the hundreds of thousands of kids roaming Russian cities – diving past you into the Moscow metro, whooping gleefully as they release yet another dog some hapless owner has left tied to a tree – are, more often than not, merely preferring the questionable allure of the streets to abuse, violence and dipsomania at home. Though after a scheme for the privatization of apartments was introduced after 1991, some parents reportedly sold up and made off, leaving an estimated 100,000 children to fend for themselves.

They shelter mostly in the attics of tenement blocks and in cellars, at railway stations and airports, in small groups with a teenage leader who acts as financial manager, housing adviser, judge and agent of punishment. Some wash cars. Some get caught up in organized crime. According to the Charities Aid Foundation, adolescent professional killers are sometimes willing to do the job for as little as 100,000 roubles (less than US$20).

It is a chilling sign of the times. But then eight out of 10 families in Russia live below the poverty line. Education, career prospects and entertainment are reserved for the privileged few. The rest are relegated to the stairwells, out of the way of parents weighed down by job losses, inflation and personal distress. A recent report in *Izvestiya*, from the Kemerovskaya region in the Urals, depicted an entire community centred around the town refuse dump which also serves as a refuge for growing numbers of scavenging kids who shelter at night in the heating plant chimney. With pay packages months overdue, the sale of discarded bottles is a surer source of income than working down a mine shaft. And they are here for the taking beside piles of decaying garbage of all kinds and, just occasionally, the body of a new-born child.

The economic transition of eastern Europe has placed the very young at the epicentre of a seismic shift. Where poverty and crime has risen they have been its chief victims. For underworld networks, drug smugglers and paedophiles, the map of Europe and Asia has been redrawn. The collapse of the Soviet Empire opened new supply routes for drugs from Pakistan and Afghanistan via Russia and the new independent states, and aided the proliferation of smuggling rings from Tallinn to Rangoon. These days drugs are sold by old ladies outside the Lubianka (once the KGB headquarters) to addicts and to kids. The collapse of the Berlin Wall has drawn paedophiles to the banks of the Danube and to public spots in Warsaw or Prague. Teenagers from the Ukraine or Romania appear in the cities of central Europe for a spell of prostitution and subsequently vanish. The tales Russian street children tell of violence, sexual harassment or arbitrary detention find easy echo in Bucharest, Budapest or, as a recent Human Rights Watch report on police brutality against the children of Bulgaria amply documents, in Sofia.

In the early 1980s, Gabor Demszky was an underground publisher and founder of SZETA, the first independent social welfare organization in Hungary. Subsequently he spent six months in prison and today he is mayor of Budapest. He elaborates conscientiously on rationalization of expenditure and public transport problems, and only when pressed begins to speak of attitudes that characterize the economically polarized societies of central and eastern Europe: inadequate social and economic mobility, lack of tolerance, raging competition and inflexibility. 'Young professionals, talented people make fortunes, but they don't understand the problems of the rest,' he announces with sudden animation. 'In this yuppie subculture, there isn't much social feeling, solidarity, or sensitivity. This is also true of the new bourgeoisie. There is absolutely no openness and no understanding of social tensions.' The same is true of the 'new Russian' social and political culture, with the Kremlin still, as ever, nominating the winners and consigning its losers to limbo.

Statistics acknowledge that between 1992 and 1994 child crime more than doubled in Russia. Young offenders are left to await trial for up to three years in Interior Ministry investigation cells built for four inmates and shared by up to 15. There is seldom opportunity to exercise; violence, rape and murder are rife because prison guards prefer not to intervene in disputes between prisoners. An arbitrary decision by a prison guard can have a 15-year-old stripped and despatched to an unheated isolation cell with no light and a soaking floor for between five and 10 days. Later, if convicted, adolescents have to endure educational labour colonies ruled less by official administrators than by internal hierarchies in which inmates are classified within their own community as masters, lackeys or slaves according to strength, wit and will. 'Slavery', of course, implies routine taunts, humiliation and rape.

The investigation cells and educational labour colonies are as much of an insult to east European democracy today as labour camps were to the original Communist Utopia. To children without family relationships, a community or a welfare state to help give shape to the world, democratization has offered a vacuous universe with neither order nor rationale. Deprived of cultural or educational grounding, and of any credible political, economic or social point of reference, the unwanted children of eastern Europe live on a plane of shifting sands. And who, after all, would dare to blame them if, one day, they come to elect a life 'in chorus' which will relieve them at last of their present terrible torment of coming to a free decision themselves?

March/April 1997